The Asian Pacific Rim and Globalization

Enterprise, governance and terri

Edited by
RICHARD LE HERON
University of Auckland, New Zealand

SAM OCK PARK
Seoul National University, South Korea

Avebury

Aldershot · Brookfield USA · Hong Kong · Singapore · Sydney

Published by
Avebury
Ashgate Publishing Ltd
Gower House
Croft Road
Aldershot
Hants GU11 3HR
England

Ashgate Publishing Company
Old Post Road
Brookfield
Vermont 05036
USA

A CIP catalogue record for this book is available from the British Library

1 85628 894 3 ✓

Reprinted 1996, 1997

Library of Congress Catalog Card Number: 95-75576

Typeset by
Toni Snowball-Kui
Palmerston North

Printed and bound by Athenæum Press Ltd.,
Gateshead, Tyne & Wear.

THE ASIAN PACIFIC RIM AND GLOBALIZATION

Also in the series:

The Industrial Enterprise and Its Environment: Spatial Perspectives
Edited by Sergio Conti, Edward J. Malecki and Päivi Oinas
ISBN 1 85628 876 5

Environmental Change: Industry, Power and Policy
Olga Gritsai and Michael Taylor
ISBN 1 85972 161 3

90 0470024 0

Contents

List of figures

List of tables

Contributors

Claes Alvstam, Professor of Economic Geography, Swedish School of Economics and Business Administration, P.O. Box 479, FIN-00101, Helsinki, Finland and Director of the Centre for East and Southeast Asian Studies, University of Göteborg, Brogatan 4, 5-41301, Göteborg, Sweden.

Graham Humphrys, Senior Lecturer, Department of Geography, University of Wales, Swansea, Singleton Park, Swansea SA2 8PP, United Kingdom.

Won Bae Kim, Fellow, Program on Population and Adjunct Professor, Department of Urban and Regional Planning, University of Hawaii, V777 East-West Road, Honolulu, Hawaii 96848, United States of America.

Richard Le Heron, Professor, Department of Geography, University of Auckland, P.O. Box 92019, Auckland, New Zealand.

John McKay, Director, Monash Asia Institute, Monash University, Clayton, Victoria 3168, Australia.

Geoff Missen, Senior Lecturer, Department of Geography, University of Melbourne, Parkville, Victoria 3052, Australia.

Yoshihiro Miyamachi, Lecturer, Department of Economics, University of Oita, Oita 870-11, Japan.

Sam Ock Park, Professor, Department of Geography, Seoul National University, Seoul 151-742, South Korea.

Paul Parker, Assistant Professor, Department of Geography, Faculty of Environmental Studies, University of Waterloo, Waterloo, Ontario N2L 3G1, Canada.

Jamie Peck, Lecturer, School of Geography, University of Manchester, Manchester M13 9PL, United Kingdom.

Peter Rimmer, Head, Department of Human Geography, Research School of Pacific and Asian Studies, The Australian National University, Canberra, ACT 0200, Australia.

Leo van Grunsven, Senior Lecturer, Section of International Economics and Economic Geography, Faculty of Geographical Sciences, Utrecht University, Heidelberglaan 2, P.O. Box EO 115, 3508 TC Utrecht, The Netherlands.

Shuang-Yann Wong, Lecturer, Geography Division, National Institute of Education, Nanyang Technological University, 469 Bukit Timah Road, Singapore 1025.

Acknowledgements

The Editors offer a special thanks to the publication team whose efforts brought the book to final completion. In particular, the following were invaluable: Ian Cooper (University of Auckland), for extensive editorial advice and assistance, including indexing; Toni Snowball-Kui for word-processing the text and tables to the camera ready state; Jonette Surridge (University of Auckland) for preparing the figures and advice on layout; Edwina Brafield and Pam Haydon for typing drafts of Chapter 9 and the index and assisting with facsimile communications and Kiri and Erena Le Heron with index pagination.

The book had its genesis at the Tokyo meeting of the International Geographical Union Commission on 'The Organisation of Industrial Space' in 1993. The comments and suggestions of participants were very helpful in assisting the Editors identify the themes which form the book's content. Sergio Conti and Ed Malecki from the Commission's Executive gave encouragement throughout the project.

Richard Le Heron   Sam Ock Park
University of Auckland   Seoul National University

Abbreviations

AFTA	Asian Free Trade Association
APEC	Asia Pacific Economic Cooperation
ASEAN	Association of South East Asian Nations
BIDA	Batam Industrial Development Authority (Indonesia)
BRU	Brunei
CCD	Colour Crystal Display
CIS	Computer Information Systems
DRAM	Dynamic Random Access Memory
EAEC	East Asian Economic Caucus
EAIT	External Affairs and International Trade (Canada)
EC	European Community
EOI	Export Oriented Industrialization
EPZ	Export Processing Zone
ERSO	Electronics Research and Service Organization (Taiwan)
EU	European Union
FDI	Foreign Direct Investment
FPG	Formosa Plastic Group
GATT	General Agreement on Tariffs and Trade
GDP	Gross Domestic Product
GNP	Gross National Product
G7	Group of Seven
HKG	Hong Kong
IBRD	International Bank for Reconstruction and Development
IC	Integrated Circuits

IND	Indonesia
IDIC	Industrial Development and Investment Centre (Taiwan)
IMF	International Monetary Fund
ISI	Import Substitution Industrialization
IST	Industry, Science and Technology (Canada)
ITRI	Industrial Technology Research Institute (Taiwan)
JAP	Japan
JETRO	Japan External Trade Organization
JIT	Just in time
JSEDC	Johor State Economic Development Corporation (Malaysia)
KMT	Kuomintang state in Taiwan
LCD	Liquid Crystal Display
LE	Large Enterprise
MAL	Malaysia
MFN	Most Favoured Nation
MITI	Ministry of International Trade and Industry (Japan)
MSR	Mode of Social Regulation
NAFTA	North American Free Trade Agreement
NIC	Newly Industrializing Country
NIE	Newly Industrializing Economy
OECD	Organization for Economic Cooperation and Development
PAP	People's Action Party (Singapore)
PCB	Printed Circuit Board
PIL	Philippines
PRC	People's Republic of China (China)
R & D	Research and Development
REZ	Regional Economic Zone
ROC	Republic of China (Taiwan)
ROK	Republic of Korea (South Korea)
SCHTEZ	South China-Hong Kong-Taiwan Economic Zone
SEOI	Secondary Export Oriented Industrialization
SEZ	Special Economic Zone
SIJORI	Singapore-Johor-Riau Growth Triangle
SIN	Singapore
SISI	Secondary Import Substitution Industrialization
SITC	Standard International Trade Classification
SME	Small and Medium Sized Enterprise
THA	Thailand
TIER	Taiwan Institute of Economic Research
TNC	Transnational Corporation
TNT	Thomas Nationwide Transport
US	United States
YSR	Yellow Sea Economic Zone (also Yellow Sea Rim)

1   Introduction: Geographies of globalization

Richard Le Heron and Sam Ock Park

Introduction

At the end of the twentieth century, the Asian Pacific Rim occupies a special place in world opinion and thought. For more than two decades the centre of gravity of world economic activity, as measured by aggregate economic indicators, has increasingly edged away from the Atlantic into the Pacific area (*Time International*, 22 February, 1993). With this has come a gradual transformation of perceptions about the perimeters of Asia and the Pacific, culminating in the 1980s and 1990s in a serious questioning of the terms used to denote the Asia-Pacific area and the various combinations of nation-states included in particular definitions (Drakakis-Smith, 1992; Hodder, 1992; Palat, 1993). The initial mapping of the Atlantic axis idea onto the Pacific, with its overtones of cartographic elegance and simplicity and implied structural connectivity, was soon supplanted by a series of competing terms which added further to the impression of unity and cohesion. Terms such as 'Pacific Rim', 'Pacific Basin', 'Asia Pacific', 'Pacific Asia' and the 'Asian Pacific Rim' began to appear in the literature. All terms implied in varying ways an inner geography of homogeneity, commonality of interests, equality of involvement, similar historical experiences, equivalent contemporary experiences, a shared future and mutually determined prospects. Thinking in this vein has been reinforced by the suggestion that the twenty first century will be the dawning of the Pacific Age or could be the 'Pacific Century', a myth which confers causal powers to an arbitrarily defined area and postpones scrutiny of the influences behind world patterns of growth that are attracting attention. Despite the errors associated with the Pacific Century mythology, its appeal in many quarters stimulated geographic research on the area. Fortuitously, the interest coincided with a significant reassessment internationally of the theoretical categories of industrial geography, a development that has seen a gradual but nonetheless significant reorientation in the research of industrial geographers and some differentiation in research practice[1]. In recent years attempts have been made to render more visible the historic-geographic forces behind the growing importance of the Asia-Pacific area in the global economy and to expose the heterogeneity of formative influences shaping change and perceptions about change[2].

1

Despite the insight that has come from more critical interpretations about the nature and significance of developments connected with the broader Asia-Pacific region, research has thrown up as many questions as answers. Indeed, to consider the territoriality of the global economy and the significance of different geographic and historical processes is to immediately question categories presently used to discuss the history of capitalism (Conti, 1993, 1994; Fagan and Le Heron, 1994; Le Heron and van der Knaap, 1994a). And to seek to represent dimensions of the contemporary organization of industrial activity in such a manner is to cast doubt on the adequacy of analytical conventions and method lying behind earlier interpretations of capitalism's historical geography. In the mid-1990s the theoretical work of industrial geographers is challenging much of the 1980s orthodoxy about the nature and progression of industrialization, globalization and industrial restructuring (Dicken, 1994; Le Heron, 1993; Scott, 1992; Storper, 1992). Fresh empirical research, informed by and informing theory, is providing increasing evidence which suggests that *some* historically new lines of integration, anchored in enterprise behaviour and investment patterns, are discernible in the Asian Pacific Rim.

Theme - The Asian Pacific Rim and Globalization

The book's title fuses two influential metaphors, both of which have contentious elements. Together they make up a backdrop of 'metatheory' conditioning thinking about the geography of industrial change, encouraging particular lines of enquiry, at the same time as squeezing out other threads of research. Because of the relative novelty of a study dealing with globalization in the Asian Pacific context, it is important to establish reasonably precisely the scope of the book and the nature of the theoretical and empirical claims that might or might not be made from the work.

The Asian Pacific Rim

Many industrial geographers contend that developments in world capitalism in particular influence which portions of the world are deemed to be especially important and what segments of economic activity are considered especially significant in shaping networks of interaction at different levels. Decisions on the former stem from a growing appreciation of the importance of historical shifts of different scales in the history of capitalism, while those on the latter draw upon increased understanding of the patterns and regimes of capital circulation which distinguish capitalist history. In each instance the tentative formulations of theory have been turned into relatively definite statements of 'implied fact' which serve to inform and guide further theoretical and empirical effort. There are risks in uncritically accepting any labelling, when the root ideas themselves have relatively uncertain status. Two risks are especially relevant. First, to use either the Asian Pacific Rim or the global economy as organizing devices to 'steer' research is to possibly prejudge how interactions and their accompanying geographies might be interpreted. Interactions might be seen as creating geographies involving the Asian Pacific Rim as an area or geographies which are largely internal to the Asian Pacific Rim. Deciding to highlight the Asian Pacific Rim and by implication its wider role (in the global economy) is thus not an inconsequential matter. Rather an argued case must be made to justify its selection as an 'arena' to illustrate historically important interactions shaping the spatiality of capitalist industrialization. Second, by beginning with an area designated as the Asian Pacific Rim (inevitably constructed from a grouping of countries) there is a temptation to draw on national level data to probe interactions. The way in which interactions are regarded and studied, however, affects both how 'geographies' are identified and how evaluations are made of patterns revealed from investigation and analysis. Feminist analysis warns, for instance, that much industrial geography excludes other formative processes, not necessarily by deliberate design, but because of incomplete and inadequate conceptualisation of the relevant processes responsible for particular patterning and outcomes (Gibson and Graham, 1992; Graham, 1992). The view that geographies are socially created is thus a double claim; their reality is created from social interaction and from the interpretative lenses used by researchers.

Most scholars agree that a distinctive feature of capitalism is its tendency to undergo internal transformations. This tendency reinforces a fluid mosaic of geographic unevenness which is another recognizable characteristic of capitalism. Although the spatiality of this proposition is broadly sensed, it has not been matched by longitudinal and geographical summaries of the main interconnections which are implied by and underpin major transformations (Le Heron and van der Knaap, 1994b). This may owe something to an insensitivity to historical shifts, in everyday experience and in research practice. But a much more critical matter needs to be confronted than simply that of being more aware of the macro shifts in which analysis might be set. The general difficulty of identifying transformative developments *while they are happening* poses problems for industrial geographers, as it does for any group of researchers or individual researcher. If the industrial scene of the 1990s is partly definable by significant flexibility in the organization of industrial activity, then it is especially important that dimensions of various dynamics be 'identified' and 'represented'. The vexing difficulty is finding simple and manageable methods to enable indicative analyses of the plurality, indeterminancy and general open-endedness of organizational options associated with contemporary industrial change.

The outstanding performance of Japan as a national economy and Japanese enterprise internationally has necessitated serious examination of the origins of its successes, especially since Japanese investment is an integral part of the Asian Pacific scene in the 1990s. The explanatory argument rests on the emergent and major role of the Japanese economy and Japanese investment around the world. For many the evidence is compelling, but a cautionary note does need to be sounded in terms of the geographic reach, nature and dynamic of the networks of capital circulation about which industrial geographers are particularly interested. Several questions must be asked. Is the assessment portrayed above eurocentric, with for

3

example a 'hidden' bias towards including Japanese investment (because perhaps it is better monitored) than say Chinese investment (perhaps considered inappropriate for geopolitical and racial reasons)? What are industrialists, politicians, unionists, researchers and so on in the nations making up the Asian Pacific Rim actually saying about the Rim? What makes up the institutional settings which are forging and filtering similar and different ideas about appropriate investment foci? What currents of opinion can be documented over time? Are any changes in conception, valuation of importance and advocacy linked to the diffusion of governmental restructuring policies and strategies or have they had distinctive internal origins and promoters? Are cultural evaluations, sourced country-by-country or from different ethnic groups, submerged beneath the apparent 'neutrality' of the language of economics or should cultural evaluations be seen as more appropriately, intercultural in nature? The matrix of valuations of investment arenas is obviously potentially quite large, but the crucial importance of clarifying the general climate and context of investment behaviour, especially with respect to longer term shifts in 'national' and 'regional' investment orientation engendered by guiding metaphors deserves scrutiny.

Globalization

Just as ideas about the saliency of the wider Asia-Pacific require unpacking, so too do those about globalization. Again the Anglo-American stamp upon the intellectual heritage of globalization as a theoretical concept and the global economy as an empirical concept may need tempering with a view of capitalist industrialization which is de-centred away from mainly European interpretations (Pieterse, 1994). Recent work also contains scepticism about the global economy concept and aspects of the globalization thesis (Thrift, 1992). With the primary interest of documenting how and why and in what ways and to what degree industrial interactions of different places are incorporated into webs of wider interactions, the book must confront these criticisms. A main disagreement in the literature involves a rejection of any suggestion that the global economy and the globalization tendency of capitalist industrialization should be seen as totalizing and homogenizing in nature. By voicing this concern the critics mean that the global economy is really a conceptual label for the set of propulsive institution-mediated investment connections amongst places in the world (Le Heron, 1993). In this more open conception not all interactions are necessarily global in expression or extent, and, moreover, not all investment interactions should be construed as being part of the global economy. What is often overlooked, however, are newly emergent and diverse enterprise or organizational capacities that, according to the globalization perspective, are integral to an understanding of emergent contemporary industrial interactions. Organization capacity, whether seen from the standpoint of individual entities or in terms of patterning springing from the interactions of many organizations, places heavy strain on the research conventions of industrial geography.

4

Theme - enterprise, governance and territoriality

One major shortcoming of the globalization literature is the paucity of studies dealing with the interconnections between globalization and enterprise change in different settings. This is somewhat surprising as enterprise strategy and behaviour in fact underpins much of the patterning which globalization research attempts to interpret. The subtitling of the book, 'Enterprise, Governance and Territoriality', endeavours to make more explicit the treatment and approach followed by contributors. The approach is primarily translatory rather than overtly explanatory. It diverges from accounts that attempt to argue that governance and regulation should be put aside, leaving enterprise to fend for itself. Instead it recognizes that enterprise and governance form a relation, that is they are mutually constituted by and constitutive of each other, and as such, should be examined in tandem. In stressing the interconnections between 'context and agency' the book is able to make some progress in holding together the actuality of industrialization policy and enterprise strategy and adjustment. As a result the book differs from studies concerned with spelling out normative models of enterprise behaviour which are seen as universally applicable, irrespective of context or mix of enterprises.

Openness and emerging coherence

A broad argument of the globalization perspective is the view that the trend towards greater openness and unleashing of the enterprise-system (amounting to a borderless economy on a world scale populated by players facing new sorts of constraints on investment behaviour) is accompanied by (even defined by) historically-specific patterns of differing levels of complexity which are products of structured stability and coherence (Cloke and Goodman, 1992; Conti, 1993; Le Heron, 1993). This argument differs from the debate over the interdependence between regulatory and accumulation processes, though it does draw from and impinge upon it. The argument's significance lies in the translational guidance it embodies. The phrasing 'structured coherence' is especially apt as it keeps structure and agency together and it also signals the urgent task of working out a general methodology to advance the investigation of 'structuring' organizations and structured 'organization', two interrelated sides of structure and agency.

The research focus of trying to comprehend the organization of industrial space means the process by which dimensions and examples are chosen is probably as important to the 'mapping' of interactions as the techniques and procedures of analysis. The process of choosing is of course a theoretical, conceptual and translation exercise which is intimately tied into researcher's responses to popular news coverage. The risk of inadvertently or uncritically transferring ideas from one setting to another is always high (the ideal-type problem) and the determination of interactions for and from analysis heavily dependent on the background and experience of researchers.

Extending the 'Geography of Accumulation and Regulation' framework

A geography of accumulation framework provides *a* way to situate a range of theoretical initiatives within the orbit of industrial geography. Four strands of theoretical work bear upon this study: work on the circuits of capital; studies of the regulation of capital; perspectives on techno-economic and socio-institutional regimes; and inquiry concerned with regional nexa of accumulation and regulation. The four strands are interconnected but have usually received separate theorization. Figure 1.1 is a tentative depiction of how a range of theoretical and empirical issues can be intertwined into a framework focusing on the organization of industrial territoriality. The figure reflects a view that local developments relating to *both production and consumption* must be regarded in an historical sense as embedded in the context of higher order circuits of capital, state regulation and technological orders. That is to say the idea of processes, central to the circulation of capital notion, is a way to indicate the expression and historical significance of interactions. This is not to say that meaning is 'imposed' or 'deduced' by assuming a hierarchy of processes. Assessing significance is a more subtle and complex process, springing from the fusion of globalization and localization. State policy enters as a mediating membrane over the development of technological and organizational forces and capacities and attendant labour processes. The geography of interactions is thus a template of revealed and perhaps present perceptions of investment-labour potential. But the thrust of Figure 1.1 is that the organization of industrial space metaphor is at heart, to quote Storper (1992, 91), an argument that 'localized production systems are central to contemporary global economic development'. The global economy may be seen in this light, according to Storper, as consisting, in important measure, of a mosaic of specialized technology districts, the emergence of which rest on period-specific conditions.

The Storper position is, however, a truncated explanation of the integrative tendencies of the global economy. The geography of accumulation framework fully acknowledges the links between production and consumption that hold together the capitalist order. Just as techno-economic systems, in socio-institutional settings are anchored in 'technology districts', so too, are they coupled to 'districts of consumption' (e.g. metropolitan centres, shopping malls and centres and other specialized zones in metropolitan and other centres). *The regional geographies of product-based technological learning needs to be counterbalanced with the regional geographies of consumer-centred experiential learning.* Organized industrial space may be better understood if the span from production to consumption is more fully considered.

This assessment of the dynamic of contemporary capitalist industrialization introduces extra data demands, especially for information on the corporations and governance arrangements associated with particular technology districts, technology systems and locales of consumption. The bold portions of Figure 1.1 contain suggestions about useful empirical questions. These form part of a preliminary

PERSPECTIVES	Capital Circuits	Regulation	Technology	Regions
TRADE	Patterns and main axes of international trade **Export and import Specialization**	Constraints on development of production-consumption links **Trading blocs, state trade policy, cultural norms/preferences**	Production sequences behind intra and inter trade **Main industries and organisations, strategies of key organisations**	Infrastructure supporting export and import trade **Main organisations and networks**
FINANCE	Patterns and axes of external and internal investment **Investment flows, public/private funds, investment combinations**	Environment for investment in different circuits **State development and investment policy, investor traditions, behaviour and strategies**	Production sequences affected by investment **Main industries, key intermediaries, banks, corporates, perception of industry risk**	Local attitudes towards financial risk **Main organisations and networks**
PRODUCTION	Patterns and axes of production organisation within and amongst countries **Main commodity production systems, patterns of integration**	Environment for technology development and adoption **State technology policy, industry biases in regulation**	Technological bases of production sequences and consumption preferences **National science and technology infrastructure, sources of technology in industries, technological leaders, advertising**	Conventions supporting technological dynamism and consumption norms **Main organisations and networks**

Figure 1.1

Scheme for exploring the organization of industrial space (a Geography of Accumulation and Regulation framework).

7

research agenda, but leave scope for later assessment of which interactions and patterns are noteworthy or significant.

Restructuring for survival in the Asian Pacific Rim

During the post-war period until the 1980s, Asian countries in the Asian Pacific rim area were experiencing difficulties in economic cooperation due to political barriers and the differences in regulatory and economic systems. However, recently there has been a considerable level of cross-border economic cooperation and development in industrial spaces in the Asian Pacific rim area. Asian NIEs (Hong Kong, Singapore, South Korea, and Taiwan) have been the major players among those in the area in enhancing external trade and direct foreign investment. The recent increase in trade volumes and investment by the Asian NIEs in the Asian Pacific rim area can be regarded as the result of restructuring for survival due to the changes in international politics and their competitiveness in global competition.

Restructuring is not just sectoral or regional shifts of industry but rather underlying changes of organization and technology of production, of labour relations, as well as of relations between firms (Todling, 1994). The process of restructuring for survival can be clearly identified from industrial restructuring of the Asian NIEs in recent years. After three decades of rapid industrial growth, the Asian NIEs are currently undergoing industrial restructuring. Since the late 1980s, the Asian NIEs have become vulnerable to the changes in domestic and international environments. These changes include rapid increase in wages, labour shortages in production, price and exchange rate fluctuations, increasing competition in export markets, and protectionist tendency in major world markets (Park, 1994).

The Asian NIEs are now facing new problems and challenges in global competition. The severe rivalry between US and Japan and the development of macro-regional trading blocs deter the entry of the Asian NIEs into major world markets. The rise of low-cost economies of China and the ASEAN-4 have made the Asian NIEs more vulnerable. How to respond to these problems is the immediate issue for their own survival.

The most important triggers of the industrial restructuring in major cities of the Asian NIEs are rapid increases in wages and labour shortages in production (Ho, 1993; Lim, 1993; Lui and Chiu, 1993; Park, 1993). The role of state was critical for industrial changes and spatial restructuring in the rapid industrialisation phase of the Asian NIEs during the 1960s through the 1980s (Markusen and Park, 1993; Song, 1990). Government policy is still significant for industrial changes and restructuring. In South Korea, for example, government policy focuses on the support of structural adjustments since the mid-1980s due to the emergence of low-cost foreign competitors and soaring domestic costs. While government is still an important element in industrial restructuring of the Asian NIEs, recently firm level competitive strategy is attracting lots of attention as a solution for the recent problems since government policy is limited in regaining competitive advantage.

Confronted with the erosion of competitive advantages, especially in the labour intensive industries in the NIEs, firms have responded dynamically in the restructuring process. The dynamic restructuring process embraces or combines changes in technology, location, organization, and local labour markets (Park, 1995). Firm's competitive strategy in developing technology, selecting location, controlling labour, and organizing production systems have become more important than before in the dynamic restructuring process of the Asian NIEs (Clark and Kim, 1995).

Utilization of flexible labour such as part-time or temporary workers and foreign workers has been adopted as major firm strategy on labour in order to overcome problems with high wages and labour shortages in manufacturing in Hong Kong, Singapore, and Seoul metropolitan area (Ho, 1995; Chiu and Lui, 1995; Park, 1995). Subcontracting has been adopted as a competitive strategy by most of the firms in the major cities of the Asian NIEs. The main reason of the subcontracting strategy is lowering wages and labour costs, and accordingly, the subcontracting strategy is directly related to labour strategy (Ho, 1995; Park, 1995). Because of high wages and labour shortages, overseas investments in plants or factories are considered as appropriate locational strategy by many firms in the labour intensive industries.

A considerable proportion of the firms in the major cities in the Asian NIEs have introduced new technology as part of their competitive strategy. Firm strategies on labour and organization are regarded as short term adjustment strategies or short term restructuring for survival responding to the problems of high wages and labour shortages in the Asian NIEs. However, major purposes of the introduction of new technology are to increase productivity and improve quality along with cutting costs. Productivity increase is the most important reason for the introduction of new technology and cost related factors are relatively less significant in the technology strategy compared to other firm strategies (Clark and Kim, 1995). Firm strategy on technology is a strategy of long term restructuring for survival which can ultimately contribute to the improvement of quality of life in the Asian NIEs and other Asian Pacific Rim countries. Direct overseas investment strategy is also important for the future role of the Asian NIEs in the Asian Pacific Rim area.

Organization of the book

The Asian Pacific Rim and Globalization is one response by a group of industrial geographers to help clarify the dimensions, directions and spatiality of contemporary industrialization. It is concerned with two interdependent themes; the changing course of industrialization and enterprise in Asian Pacific countries over the last quarter century and the development of ideas for the analysis of such industrial change. Both these themes are in their own right highly problematic, yet by exploring them together, important insight can be obtained into the dynamics of the global economy. The book argues that from the complexities of 25 years of nationally organized industrialization in the Asian Pacific Rim distinctive cross-border patterns of regionalization are *beginning* to emerge (Figure 1.2). The book

9

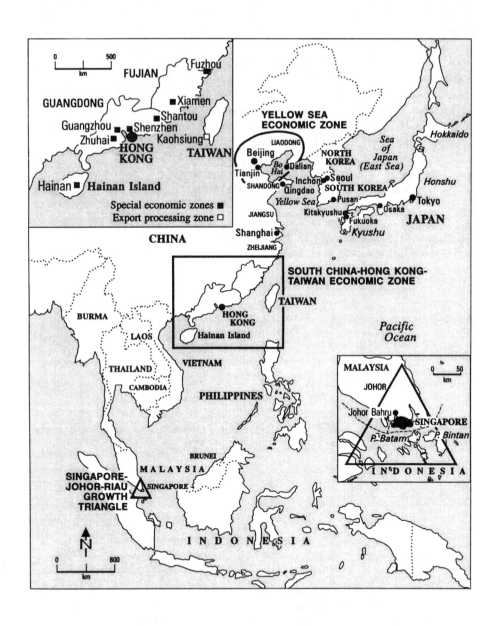

Figure 1.2
Location map of Asian Pacific Rim.

sets the foundations of industrialization policy in the wider context of national socio-institutional structures and explores the role of national enterprise structures in shaping business strategy and government policy. It provides new insight into and evidence on the patterns and geography of integrative tendencies in the global economy which are persistently transcending national boundaries.

Chapter 2 starts the exploration of the plurality of globalization by examining the theme of 'state' as context and 'organizations and enterprises' as agents. The approach adopted by Peter Rimmer is a comparative and critical analysis of the geopolitical and nationalist origins of four NIEs. This conceptual framework helps reveal state policy relating to industrialization as a powerful influence in shaping investment patterns in the Asian Pacific Rim, in the post-World War II long boom and during the restructuring era, when the rest of the world is in the grips of deregulation and privatization. An important aspect of Rimmer's approach is the way he positions developments in state policy regarding industrialization in relation to theoretical ideas prevailing in particular periods. The patently Western face to early views about industrialization is replaced by revisionist views, which while accenting the autonomy of the nation-state, still represent extensions of development models originating from the West. In spite of the succession of theoretical refinements to industrialization policy, differentiation in state and enterprise strategy has begun to be noticeable in the NIEs. Rimmer's chapter brings us to a point where we can seriously ask whether the pursuit of Western industrialization in the NIEs has been more open-ended in character than perhaps previously surmised. Rimmer's review is suggestive of indeterminacy in the adoption of industrialization models, multiple determinacy of policy formulation, heterogeneity as a feature of policies forming the context for enterprise and diversity and transmutative strategies on the part of enterprises. These tentative ideas amount to a hybridization view of globalization, by which the complexity of the Asian Pacific context can be revealed through analysis and incorporated more fully in discussion.

In Chapter 3 Jamie Peck and Yoshihiro Miyamachi consider post-1945 Japanese growth and crisis from various regulationist perspectives. Their chapter begins by questioning the validity of Anglo-American assessments of Japanese industrialization since 1945 which have generally applauded the successes of the Japanese economic growth model, without examining either its social origins or the manner in which the model has been inserted into different theoretical discourses. They set themselves a challenging task, to reveal firstly how the specificity of Japanese industrialization, manifest in state policy and state-capital-labour relations, can be better understood by application of 'regulation school' propositions, and secondly, how such an inquiry using regulationist perspectives ensues a reconsideration of the premises and methods of the theoretical systems enlisted to help with the interpretation of the Japanese experience. Their discussion, involving a gradual deconstruction of Western-rooted regulation theory and an equally gradual reconstruction of post-1945 Japanese economic history, is facilitated by a thorough airing of the Japanese case, through Western and non-Western eyes. They argue that the particular conditions emanating from state-policy and the organizational developments nurtured in the Japanese context are non-replicable and derived from very particular economic and institutional conditions. Thus, despite the attractiveness of the Japanese model as a 'different' model for growth, such hope appears to be misplaced. The distinguishing feature of a 'different' developmental history seems to be a general outcome in the latest era of capitalism and the ingredients of differing development histories are context bound and non-transferable.

Chapters 4 and 5 situate enterprise and agency in the context of actual state policies on industrialization. John McKay and Geoff Missen consider the divergent situations of Taiwan and South Korea. Their chapter illustrates that industrialization policy implicitly involves enterprise policy. Depending on the inter-cultural underpinnings of socio-economic transformation and inter-nation links, the scope and trajectory of enterprise structure can be markedly influenced. The comparison of evolution in Taiwanese and South Korean enterprise patterns and interactions is particularly illustrative because it identifies how adjustments in state industrialization policy are tied in part into perceptions about the international advantages and disadvantages of national enterprise structures. In a similar fashion, Paul Parker's outline of state-led and corporate-initiated strategies for organization of various spheres of industrial activity, within Japan and abroad, demonstrates a complexity to Japanese response to world competitive pressures. Restructuring for survival, in the emerging global economy, either by Japan in the immediate post-World War II period, or later, by Taiwan and South Korea, cannot be reduced to a discussion of the spread of industrialization models or enterprise strategy. Both Chapters 4 and 5 sketch accounts which are anchored in the accumulation and regulatory conditions of particular nation-states, and are sensitive to the wider geopolitics and geoeconomics of national differences. Indeed, these chapters, like the two earlier chapters on industrialization, contain some shifts in method which deserve mention. Three aspects are especially pertinent. First, Chapter 4, in particular attempts to demonstrate how issues such as firm size and restructuring are intertwined with the dynamics of accumulation and regulatory regimes and that regime dynamics are shaped from a complexity of influences operating at different geographic scales. Second, enquiry should not be reduced to culturally-based arguments as this approach is far too restrictive, failing to recognize or adequately state the constraining nature of capitalist investment pressures. Third, precisely because the chapters have addressed the specificity of processes associated with each nation-state, the interdependence and interpenetration interactions and outcomes in the Asian Pacific Rim can be considered. Globalization pressures are a mixture of pressures for convergence and difference.

The structural characteristics of each nation-state retain dimensions of earlier industrialization policy and enterprise behaviour. In spite of a temptation to follow the Japanese model, the very absence of a single and unambiguous understanding of the model and its particular social foundations, means that the prospects of different economies and societies becoming, more like each other, and each of them more like Japan, are probably much less likely than most would suppose. Further, the evidence from Chapters 6 and 8 introduces the growing incorporation of China into the global economy, and with this development, a potential refocusing of industrialization and enterprise strategy in many countries. In the evolving scene of the Asian Pacific Rim, the extent to which the developmental structures of each country continue as Paul Parker argues, to provide a base for future initiatives, should form the focus of any enquiry seeking to delineate the plurality of contemporary (and perhaps past) globalization.

In the economic geography literature on globalization integrative tendencies are identified as a distinguishing feature of the 1980s and 1990s. However, this interpretation does need to be empirically substantiated. Chapters 6 and 7 pursue the globalization theme by investigating, firstly, the emerging patterns of intra-regional trade and investment in the Asian Pacific Rim and, secondly, the patterning connected with Japanese industrialization, enterprise behaviour and developmental path. The chapters focus on the outcomes of investment, in the case of the general Asian Pacific Rim review by Claes Alvstam, over approximately 25 years, and in the case of the longitudinal analysis of Japan by Graham Humphrys, more than a century. Chapter 6 provides a preliminary view of dimensions of integration across territories, with increasing evidence that China is a major site in investment and trade interactions involving Asian Pacific Rim countries. This observation should not be regarded, however as a claim that this necessarily authenticates the use of the term Asian Pacific Rim. It does, nonetheless, suggest that when the nation-states of the Rim are examined with reference to their historical and geographic experiences, some sense can be made of incipient interactions amongst especially China, Japan, Taiwan and South Korea. Chapter 6 can be read alongside Chapters 2-5, as the trade and investment data are aggregate summaries of interactions which are occurring in the context of state and enterprise policy, discussed earlier in Chapters 2-5. Likewise, Chapter 7, which examines the infrastructure blueprint constrained and assisted Japanese industrialization and the rise of Japanese-originated corporates, can be usefully read as a companion piece to Chapters 3 and 5.

Globalization is a metaphor which implies interactions amongst processes operative at a variety of geographic levels. This theme is explicitly explored in Chapter 8 where the interconnections between integrative tendencies and regionalization are considered. Bringing the ideas of integration and regionalization together does reflect possible idiosyncrasy in the Anglo-American literature over the spatiality of capitalism. However, Leo van Grunsven, Shuang-Yann Wong and Won Bae Kim, attempt in a manner akin to Jamie Peck and Yosihihiro Miyamachi, to combine local knowledge and understanding with a critical view of international concepts and theories. In adopting this approach which as strong parallels to that outlined in Pieterse (1994), Chapter 8 contains insight from local learning and from extra-local or translocal learning. The wide scope of Chapter 8, from the Yellow Sea Economic Zone to the Singapore-Johor-Riau triangle, demands increasing recognition of the methodological potential of making visible inward-looking and outward-looking views of territoriality. In fact, a major argument of *The Asian Pacific Rim and Globalization* is that what is going on in the Rim countries can be usefully interpreted by sketching more fully how nation-states and sub-national areas are mixtures of wider as well as local influences. Attempting to portray the mixing of inward and outward cultures has its own transformative qualities. As was shown in Chapter 3, critical applications of theory to differing contexts can alter the conception of both what is happening and how change might be studied.

The book concludes with a short discussion by Richard Le Heron and Sam Ock Park on some of the implications of the book's findings and approaches for theoretical and policy initiatives.

Notes

1. At the International Geographical Union Congress, Sydney, Australia, in 1988, a symposium was held on the theme 'The Pacific Century'. Speakers at the symposium were Development Studies and Industrial Geography specialists. It was several years before journals normally carrying articles by industrial geographers began to contain noticeable numbers of papers combining 'industrial' and 'development' perspectives and focusing on parts of the world other than Europe or North America.
2. The special issue of *Environment and Planning A* in 1993 is one example.

References

Chiu, S. and Lui, Tai-Lok 1995: 'Hong Kong: restructuring under unorganized industrialism', in Clark, G.L. and Kim, Won Bae (eds) *Asian NIEs and the Global Economy: Industrial Restructuring and Corporate Strategy*. Baltimore, The John Hopkins University Press, in press.

Clark, G.L. and Kim, Won Bae (eds) 1995: *Asian NIEs and the Global Economy: Industrial Restructuring and Corporate Strategy*. Baltimore, The John Hopkins University Press, in press.

Cloke, P. and Goodwin, M. 1992: 'Conceptualising countryside change: from Post-Fordiam to structured coherence', *Transactions Institute of British Geographers*, 17, 321-336.

Conti, S. 1993: 'Four paradigms for the enterprise system'. Paper presented to the International Geographical Union Commission on the Organisation of Industrial Space, Tokyo, July 26-30.

Conti, S. 1994: 'Industry and environmental challenge. Focus on industrial transition in the post-socialist countries. Some interpretative suggestions.' Paper presented to the International Geographical Union Commission on the Organisation of Industrial Space, Budapest, August 16-20.

Drakakis-Smith, D. 1992: *Pacific Asia*. London, Routledge.

Fagan, R. and Le Heron, R. 1994: 'Reinterpreting the geography of accumulation: the global shift and local restructuring', *Environment and Planning D: Society and Space*, 12, 265-285.

Gibson, K. and Graham, J. 1992: 'Rethinking class in industrial geography: creating a space for an alternative politics of class', *Economic Geography*, 68(22), 109-27.

Graham, J. 1992: 'Post-Fordism as politics: the political consequences of narratives on the left', *Environment and Planning D: Society and Space*, 10, 393-410.

Ho, Kong Chong 1993: 'Industrial restructuring and the dynamics of city-state adjustments'. *Environment and Planning A*, 25, 47-62.

Ho, Kong Chong 1995: 'Manoeuvring in the middle league: industrial restructuring and firm strategy in Singapore', in Clark, G.L. and Kim, W.B. (eds) *Asian NIEs and the Global Economy: Industrial Restructuring and Corporate Strategy*. Baltimore, The John Hopkins University Press, in press.

Le Heron, R. 1993: *Globalized Agriculture Political Choice*. Oxford, Pergamon.

Le Heron, R. and van der Knaap, B. 1994a: 'Industrial spaces as contexts for human resource development', in van der Knaap, B. and Le Heron, R. (eds) *Human Resources and Industrial Spaces. A Perspective on Globalization and Localization*. Chichester, John Wiley, 3-27.

Le Heron, R. and van der Knaap, B. 1994b: 'Building blocks for an industrial policy and planning framework', in van der Knaap, B. and Le Heron, R. (eds) *Human Resources and Industrial Spaces. A Perspective on Globalization and Localization*. Chichester, John Wiley, 229-241.

Lim, Jung Duck 1993: 'Urban growth and industrial restructuring: the case of Pusan'. *Environment and Planning A*, 25, 95-109.

Lui, Tai-Lok and Chiu, S. 1993: 'Industrial restructuring and labor market adjustment under positive non-interventionism'. *Environment and Planning A*, 25, 63-79.

Markusen, A.R. and Park, Sam Ock 1993: 'The state as industrial locator and district builder: the case of Changwon, South Korea'. *Economic Geography*, 69, 157-181.

Palat, R. (ed) 1993: *Pacific-Asia and the Future of the World-System*. Westport, Connecticut, Greenwood Press.

Park, Sam Ock 1993: 'Industrial restructuring and the spatial division of labor: the case of the Seoul metropolitan region, the Republic of Korea'. *Environment and Planning A*, 25, 81-93.

Park, Sam Ock 1994: 'Industrial restructuring in the Seoul metropolitan region: major triggers and consequences'. *Environment and Planning A*, 26, 527-541.

Park, Sam Ock 1995: 'Seoul (Korea): city and suburbs', in Clark, G.L. and Kim, W.B. (eds) *Asian NIEs and the Global Economy: Industrial Restructuring and Corporate Strategy*. Baltimore, The John Hopkins University Press, in press.

Pieterse, J.N. 1994: 'Globalization as hybridisation'. *International Sociology*, 9(2), 161-184.

Scott, A. 1992: 'The Roepke Lecture in Economic Geography. The collective order of flexible production agglomerations: Lessons for local economic development policy and strategic choice', *Economic Geography*, 68(3), 219-233.

Song, Hyung-Nak 1990: *The rise of the Korean economy*. New York, Oxford University Press.

Storper, M. 1992: 'The limits to globalization: technology districts and international trade', *Economic Geography*, 68(1), 60-93.

Thrift, N. 1992: 'Muddling through: world orders and globalization', *Professional Geographer*, 44, 3-7.

Todling, F. 1994: 'Firm strategies and restructuring in a global economy'. Paper presented to the Regional Conference of the International Geographical Union, Prague, August 22-26.

2 Industrialization policy and the role of the state: Newly industrializing economies

Peter Rimmer

All of the East Asian high-growth systems have been characterized by soft or quasi-authoritarian political structures (de facto one-party systems in Japan and Taiwan, colonialism in Hong Kong, and patrimonialism of the charismatic and military varieties, respectively, in Singapore and Korea), and guided market economies (Johnson, 1986, 383).

Introduction

This chapter examines industrialization policy and the role of the state in the four Newly Industrializing Economies (NIEs) - Hong Kong, Singapore, South Korea and Taiwan - that lie athwart the sealanes from the Sea of Japan to the Straits of Malacca. Strong views have been advanced that state policy in relation to industrialization has been, and still is, a powerful influence in shaping investment patterns in the Asian Pacific Rim at a time when the rest of the world is in the grip of deregulation, reregulation and privatisation. Before these claims can be investigated the theme of the 'developmental state' as context and 'organizations' as agents needs to be explored.[1] This requires a comparative and critical analysis of the geopolitical and nationalist origins of the four NIEs.

Such an analysis is, however, problematical. A separate consideration of Hong Kong, Singapore, South Korea and Taiwan in single-economy studies overemphasizes their uniqueness. When all four economies are considered together, analysts hyper-theorise by accentuating their remarkable similarities, overstressing the homogeneity of the East Asian region, overconcentrating on their 'export-based' success, and overgeneralising the NIEs model to the rest of Pacific Asia (Jeon, 1990). The nature and strength of the state in the four economies, however, has varied over time as has their adoption of industrial policies - import-substitution industrialization (ISI); export-oriented industrialization (EOI) involving labour-intensive manufactures; and the simultaneous secondary import-substitution industrialization (SISI) and secondary export-oriented industrialization (SEOI) involving intermediate and capital goods in the former and more capital and technology-intensive products in the latter (Wong *et al.*, 1991). To overcome this dilemma and to detect some of the differences, changes in the nature of the state and the formulation of industrialization policies are examined at different dates. Ideally, 1935 should have been considered to examine the colonial roots and thousand-year histories of the NIEs, as they still influence the state and industrial policies (Amsden, 1985; Jeon, 1992). However, attention is restricted here to exploring the post-war period by concentrating on three dates - 1965, 1985 and 1995 (Table 2.1).

In 1965 the relationship between the state and organizations in the four economies under review is considered by examining ISI policies and initial expressions of EOI. In 1985 interest is centred on the role of the state and its agents in the shift from EOI policies to the SISI and SEOI policies. In 1995 attention is focused on the changing nature of the states and the divergence of their industrialization policies. An assessment is then made of the claims that the nation-state has been much more supportive than has perhaps been realised and continues to play a very formative, though changing, role. Before examining the historical experience of industrialization in the four economies the notion of the developmental state is introduced.

The developmental state

Japan's state-led, industrialization experience prompted Chalmers Johnson (1982) to fashion the concept of the 'developmental state'. It is characterised by an elite and talented economic bureaucracy, an authoritarian political regime and close state-big business relationships. The last element is critical. Not only does it highlight the state as 'context' and business organizations as 'agents' but it underlines that industrialization policy is of paramount importance. The state is involved with the protection of domestic industry, the development of strategic industries and with creating the economic structure that ensures international competitiveness. It is not merely concerned with regulating industrial activities but with actively directing the entire industrialization program in the national interest.

Having defined national strategies or development goals (e.g. high-speed growth) the state then influences, pressures or cajoles business groups as its agents to meet the goal set. Although the state owns key industries (e.g. airlines, banks and railways), the government-big business relationship is crucial. While the economy is primarily in the hands of private enterprise and operates in a competitive market, the state has the power to rationalise the detailed operations of individual enterprises in order to achieve its declared goals. Where gaps in the overall industrial structure are identified as being inimical to economic growth, the state will use a variety of mechanisms to plug them (e.g. import restrictions, subsidies and administrative guidance).

In more refined versions of the developmental state the close state-big business relationship has been seen as tantamount to a quasi-internal organization which operates in two ways: an internal capital market through which the state exerts its influence over the private sector by regulating credit through preferential lending to different sectors and industries; and a subtle parabureaucratic network of long-term ties exercised through consultations between the ruling elite and key representatives of the private sector (Shin, 1991). These collective policy-making arrangements are deemed not only to develop efficient policies but to contribute towards a superior performance, provided they are acceptable to a broad-based coalition of the dominant forces within society. The quasi-internal organization is not unlike a multidivisional firm in which the central policy-making apparatus functions as the head office and the business groups as divisions (Lee, 1992). If the multidivisional firm is an efficient organization, it follows that the internal organization forged between the state and its agents has a similar quality.

Table 2.1
Growth rates of Gross Domestic Product at market prices
(US\$ constant: 1987 = 100)

	1960-65	1965-85	1985-92
NIEs			
Hong Kong	11.7	8.5	6.5
Singapore	4.9	9.2	8.2
South Korea	6.5	9.1	9.2
Taiwan	9.8	9.1	9.1
Average	8.3	9.0	8.6
ASEAN-4			
Indonesia	1.7	6.8	6.3
Malaysia	6.8	7.2	5.2
Philippines	5.2	4.9	3.6
Thailand	7.4	7.0	10.1
Average	4.4	6.4	6.7
European Commission	5.0	3.0	2.7
Japan	9.7	5.7	4.4
North America	4.7	2.6	2.3

Note: Growth rates calculated using least squares method.
Source: International Economic Data Base, The Australian National University, and World Bank World Tables (pers. comm.).

The developmental state has been the key determinant in Japan's economic miracle. Its trappings of an elite bureaucracy and quasi-authoritarian and corporatist state have been readily identifiable in Singapore, South Korea, Taiwan and, more controversially, in Hong Kong (Johnson, 1986, Castells, 1992). They are evident in the limited opportunities for the expression of popular sentiment and the workings of state-sponsored interest groups involving both bureaucrats and corporate representatives (Wade, 1990). Industrialization policy was also of paramount importance in these economies. The classic Japanese state-big business relationship, however, was not replicated. Each state used different agents to carry out industrialization policies. These variations in industrial structure are elaborated upon by exploring the 'developmental state' as context and 'organizations' as agents in a comparative analysis of the geopolitical and nationalist origins of the four economies under review in 1965, 1985 and 1995. At each date attention is focused on prevailing geopolitics, industrialization policies and the state, and key theoretical interpretations which guided the formation and implementation of key industrialization policies.

Industrial awakening, 1965

In 1965 the so-called developmental state was in place - the Park regime in South Korea, the Kuomintang (KMT) state in Taiwan, the PAP state in independent Singapore and the colonial state in Hong Kong. Already they had embarked on an industrialization program to guarantee their legitimacy.

Geopolitics and nationalist origins

In 1965 the prime effort of the states was still focused on ensuring the survival of their economies conceived in the geopolitics of the Cold War in East Asia. South Korea had been left devastated after its battle with the communist regime of North Korea in the Korean War (1950-53) which followed the dismemberment of the former Japanese colony (1910-45). Taiwan had become the refuge of the retreating Kuomintang armies following the communist Chinese Revolution (1947-49) and the nationalization of Japanese assets in the former colony (1895-1945). Singapore had achieved self-government from Britain in 1957 but its entrepôt function had been threatened by the Indonesian Confrontation (1963) and separation from Malaysia (1963-65). Hong Kong's status as a British Colony (since 1842) had been subject to continuing review, and its entrepôt function endangered after the Chinese Revolution and the embargo on trade with China imposed by the United Nations during the Korean War. The continued survival of the four economies, however, had been guaranteed by United States' aid to South Korea and Taiwan, and by British support for Singapore and Hong Kong. Once these 'vassal states' had made their contribution to their 'sovereign states' they had considerable autonomy to conduct their rapid industrialization policies (Castells, 1992, 63). Fortuitously, their initial 'take-off' coincided with the long, post-war boom (Henderson and Appelbaum, 1992).

Industrialization and the state

By 1965 Singapore, South Korea and Taiwan had 'caught up' with Hong Kong's emphasis on EOI. Since the 1950s Hong Kong had concentrated on the export of labour-intensive products whereas the other three economies had combined ISI policies with central, authoritarian power. A politically strong state could push through domestic policies despite opposition, and implement them through government agencies and state-owned enterprises. The South Korean state had used preferential loans and access to new technologies to coopt diversified business groups (*chaebol*) to carry out its ISI policy. In Taiwan the state used state-owned banks and industries, together with American aid, to develop an import substitution policy (1953-57), enlisting private interest groups closely connected to the KMT as its agents (e.g. Far Eastern Textiles and Yue Loong Motors). Preference for trade and port development at the expense of indigenous, small-scale manufacturers had been marked in Singapore, and the PAP state's belated emphasis on ISI was stifled by its separation from Malaysia in 1965.

In 1965 the initial emphasis on import-substitution in Singapore, South Korea and Taiwan had given way to more outward-looking policies. In South Korea industrialization policy had shifted from import-substitution towards export promotion by designating light manufacturing activities as strategic industries (e.g. textiles and consumer electronics). Similarly, in Taiwan the domestic market for import-substitution products had been quickly exhausted and an outward-looking policy, initiated in 1958, had been bolstered by the opening of the Kaohsiung Export Processing Zone (1961). In Singapore an alternative to ISI policy had been formulated by the Economic Development Board to attract foreign firms - national savings, grants and subsidies being used to establish priority industries such as shipbuilding and iron and steel (Ho, 1993). In Hong Kong, however, the colonial state had been closely associated with financial and commercial sectors and remained aloof from industrial development focused on the export of labour-intensive products - wigs and plastic flowers blooming in the early 1960s.

In South Korea the change towards an outward-looking industrial policy was reinforced by regulations governing wages, and by the suppression of trade unions, and was implemented through government use of preferential credit to dictate priority industries to a small number of domestic conglomerates such as the Daewoo, Lucky-Goldstar and Samsung Groups. Taiwan's outward-looking industrialization policy was centred on plastics, synthetic fibres, and electronic components which capitalized on existing technical capabilities, low-cost female labour, and foreign investment from the United States and Japan. In Singapore preferential loans, remission of tax profits and other incentives were offered to encourage labour-intensive, export-oriented manufacturing. These outward-looking policies ran counter to the accepted western wisdom of development of the mid-1960s.

Theoretical interpretations

Underdevelopment was attributed to the failure of the market mechanism. ISI was prescribed by economic nationalists to offset the decline in primary exports. As the benefits of ISI outweighed costs once market demand was satisfied in Singapore, South Korea and Taiwan, World Bank advocates for EOI started to challenge the old orthodoxy (Chowdhury and Islam, 1993, 42-6). The new policies suggested that the blockages to development were self-imposed.

'Take-off' could be achieved by removing those internal cultural forms and social structures - including interference by the state - that distorted capital and labour markets and the acceptance of new technology. This modernization argument appeared to be vindicated by the results of integrating the four economies into the world market - a transformation discrediting dependency theorists who offered the stark choice of either persistent underdevelopment or revolution.

Export-oriented industrialization, 1985

By 1985 the once poor, East Asian developmental states had become economies specialising in the export of labour-intensive manufactures in a world economy. Their sustained hyper-growth rates of economic growth since 1965 had exceeded the average for both developing and developed market economies, earning such epithets as the 'gang of four', the 'four little tigers' or 'dragons' and, more soberly, NIEs (or the JAPNIEs to denote their status as the 'New Japans').

Geopolitics

Since the mid-1960s the development of the NIEs coincided with a decline in the economic and political hegemony exercised by the United States. Yet the United States had not only provided a market for the NIEs but had been the bulwark against the spread of communism. All of the economies had been buoyed by the Vietnam War (early 1960s-75) due to contracts for goods and services. Although there had been adverse effects from the progressive reduction of United States' aid and political support during the post-1970s recession (1973-82), the United States remained the major market (Chow and Kellman, 1993). As the influence of the United States weakened, dependence on Japanese trading companies, machinery and components, and technology increased. Progressively, the accumulation of a trading deficit with Japan more or less offset the surplus with the United States. Taiwan had a special dilemma as it had been expelled from the United Nations in 1971 and forced out of the World Bank and International Monetary Fund a decade later.

Industrialization and the state

Within this geopolitical framework the developmental states sought legitimacy by becoming the instruments of economic development. South Korea under the Park and Chun military regimes brought about high-speed EOI by presidential decree rather than by the market. The state coopted the *chaebol* as its agents and repressed labour (particularly female workers), and this was done with the broad concurrence of the upper middle class and other social groups. In Taiwan the KMT state brought about a similar result through a different set of agents - 'the triple alliance' of state technocrats, foreign investors, and domestic mainlander and comprador business groups (e.g. Taiwan Cement and Taitung). Singapore's PAP state used multinational firms as its agents to bring about EOI by guaranteeing them a cheap and docile workforce through increased female participation and imported foreign labour from Europe, Japan and the US. In Hong Kong the colonial welfare state provided the trade information and social subsidies that enhanced the flexibility and competitiveness of its architypal small businesses (Castells, 1992). After 1970 the general downturn of the world economy saw many textile, garment and electronics firms in Japan and other advanced capitalist countries relocate their low-cost manufacturing sectors to take advantage of cheap, non-unionised and predominantly female labour in the NIEs.

Throughout the 1970s the NIEs pursued industrial deepening and moved away from labour-intensive, simple manufacturing activities to a variety of more complex and skill-intensive ones. In 1973, at President Park's behest, South Korea overrode the scepticism of the Economic Planning Board and shifted from an export-promotion strategy based on labour-intensive light industries (e.g. textiles) to one of capital-intensive, heavy and chemical industries such as iron and steel, machinery, non-ferrous metals, petrochemicals and shipbuilding. Under Taiwan's 'bureaucratic capitalism' the large, state-sector enterprises owned by the mainland-dominated government and the KMT took the lead in establishing risky, capital-intensive, heavy and chemical industries (petroleum, steel and shipbuilding). This was embarked upon as part of a US$8 billion second import-substitution program comprising ten major industrial projects in the 1970s (e.g. Kaohsiung Shipyard). The myriad of Taiwanese-dominated, small and medium producers participated in Original Equipment Manufacturing (OEM) subcontracting agreements with Japanese and United States' firms in a more informal and market-conforming way. Singapore, using government revenue and local savings, had developed through its Economic Development Board an offshore production platform to attract foreign multinationals manufacturing electronic and electrical products, food and beverages, industrial machinery and chemicals, and petroleum and pharmaceuticals. Hong Kong's distinctive, family-based light-industrial enterprises had continued to thrive, helped by an influx of relatively unskilled migrants from China during the 1970s, weak unionism and the opportunities provided by China's open-door policy. Larger domestic and overseas-owned factories relied on subcontracting for the international consumer market, particularly in garment-making and electronics - radios, electronic watches and calculators (Lui and Chiu, 1993). Obviously, there had been little support for the adage that specialization on a narrow range of industries enhanced economic growth. Marked structural change had occurred in the NIEs with more than 20 per cent of GDP in each state being derived from manufacturing in 1985.

A battery of market-violating measures had been used by the elite bureaucracies to achieve export success (e.g. subsidies, preferential access to credit and investment incentives). In South Korea the *chaebol* were granted infant-industry status in new industries guaranteeing them a monopoly position and protection from overseas competition - a situation reinforced by government-controlled preferential bank credit, export subsidies, market protection, tax exemptions, infrastructural services and access to foreign loans. In Taiwan the export drive had been sustained by large-scale, public investments, including those in state-owned enterprises, together with extensive support for small and medium-size exporters. Also tax exemptions, tax holidays and unlimited repatriation of profits were used to attract foreign investments from the United States and Japan with additional incentives for locating in any of Taiwan's three export-processing zones. Singapore's industrial restructuring program was more free-market oriented, using higher wages and training schemes to propel domestic and foreign entrepreneurs towards skill-intensive activities such as electronics. Considerable control over the economy, however, was exercised through compulsory employer and employee contributions to the Central Provident Fund. Hong Kong did not have an explicit industrialization policy but facilitated development through a massive public housing program which, like Singapore, supported the reproduction of labour power. This policy made low-wage, labour-intensive activities a feasible proposition, though manufacturing declined in absolute terms after 1981 (Ho and Kueh, 1993). Government intervention, therefore, had subverted the operation of the free market in allocating resources within the NIEs (Amsden, 1989; Bradford, 1987).

By 1985 the four states had to resolve new dilemmas created by export-orientation and exposure to the recession of the early 1980s. In South Korea the industrial power of the *chaebol* and the undermining of small and medium-size firms had widened regional disparities between the prosperous Seoul-Pusan axis and the neglected west coast provinces (Chollas). Overcapacity problems in the heavy and chemical industries, coupled with higher wages and an overvalued currency, had weakened international standing of Korean exports. To compensate, a greater role for the market was incorporated in a financial and import liberalization programme. In Taiwan the incremental approach to industrial adjustment, together with greater political stability than that of South Korea led to targeting strategic industries (machinery, electronics and chemicals), and preferential financing. In Singapore the multinationals were reluctant to support the PAP state's strategy of forcing up wages to encourage upgrading of industry production processes. Consequently, a decline in investment, coupled with a weakening in international demand for key manufactured goods, triggered a severe recession (1985). Hong Kong's export-oriented manufacturers, large and small, had been successful in exploiting market conditions and special niches, but their very success had triggered quantitative restrictions and trade barriers in overseas markets. It led to the relocation of production activities in the open coastal area of South China which, in turn, gave rise to the 'outward processing trade'. In dealing with the problems stemming from EOI the corporatist devices of the developmental state proved to be inadequate; edicts and bans had to give way to softer controls.

Theoretical interpretations

In 1985 the emphasis on the developmental state had not been the dominant reason behind the East Asian ascendancy. Geographical location and culture were also given short shrift. The prevailing orthodoxy was derived from mainstream, neoclassical economics and focused on 'getting prices right'. In particular, neoclassical economists were intent on emphasising that the success of the four economies between 1965 and 1985 had been due to export-oriented production, cheap labour, an undervalued currency and real competitive markets (Chow and Kellman, 1993). At best, the state was seen as having played a minor role. World Bank proponents of the EOI strategy pointed to the successful experience of the NIEs as vindication of their arguments (Chowdry and Islam, 1993, 42-6). The Bank's strategy claimed both allocative and dynamic efficiency, and the promise of equity improvements through increased employment. Coincidentally, the strategy met the needs of United States-based multinationals to resolve the high costs of unionized labour at home and capitalize on low wages in East Asia.

There was little dispute over the roles export-orientation, cheap labour and an undervalued currency played but free markets were overemphasized and the activist role of the state underplayed. Although the laws of the market did operate, they were governed by elite bureaucrats. Indeed, the neoclassical framework is not easily reconcilable with industrial policy (or interventions in financial markets). This observation, however, did not prevent the World Bank from advocating structural reform. During the late 1980s and early 1990s the neoclassical orthodoxy faltered as the unique conjuncture of external and internal conditions that contributed to the success of the NIEs disappeared. The changed conditions also threatened the legitimacy of the developmental state that had accelerated export-oriented industrialization.

Industrial restructuring, 1995

Looking back from 1995 both the industrialization policies and power structures of the NIEs had been under scrutiny for more than a decade. Protectionism in industrialized markets, internal crises within the developmental states themselves and a structural squeeze on EOI had brought about divergent industrialization policies. These changes accompanied the decline of the United States' hegemony in the Asia Pacific region and the rise of Japan as an economic power. The latter was marked by the greater dependence of the NIEs on Japanese equipment and materials (Moon, 1991). Following revaluation of the yen in 1985, there had been a flow of investment initially from Japan but later from Hong Kong, Singapore, South Korea and Taiwan to near-NIEs in South East Asia, notably Indonesia, Malaysia and Thailand.

More complex geopolitics

Since the mid 1980s the NIEs had experienced a more complex external trading environment marked by recession, protectionist sentiments and techno-nationalism in major industrialized countries. The unfair trader label accorded Japan, and resultant retaliatory measures sanctioned under the Super 301 legislation[2], had been extended to the NIEs (particularly to force South Korea and Taiwan to open up their protected agricultural markets). Foreign pressure over unfair trade practices, especially from the United States, resulted in currency revaluation - first in Japan, following the Plaza Accord of 1985, and then in South Korea and Taiwan to increase the cost of their exports. Subsequently, the pressure led to a marked reduction in export subsidies and import liberalization, particularly in South Korea and Taiwan (though South Korea kept its controls on agriculture and blanket import ban on products from Japan). The key to changing the relationship between the state and society, however, was financial liberalization which was marked, though still incomplete, in both South Korea and Taiwan (Woo, 1991). More subtle forms of state control - informal import barriers, indirect export promotion and enforcement of intellectual property rights - still remained and were likely to be the source of future tensions (Smith, 1994, 18).

Mounting competition for world markets and the development of supra-regional trading blocs (e.g. EC and NAFTA) have forced the NIEs to search for new markets in China, Russia and eastern Europe. The thaw has been sufficient to stimulate regional economic integration by involving the NIEs in schemes with provinces in China (e.g. South Korea with Shandong, Taiwan with Fujian, and Hong Kong with Guandong). This search for new markets, however, was aggravated by competition from ASEAN and China in labour-intensive industries. International pressure to open up markets, coupled with the privatization of state enterprises and banks, had deprived the state of a set of tools for guiding the economy following the breakdown of many, but not all, Cold War structures (Kim and Huang, 1991).

Industrialization and the state

Before discussing industrialization policies in the light of the new geopolitical situation, it is pertinent to note that the developmental states had been forced to lessen their authoritarian styles. These changes were designed to meet the demands arising from polarised struggles over the distribution of income and the direction of development (e.g. labour movements and grass roots environmental movements). In South Korea recurrent worker-farmer-student unrest between 1987 and 1990 had not only made collective bargaining difficult but forced changes in the military-technocratic relationship with big business. In particular, the greater bargaining power of the *chaebol* through control over mergers in financial sectors and real estate speculation had led to their alienation from the general populace. In Taiwan the effective authority of the KMT party apparatus had been reduced following the end of martial law in 1987 which had forbidden free political association. Paradoxically, the KMT party was rejuvenated under native Taiwanese leadership. Conversely Singapore had retained its authoritarian PAP state despite industrialization and embourgeoisment of its population (Rodan, 1993). In Hong Kong limited elections had been introduced. Thus, to maintain their legitimacy, the developmental states have undergone a transition towards more open or more broadly-based democratic processes (Bello and Rosenfeld, 1992). Further, they committed heavy infrastructural investment to overcome the adverse aspects of accelerated growth - pollution, congestion and housing.

These political shifts had their roots in economic changes. The NIEs had progressively lost their competitive edge due to their low labour and production costs and waning attraction to foreign investors. Higher production costs had led to the relocation of labour-intensive activities (e.g. electronics components) from the NIEs to off-shore locations, particularly in ASEAN and China, as part of a new international division of labour (Herschede, 1991). Domestic shortages of labour had been met by the introduction of lower-paid guest workers. These new challenges were posed by the complexities of their economies, and difficulties in adapting to the demands of more openness and better integration into the world economy.

As industrialization policies fashioned during the period of rapid growth had differed an identical approach was not anticipated. South Korea's actions had shifted to supporting small and medium-size industries to counter the past preoccupation with the *chaebol* and bailing out sunset industries. Heavily entrenched in shipbuilding and motor car manufacture, the *chaebol* had increased degrees of freedom to operate independently of the state. Taiwan, faced with the 'hollowing out' of its industrial base, had intervened to ensure its self sufficiency for defence purposes. Singapore diversified its traditional industrialization policy of favouring inward foreign investment from multinational corporations in chemicals and electronics. A new, more outward-oriented strategy for facilitating overseas investment by its own local firms either alone or in joint ventures with foreign groups was developed. China and Vietnam were prime targets of these initiatives. Hong Kong had continued its labour-intensive manufacturing. It had been slow to upgrade its production technology and shift to higher-value products. Many of its manufacturers, however, had relocated factories across the border, especially in the Pearl River Delta, where basic wage rates and land costs were considerably cheaper. Although the four economies were grouped together as NIEs, they were highly competitive with one another in seeking foreign investment, technology and overseas markets.

Each economy has developed its own areas of specialization. In the computer industry, for example, South Korea concentrated on semi-conductors, Taiwan on monitors, Singapore on hard disk drives and Hong Kong on peripherals (Simon, 1994). All NIEs, however, wanted to move their economies away from labour-intensive manufacturing towards more skilled, higher-value-added production. South Korea had shifted to electronics and machinery, though it maintained an interest in motor vehicles and shipbuilding as the leading edges of its industrialization program. Unlike Taiwan, South Korea adopted a less activist approach to high-technology (Smith, 1994). Taiwan's high-technology industrialization policy was centred on biotechnology, electro-optics, machinery and precision instruments, and environmental technology industries. Improvements to the quality of these products and productivity of its workforce were targeted to remain attractive to its United States, and possible Japanese, co-partners. Singapore had sought to eliminate its few remaining labour-intensive activities so as to concentrate on being a producer of higher-value-added technology-based industries. These emphasised R&D, product design and process development, creation of critical components and core products, adoption of highly sophisticated and automated manufactured products and training of highly skilled workers (Régnier, 1993, 307). In Hong Kong, electronics has superseded garments as the major activity in the Colony's 'hollowed-out' manufacturing base. The general lack of skilled scientists and engineers in the NIEs, however, led to questioning of their ability to sustain high-tech manufacturing (e.g. video-disc players and artificial computer intelligence) as they faced the prospect of accelerated deindustrialization.

The picking of high-tech winners has, to some extent, eluded the NIEs. South Korea's development of high-tech activities had been limited by the failure of the *chaebol* to foster technological innovations independent of Japan and the United States in order to boost exports of microelectronics and motor cars. Taiwan had created an integrated motor vehicle industry and self-sustaining high-tech industry but found it was extremely difficult to shift towards high-technology commodities. Symbolically, the science and industrial park at Hsinchu (established 1980) had replaced the Kaohsiung EPZ in importance, but most manufacturers were still assembling imported high-technology components. Singapore's failure to attract more than showcase R&D facilities (e.g. Apple and Matsushita) and other high-tech investments led to plans for developing it as South East Asia's financial hub and regional centre for multinationals. High technology, therefore, had not proved to be a panacea for the NIEs because it had increased their dependence on Japanese technology.

All economies had been affected by the increased significance of the services sector (e.g. communications, retailing, banking, media and construction). South Korea had an advantage in construction services (cf. Singapore in data processing and Hong Kong in film making). Taiwan had sought a more broadly-based services sector by relaxing state regulatory controls over banking, aiming specifically at becoming a regional financial centre so as to capitalise on any opportunities stemming from the reversion of Hong Kong to China (Rimmer, 1994). Singapore had become a regional operation centre and had attracted heavy commitments in exhibition, leisure and services - especially in logistics (e.g. DHL Federal Express, TNT and United Parcel Services). A concerted effort had been made to develop its telecommunications facilities. Deindustrialized Hong Kong, however, had the most highly developed service sector among the four economies which accounted for 70 per cent of its GDP and 60 per cent of its employment. Trading, financial and business services were of pivotal importance (Ho and Kueh, 1993; Stewart, 1993, 355).

The NIEs had found restructuring difficult, as a lengthy period of government direction and control had, in varying degrees, discouraged individual initiatives and participation in economic activities. Belatedly, South Korea had abandoned direct intervention and industry-specific incentives for an increased reliance on the market and a shift in emphasis to technology-intensive industries and from large *chaebol* to small and medium-size enterprises. These measures were intended to overcome 'the legacy of distorted credit markets, overly-indebted firms and a high concentration of industrial power' (Smith, 1994, 1). Taiwan's industry still remained dependent on cheap labour as its high-tech future had proved illusory, and structural transformation had been stymied by the failure of Japan and the United States to transfer advanced technologies to permit automation. The reaction has been to transfer capital to low-wage countries. Singapore's élitist government approach, together with an emphasis on multinationals, had been the prime cause of the marginalization of small entrepreneurs rather than any shortage of entrepreneurial spirit. Hong Kong had been less inhibited than its counterparts as its economic prospects and the resolution of its problems had been dictated by the China factor rather than the colonial state. Indeed, China's economic performance and its political relations, particularly its Most Favored Nation (MFN) status with the United States was of crucial importance to Hong Kong.

By 1995 the economic policies of the NIEs had diverged to meet the challenges of protectionism, internal political crises and structural change brought about by high levels of capital accumulation and development of a strong bourgeoisie. They were still subject, however, to continuing political vagaries and vicissitudes. South Korea's rapprochement with North Korea had still to be realised. Further, a redistribution of income and greater use of the domestic market as an 'engine of growth' had still to be achieved. Taiwan had elements in domestic politics asserting its own national identity. Paradoxically, Taiwan had become increasingly dependent on its economic interactions with the Mainland to the extent that it was regarded, with China and Hong Kong, as part of a Greater China Economic Community. Singapore had become a key regional operations centre for South East Asia but had made few concessions to greater political liberalization and democratization. Hong Kong's economy after integration with China in 1997 may be reduced in the most adverse scenario to an outpost for trading, banking, shipping, telecommunications and tourist services (Ho and Kueh, 1993). While the NIEs had been successful in maintaining economic growth their achievements could be undermined by sudden geopolitical changes, particularly those involving China. In seeking an alternative program, attention had to be refocused on their domestic markets.

Theoretical interpretations

By 1995 the notion of the state as the 'engine of growth' had been highlighted in the revisionist literature on the East Asian NIEs which treated capital accumulation as the principal force for economic growth (Amsden, 1985, 1989; Castells, 1992; Deyo, 1987; Gold, 1986; Jones and SaKong, 1980; Skocpol, 1985; Wade 1990). In short, the NIEs simply did not conform to the neoclassical model. To some extent this has been acknowledged by neoclassical economists whose position had metamorphosed by 1995 into the full-blown neoclassical political economy of the New Right. In this new orthodoxy, however, the role of the state has been prescribed to areas where it has a distinct advantage over the private sector. Apart from establishing a stable and predictable macroeconomic environment through fiscal, monetary and exchange-rate policies, the state's role was confined to intervention in cases of proven market failure. When that occurred, lump sum taxes and subsidies and incentives could be used to reestablish the private market. The state was confined to the provision of 'pure' public goods (e.g. public infrastructure and defence). If the state exceeded these limits 'government failure' was deemed to have occurred. The central argument was that state intervention to create socially-desirable industries generated monopoly rents. These are captured by narrowly based, rent-seeking coalitions. Each successive intervention created additional monopoly rents and retarded economic development. In a bid to counter the regressive role of the state in economic development, the New Right sought to rely on a market-driven private sector to mobilize and allocate resources to growth-promoting activities. This strategy was supported by devising simple institutional arrangements for minimising government failure.

There were abundant facts on the NIEs that fitted neoclassical, political economy theory, and the notion of 'government failure' in particular. The inference that 'market failure' had been rare, however, was unwarranted (Chowdhury and Islam, 1993, 53). If both types of failure were possible the importance of the role of the state in industrialization policy had to be conceded. Indeed, much government intervention exceeded the theory's desired norms, and favoured outcomes that would not have occurred under free market conditions. What had been distinctive was not the state's marked impact on the economy but its control over its direction by identifying and supporting particular industrial goals (Wade, 1990). Admittedly, this did not mean the state was the 'engine of growth' but it at least conceded it could be the 'handmaiden of growth'. The admission of a link between governance and economic development led to enunciation of the World Bank's (IBRD, 1993, 4, 82-6) eclectic 'market friendly' strategy (cf. Amsden, 1993). In this approach the state was accorded a reduced role in production where markets were effective but a greater role where they were ineffective (e.g. investments in people and maintenance of a competitive environment for enterprise). According to the World Bank, the importance of selective interventions in the NIEs were not, on balance, as irrelevant as argued by neoclassical critics, or as important as suggested by their statist proponents.

Developmental state revisited

In studying industrialization policy in the NIEs this Chapter has given prominence to the developmental state. A basic premise was that the state played a pivotal role for these latecomers to industrialization by stimulating and restructuring their developing economies (Table 2.2). State-led industrialization was possible where the state dominated the relationships with its economic (and social) agents. At any given point in industrialization, state power shapes the policy response to internal forces and external pressures. The policy outcomes at a given time, however, affected state power at subsequent dates and limited or created opportunities for making new policy choices (Kim and Huang, 1991).

These propositions were explored by considering the role of the state and industrialization policy in the four economies in 1965, 1985 and 1995. The time dimension was inserted to track changes in the state-business relationship within historical contexts so as to better understand the impacts of the state-business relationship on industrialization policy over time. In 1965 the strength and relative autonomy of each state had risen and led to the implementation of ISI policies in Singapore, South Korea and Taiwan before they were put on a par with Hong Kong's outward-looking export-oriented policies. By 1985 the further rise in the state's strength had coincided with a shift in the nature of state-led EOI from labour-intensive manufacturing to SISI and SEOI - a shift marked by changes in the ranks of agents doing the state's bidding. By 1995 there were signs that the strength of the state had weakened as a result of demands for greater democracy from an affluent and educated middle class (Wade, 1990). Inevitably, this weakening of state power raises questions as to the state's capability in handling conflicts between those involved in international capital and those dependent on domestic industry. States have grappled with this conflict by incorporating labour into the decision-making equation.

These broad generalizations obscure very real differences in the state-business relationships within the four economies (Chu, 1989). Only South Korea approximated the government-big business relationship (Korea Inc.) which used selective credit to realise its aims and functioned as an internal market. The policy network between the state and private firms in Taiwan had been less well-developed as it relied more on public enterprises and agencies. The subtle and informal networks, however, were not readily observable (Wade, 1990, 295). Singapore, unlike Taiwan, had relied on the state-multinational connection. In Hong Kong the hidden link between the state and the coalition of peak, private-economic organisations belied its image of a free market economy. These state-business relationships have contributed to the extraordinary growth of the four economies by twinning economic cooperation and vigorous competition under particular historical and institutional conditions (i.e. when it was possible to insulate a country's financial markets from the outside world). Competition was achieved through contests in which the élite bureaucracies were neutral umpires and success was determined by the volume of exports - the rewards were government favours (IBRD, 1993, 366-7).

Yet there is no empirical evidence that the multidivisional firm or the state-business analogue offered a superior economic performance (Chowdhury and Islam, 1993). Invariably, the state has been cast as an omniscient and monolithic entity and the private sector as a passive player. Little credence has been given to the possibility of a fragmented state - the outcome of inter- and intra-bureaucratic rivalry - negotiating with a powerful private sector. Foreign trade embodied in the EOI policies was assumed to have no connection with state autonomy, though domestic economic fortunes were tied to export growth. Further, EOI should not be correlated with authoritarianism, and state autonomy with economic growth Clearly, authoritarianism could occur under a variety of institutional arrangements and was unrelated to a particular phase of development (Robison, *et al.*, 1993). Autonomy is a prerequisite for development but requires an economic will to be developmentalist, and a particular policy orientation to guide the direction of development (Jeon, 1990, 353).

Table 2.2
Forms of state intervention in Hong Kong, Singapore, South Korea and Taiwan, c1960-1990

	Hong Kong	Singapore	South Korea	Taiwan
Directed companies into higher-value-added, higher wage and more technology-intensive forms of production using system of constraints, such as controlling credit through the banking system and/or rigging prices.		*	*	*
Legislated to discourage short term or speculative domestic and overseas investment and thus indirectly ensuring its flow into manufacturing.			*	*
Created industrial sectors through state enterprises or supply of credit and financial guarantees to private companies.		*	*	*
Created and refined technologies through government R&D and transferred them to private sector without development costs.		*	*	*
Protected domestic markets - across the board or (more recently) specific products.			*	*
Monitored world markets for export opportunities to identify new demand and encourage firms to meet them.			*	*
Used price controls to discourage domestic market exploitation in circumstances of near-monopolistic supply and created cartels to contain the price of basic foodstuffs.	*		*	
Used state ownership of land as budgetary mechanism to allow delivery of extensive welfare system while maintaining low corporate and personal taxation and negligible foreign indebtedness.	*			
Provided public housing to subsidise wages and legitimise autocratic regimes.	*	*		
Subjected companies receiving state-guaranteed credits to performance standards.			*	

Source: Based on Henderson and Appelbaum, 1992, 21-22.

32

Such qualifications make it difficult to draw unequivocal conclusions about industrialization policy and the role of the state in the NIEs. At best, the state provided the context for rapid economic growth by undertaking the necessary reforms in industrialization policy and supplying the required infrastructure. The industry-specific initiatives undertaken by the state were, however, decidedly more risky. As the importance of élite bureaucracies, authoritarianism and government-big business relations has been questioned, the usefulness of the developmental state itself is at stake. Inevitably, it is a finite model. Even if the developmental (or corporatist) tag is jettisoned, the state has continued to play a formative, if changing, role with its agents.

These reservations on the state's role in industrialization policy within the NIEs makes it difficult to distil lessons for aspiring industrializing countries in Southeast Asia - Indonesia, Malaysia and Thailand (Hewison *et al.*, 1993). Contrary to the NIEs strongly developed institutional mechanisms and inexcessive costs of intervention, there is little empirical evidence that selective interventions - forced savings, tax policies for specific investments, sharing risk, restricting capital outflow and repressing interest rates - have been as prominent or as successful in South East Asia's industrializing countries (IBRD, 1993, 242). Quite simply, the latter lack the capacity to administer and deliver the specific interventions that characterised the developmental states in the 1960s and 1970s. As witnessed by the Hicom fiasco of the 1980s, Malaysia's New Economic Policy (launched 1971) has not been conspicuously successful. Similarly, there is little evidence that state-led industrialization has been profitable for business in Indonesia. Since the mid 1980s the emphasis has been on the macro record - devaluation, customs reform and economic incentives - whereas the stress at the micro, industry-specific level has been to lessen rather than raise government intervention (Hill, 1993). A parallel can be drawn with Thailand where a tight macro economic policy has been matched by an absence of control (and chaos) at the micro-level. These experiences in South East Asia, however, may have more relevance outside the region than those in the NIEs where government intervention has resulted in higher and more equitable growth than would otherwise have occurred.

Notes

1. According to Robison *et al.*, (1993, 3) the *state* is an amalgam of social, political and economic elements organised in a particular way (i.e. it is an expression of power rather than a set of functions or groups of actors). State power (i.e. a complex set of dynamic social relationships) shapes the *state apparatus* - the coercive, judicial and bureaucratic arms of the state. The term *regime* is reserved for a particular type of state apparatus (e.g. authoritarian corporatist, dictatorship, liberal democracy). *Government* comprises the legislative and executive branches of the state apparatus and those officials, parties and individuals who control them. Thus the government can fall and the

state and regime remain stable. Further, the regime can be changed to maintain the state and social order (e.g. democratization in Korea under Roh Tae Woo).

2. The 'Super 301' clause was embodied in the 1988 Omnibus Trade and Competitiveness Act which sought to achieve reciprocal access to countries which the United States defined as unfairly restricted markets.

Acknowledgements

Yvonne Byron, James Cotton, Sandra Davenport, Hal Hill and Peter Van Dierman helped locate references, and Barbara Banks read the text and made helpful suggestions. Jane Lindsay supplied the data from the International Economic Data Bank at the Australian National University.

References

Amsden, A. 1985: 'The state and Taiwan's economic development', in Evans, P. B., Rueschemeyer, D. and Skocpol, T. (eds) *Bringing the State Back in*. Cambridge, Cambridge University Press, 78-106.

Amsden, A. 1989: *Asia's Next Giant: South Korea and Late Industrialization*. New York, Oxford University Press.

Amsden, A. 1993: 'Asia's industrial revolution'. *Dissent*, Summer, 324-32.

Bello, W. and Rosenfeld, S. 1992: *Dragons in Distress: Asia's Miracle Economies in Crisis*. London, Penguin, (first published 1990).

Bradford Jr, C. I. 1987: 'NICs and the next-tier NICs as transitional economies', in Bradford Jr, C. I. and Branson, W. H. (eds) *Trade and Structural Change in Pacific Asia*. Chicago, University of Chicago Press, 173-204.

Castells, M. 1992: 'Four Asian tigers with a dragon head: A comparative analysis of the state, economy, and society on the Asian Pacific Rim', in Appelbaum, R. P. and Henderson, J. (eds) *States and Development in the Asian Pacific Rim*. Newbury Park, Sage Publications, 33-70.

Chow, P. C. Y. and Kellman, M. H. 1993: *Trade - the Engine of Growth in East Asia*. New York, Oxford.

Chowdhury, A. and Islam, I. 1993: *The Newly Industrialising Economies of East Asia*. London and New York, Routledge.

Chu, Yun-han 1989: 'State structure and economic adjustment of the East Asian newly industrializing countries'. *International Organization*, 43(4), 647-72.

Deyo, F. C. 1987: 'Introduction', in Deyo, F. C. (ed) *The New Political Economy of the New Asian Industrialism*. Ithaca and London, Cornell University Press, 11-22.

Gold, T. B. 1986: *State and Society in the Taiwan Miracle*. Armonk NY, M. E. Sharpe.

Henderson, J. and Appelbaum, R. P. 1992: 'Situating the state in the East Asian development process', in Appelbaum, R. P. and Henderson, J. (eds) *States and Development in the Asian Pacific Rim.* Newbury Park, Sage Publications, 1-26.

Herschede, F. 1991: 'Competition among ASEAN, China and the East Asian NICs: A shift-share analysis'. *ASEAN Economic Bulletin*, 7(3), 290-305.

Hewison, J., Rodan G. and Robison, R. 1993: 'Introduction: Changing forms of state power in Southeast Asia', in Hewison, K., Rodan, G. and Robison, R. (eds) *Southeast Asia in the 1990s: Authoritarianism, Democracy and Capitalism.* Sydney, Allen and Unwin, 2-8.

Hill, H. 1993: "Indonesia', Special Issue on Economic Liberalisation: Its Meaning and Consequences'. *Asian Studies Review: Journal of the Asian Studies Association of Australia*, 17(2), 80-93.

Ho, K. C. 1993: 'Industrial restructuring and the dynamics of city-state adjustments'. *Environment and Planning A*, 25, 47-62.

Ho, Y. P. and Kueh, Y. T. 1993: 'Whither Hong Kong in an open-door reforming Chinese economy?' *The Pacific Review*, 6(4), 333-52.

IBRD [International Bank for Reconstruction and Development] 1993: *The East Asian Miracle: Economic Growth and Public Policy: A World Bank Policy Research Report.* Washington, The World Bank.

Jeon, Jei-guk 1990: 'The political economy of microvariation in East Asian development patterning: a comparative study of Korea, Taiwan, Singapore and Thailand'. PhD Thesis, The Ohio State University, Ann Arbor, UMI Dissertation Services.

Jeon, Jei-guk 1992: 'The origins of Northeast Asian NICs in retrospect: The colonial political economy in Korea and Taiwan'. *Asian Perspective*, 16(1), 71-101.

Johnson, C. 1982: *MITI and the Japanese Miracle: The Growth of Industrial Policy, 1925-1975.* Stanford, Stanford University Press.

Johnson, C. 1986: 'The nonsocialist NICs: East Asia', in Comisson, E. and Tyson, L. D'A. (eds) *Power, Purpose, and Collective Choice: Economic Strategy in Socialist States.* Ithaca and London, Cornell University Press, 381-422.

Jones, L. P. and SaKong, Il 1980: *Government, Business, and Entrepreneurship in Economic Development: The Korean Case.* Cambridge MA and London, Harvard University Press.

Kim, Jeong-hyun and Huang, Chi 1991: 'Dynamics of state strength and policy choices: a case study of South Korea and Taiwan'. *Pacific Focus*, 6(2), 83-108.

Lee, C. H. 1992: 'The government financial system, and large private enterprises in the economic development of South Korea'. *World Development*, 20(2), 187-97.

Lui, T. L. and Chiu, S. 1993: 'Industrial restructuring and labour-market adjustment under positive interventionism: the case of Hong Kong'. *Environment and Planning A*, 25, 63-79.

Moon, Chung-in 1991: 'Managing regional challenges: Japan, the East Asian NICs and new patterns of rivalry'. *Pacific Focus*, 6(2), 23-47.

35

Régnier, P. 1993: 'Spreading Singapore's wings worldwide: A review of traditional and new investment strategies'. *The Pacific Review*, 6(4), 305-12.

Rimmer, P. J. 1994: 'Taiwan's future as a regional transport hub', in Klintworth, G. (ed) *Taiwan in the Asia-Pacific in the 1990s*. Sydney, Allen & Unwin, 217-43.

Robison, R., Hewison, K. and Rodan, G. 1993: 'Political power in industrialising capitalist societies: Theoretical approaches', in Hewison, K., Rodan, G. and Robison, R. (eds) *Southeast Asia in the 1990s: Authoritarianism, Democracy and Capitalism*. Sydney, Allen and Unwin, 9-38.

Rodan, G. 1993: 'Preserving the one-party state in contemporary Singapore', in Hewison, K., Rodan, G. and Robison, R. (eds) *Southeast Asia in the 1990s: Authoritarianism, Democracy and Capitalism*. Sydney, Allen and Unwin, 77-108.

Skocpol, T. 1985: 'Bringing the state back in: Strategies of analysis in current research', in Evans, P.B., Rueschemeyer, D. and Skocpol, T. (eds) *Bringing the State Back in*. Cambridge, Cambridge University Press, 3-37.

Shin, R. W. 1991: 'The role of industrial policy agents: a study of Korean intermediate organization as a policy network'. *Pacific Focus*, 6(2), 49-64.

Simon, D. F. 1994: 'The orbital mechanics of Taiwan's technological development: an examination of the 'gravitational' pushes and pulls', in Klintworth, G. (ed) *Taiwan in the Asia-Pacific in the 1990s*. Sydney, Allen & Unwin, 195-216.

Smith, H. 1994: 'Korea's industry policy during the 1980s'. *Pacific Economic Papers No. 229*. Canberra, Australia-Japan Research Centre.

Stewart, S. 1993: 'Unchaining the invisible giant: The growing trade in services in Asia and the Pacific'. *The Pacific Review*, 6(4), 353-63.

Wade, R. 1990: *Governing the Market: Economic Theory and the Role of Government in East Asian Industrialization*. Princeton, Princeton University Press.

Wong, T. Y. C., Chen, E. K. Y. and Nyaw, Mee-Kau. 1991: 'The future of industrial trade development in the Asian Pacific: An overview', in Chen, E. K. Y., Nyaw, Mee-kau. and Wong, T. Y. C. (eds) *Industrial and Trade Development in Hong Kong*. Hong Kong, Centre of Asian Studies, University of Hong Kong, ix-xxxiii.

Woo, Jung-en. 1991: *Race to the Swift: State and Finance in Korean Industrialization*. New York, Columbia University Press.

3 Reinterpreting the 'Japanese miracle': Regulationist perspectives on post-1945 Japanese growth and crisis

Jamie Peck and Yoshihiro Miyamachi

Since the breakdown of the golden age of Atlantic Fordism, western academic commentators, policy-makers and business ideologues have been scanning the globe for alternative post-Fordist growth models. This search has often led them to Japan. The Japanese model's attraction is partly due to its export strength and continuing growth capacity, but partly also to its very *difference*. The model appears to epitomise a distinctly *non*-Fordist growth pattern, based on flexible manufacturing and the employment of multiskilled workers. As a result the model has been elevated to a unique position within post-Fordist discourses. Japanese techniques and practices, it has appeared, may provide a way out of the crisis of Fordism.

In the expectation that what is *different* must be the thing to emulate, attempts have been made to decant the desirable features of the Japanese model, to bottle them and export them to the West. Perhaps the most potent of these elixirs, sold under the brand name of 'flexible specialization', offers the promise of economic rejuvenation on the basis of the new-found secret ingredient, *flexibility* (Friedman, 1988; Piore and Sabel, 1984). As the extracted essence of Japanese production, flexibility is endowed with remarkable restorative qualities. Japanese-style flexibility would, we were promised, soothe the aching limbs of 'rigid' Fordism. As Lipietz, (1992a, 321) has, however, observed:

> Taking examples from Japan ... the flexible specialisation thesis reduces ... debates about post-Fordism to the identification of a single development path which is technologically determined by the introduction of new flexible machines and appears as a mere inversion of the Fordist industrial paradigm: flexible instead of rigid social legislation, and workers' involvement instead of direct control. The second aspect (which is obviously progressive) is used to justify concession-making on the first aspect.

This chapter argues that the essence of Japanese competitive success is less easy to extract, that it is deeply embedded in the social institutions of Japanese capitalism, and that it cannot be siphoned off into generic models of flexible specialization. Such models foster the impression that Japanese techniques - and successes - can be unproblematically emulated in other places, that the 'secret' is basically a technological one and therefore a transplantable one. While this 'secret' may seem to lie on the factory floor, it is in fact intricately and essentially connected to the wider institutional and social fabric. Abstracted from this context, 'Japanese techniques' take on different meanings and have different effects.

An *explanation* of the Japanese model, then, requires more than an essentialist reading of the Japanese factory, but an integrated and holistic analysis of the pattern of Japanese accumulation. This chapter moves some way towards this goal by examining regulationist analyses of Japan. The methodological framework of regulation theory, we argue, provides a way of moving beyond the limited reach of production-centred accounts of the 'Japanese miracle', because critical emphasis is placed upon macro-economic relations, class struggles and the complex of institutional forms and social mores captured in the French notion of *régulation*. Regulationist analyses offer the promise of contextualising - socially and institutionally - the 'Japanese miracle', while being less prone to partial and/or celebratory accounts. According to the Japanese regulationist Yamada, the approach provides a basis for moving beyond those

> one-sided view[s] of the Japanese model in which we either admire its efficiency or deplore its unfairness. Instead, we must explore the particular socio-economic mechanisms of *régulation* through which these two aspects [efficiency and unfairness] are connected. [The key regulatory question is:] What is it that connects efficiency and injustice in Japanese capitalism? (1991, 172).

Understanding the Japanese development path, then, means investigating simultaneously the ways in which its 'dark side' (of societal segmentation) and its 'light side' (of competitive strength) are connected.

Yet while regulationist analyses may point the way to a more nuanced and integrative interpretation of the Japanese experience, confrontation with the Japanese model also raises critical questions about the architecture of regulation theory itself. In particular, the Japanese experience calls into question some of the received regulationist thinking on the nature of Fordist growth and crisis. For the French regulationist Coriat (1992), analysis of the Japanese model meant 'turning thinking on its head'. These issues are addressed explicitly in the conclusion to the chapter. We begin by outlining the regulation approach, moving on to examine the nature and dynamics of Japanese growth, both before and after the 1970s crisis. Subsequently, the chapter focuses on the interpretation of the crisis itself, and the important issue of forms of social regulation.

The regulation approach

Regulation theory provides a conceptual framework for understanding processes of capitalist growth, crisis and reproduction. It focuses on relationships, couched largely at the macro-economic level, between the process of accumulation and the ensemble of institutional forms and practices which together comprise a mode of social regulation (MSR). Systems of accumulation and MSRs which are structurally coupled together in a stable fashion are the basis for what regulationists term *regimes of accumulation*. These refer to particular capitalist development paths - defined in terms of historical phases and patterns of development - which are characterised by economic growth and under which (immanent) crisis tendencies are contained, mediated, or at least postponed. MSRs represent temporary institutional 'fixes'; they do not neutralise crisis tendencies completely. Eventually, the ability of a MSR to mediate, accommodate and absorb crisis tendencies is exceeded and the regime of accumulation breaks down.

Regulation theorists focus on the material, historical, geographical and - perhaps above all - *institutional* specificities of capitalist development. They confront the paradox that that crises may not *only* be way-stations on the path of terminal decline, but that - in terms of the actualities of capitalist development - they may also play a rejuvenating role, literally re-structuring the accumulation process. Two forms of crisis are central to the theory:

- *Conjunctural* crises may be resolved within individual regimes but usually require some modification of the MSR, say, in the form of reform of state policies or shifts in the spatial organization of the economy;
- *Structural* crises are terminal for regimes, reflecting the 'exhaustion' of the prevailing MSR; such crises can only be resolved through the establishment of a new structural coupling between an MSR and the accumulation system, a process conditioned by theoretically-indeterminate class struggles.

Central to the process of crisis containment, for regulation theorists, is the role played by the MSR, which defines 'the social context in which expanded economic reproduction occurs' (Jessop, 1992b, 50). MSRs are not determined functionally by the requirements of the accumulation process. Lipietz (1987, 15) maintains that these are the result of '*chance discoveries* made in the course of human struggles'. The complex processes through which MSRs are formed around particular accumulation trajectories, then, is in essence a political process, one which is reducible neither to some functionalist response to the 'needs of capital', nor to conscious action on the part of capitalist states. While somewhat ill-specified, the MSR defines what is perhaps the central thrust of the regulationist project. It defines the means by which particular forms of capitalist development are sustained, by which crisis tendencies are (temporarily) contained, and by which the historical and geographical particularities of the accumulation process are captured within the framework of the theory. According to Jessop (1992b), the MSR provides the most sound basis on which a regime of accumulation should be defined (rather than the labour process or the pattern of accumulation).

The tools of regulationist analysis were forged through studies of the golden age of (Atlantic) Fordism and to a certain extent have been shaped by these antecedents.

The Fordist regime of accumulation, dominant in north America and in much of northern Europe around 1945-75 was based on the harmonious coupling of an *intensive* accumulation system with a *monopolistic* MSR. Under the intensive accumulation system, technical change within the labour process provided the basis for substantial productivity gains, which in turn permitted real incomes to rise and a mass market for consumer goods to emerge. The propulsive industries of Fordism - producing cars, consumer durables and capital equipment - combined flow-line production methods with deskilled labour utilisation, serving mass markets with standardised, high-volume products. Both productive capacity and the labour force were utilised fully, while aggregate demand and profit levels remained relatively stable. Alongside this accumulation system, a monopolistic MSR was organised around the Keynesian welfare-state and a stable international monetary order, within which the United States performed the role of global hegemon. Underwritten by and stabilized by the Keynesian welfare-state, the essence of the 'Fordist equation' was according to Altvater (1992) the virtuous relationship between productivity growth (driven by technological change and Taylorist labour process reforms) and rising real wages (the foundations upon which mass consumer markets were constructed).

In the late 1960s, this Fordist growth pattern began to falter, as rates of productivity growth and capital investment slowed, and as worker resistance to the dehumanising effects of Taylorism spread. In this sense, the crisis of Fordism was an 'internal' one - resulting from the growth regime's internal contradictions - but it was exacerbated by a series of 'external' shocks. For Lipietz (1987), the most significant of these exogenous shocks was the rise of Japanese competition (which eroded market shares and destabilised monopoly producers), the oil crises (which as well as increasing costs contributed to the unfolding stagflationary crisis of the Keynesian welfare-state), and rising international indebtedness (which triggered global financial instability and a spiral of deregulation). The supply-side internal crisis of Fordism was consequently aggravated by a demand-side international crisis, leaving the regime 'caught between a fall in profits (because of the unresolved crisis of the labour process) and a drop in demand (because there was no effective international mode of regulation); its lingering death was characterised by alternating attempts to prop up demand, which foundered upon a supply-side crisis, and efforts to restore profit margins, which came to grief because of weak demand' (Lipietz, 1992b, 19).

The Fordist crisis, according to regulation theorists, remains essentially unresolved. While some have used the language of the theory to speculate about an emerging post-Fordist or flexible regime of accumulation, the theory in fact contains no guarantees that a coherent post-Fordist regime will rise from the ashes of Fordism. The political-economic turbulence and experimentation which has accompanied the breakdown of Fordism may be characterized by a great deal of what might be termed 'tactical flexibility', but it would be a mistake to transpose the conditions of the continuing Fordist crisis onto some prematurely drawn post-Fordist regime. The period of searching continues; a search in essence for a new 'institutional fix' and a new *sustainable* pattern of development (Lipietz, 1992b; Peck and Tickell, 1994). Implicitly underlining the extent to which the Japanese development model was theorised as 'external' to the Fordist system, Japan is widely cited as the source of putative post-Fordist 'solutions' to *some aspects* of the Fordist crisis (Curry, 1993), although an important distinction clearly needs to be made between drawing lessons from the Japanese experience and *explaining* this experience.

Japan in the golden age: Fordist or not?

Emerging from the political and economic turmoil of the immediate post-War period, Japan enjoyed a remarkable phase of uninterrupted and strong economic growth between 1955 and 1973, after which the growth pattern slowed. The mere historical coincidence of this expansion with the golden age of Fordism, however, is not a basis to characterize the Japanese pattern of growth as Fordist. The Japanese growth pattern of the 1950s and 1960s differed in important respects to Atlantic Fordism. Acknowledging this, regulationists tend to refer to the country's growth pattern as 'hybrid Fordism'. Boyer argued that the Japanese production system during the high-growth period was based around assembly line production and product differentiation, realising significant increases in labour productivity. Japan's Fordism was characterised as hybrid in the sense that, while it surpassed Atlantic Fordism in terms of production efficiencies, it under-performed in terms of income distribution. Yamada (1991, 166-7) defines the system in the following terms:

> During the period of rapid growth, Japan exhibited four notable characteristics: (i) high levels of productivity growth (ii) indirect indexation of wages to productivity (iii) an uneven wage distribution (wage inequality amongst workers) and (iv) inadequate redistribution of the social wage (an under-developed welfare state). It constituted, so to speak, Fordism without social justice. ... Japan during the rapid growth period combined a beyond-Fordist (or post-Fordist) labour process with a pre-Fordist management-labour compromise.

While Yamada's (1991) interpretation is centred, following the analytical priorities of Parisian regulation theory, on the wage labour nexus, his account is generalized to a macro-economic definition of hybrid Fordism as the co-stabilization of a mass production-consumption system and a labour-management compromise under which wages are indexed indirectly to increases in productivity at the expense of acceptance of a form of Taylorist-Fordist work discipline.

In terms of the labour process, the issue of Japan's compatibility (or otherwise) with the Fordist ideal-type turns on the extent to which the dominant work system during the high-growth period could be characterised as Taylorist. While Kenney and Florida (1988) argue that the Japanese labour process was never Taylorist (taking instead a distinctively *non*-Taylorist path after the Second World War in which mental and manual work were integrated, and deskilling tendencies overcome), Schonberger (1982: 193) was certainly in no doubt that 'the Japanese out-Taylorize us all'. Similarly, Dohse *et al* (1985) insist that the Japanese labour process is a form of Taylorism, minus union opposition. Corroborative evidence for this Taylorist reading includes Maruyama's (1989) study of management systems in the 1960s, which found little shopfloor evidence of multiskilling, the use of work teams or quality circles, and Ogawa's (1983) parallel research on labour organisation, which revealed that production was organised on the basis of assembly lines and dedicated-task machinery. Similarly, Uni (1991) maintains that flexible working practices (including multi-task technology) were not introduced until the early to mid-1960s, at which time capital and labour began to establish a new set of industrial relations principles around the integration of mental and manual work. Although there is no comprehensive study of the post-War evolution of the Japanese production system from a regulationist perspective, these studies seem to indicate that the 1960s witnessed a transition from a labour process based broadly on Taylorist principles, towards a non- or post-Taylorist system which was not to stabilise until the late 1970s. The hybrid Fordist era, in other words, was a period in which Taylorism was adjusted to the needs of the emerging mass production system in Japan.

Central to regulationists' definition of intensive accumulation is the observation that the rise in real wages under Fordism created the basis for the formation of mass consumer markets. Despite the fact that real wage rises in Japan were to a certain extent restricted to its labour aristocracy, rather than being generalised across a large portion of the working class as in classic Fordism, Uni (1991) has suggested that the conditions prevailing in Japan during the high-growth era were adequate for the creation of an *internal* mass market. Itoh (1992) concurs that the basis of Japan's rapid growth during the Fordist era was the growth of domestic demand, in this case from three sources - from wage workers (for consumer goods), from the rural sector (for agricultural machinery and consumer goods), and from large businesses (for capital and equipment goods). While Itoh finds the Japanese experience broadly consistent with the Fordist model, he rightly draws attention to the comparatively weak link between productivity growth and real wage growth.

Tohyama (1990) concedes that Japan's macro-economic circuit during the high-growth phase was constructed around mass production and mass consumption, but points out that economic expansion during this period was driven not by wages (as in the classic Fordist model) but by Japan's exceptional rate of profitability growth. This led to a massive increase in capital investment in many ways consistent with the regulationists' account of extensive accumulation. In contradistinction to the intensive Fordist model, extensive accumulation is oriented to the capital goods (Department I) market rather than the consumer goods (Department II) market. Coriat (1992) has taken this argument further, characterising Japan's high-growth accumulation system as *non-Fordist, yet intensive*: based on high productivity, an organic relationship between the capital goods and consumer goods sectors, and oriented to the domestic market. For both Tohyama and Coriat, the high-growth

42

period was not classically Fordist (strictly defined in terms of wage indexation), but represented a nascent *Toyotist* model, subsequently to stabilise in the 1970s.

Such revised interpretations pose significant questions for the conceptualisation of intensive and extensive accumulation systems with regulation theory. While there is not a consensual position, most regulationists favour a version of the hybrid Fordist reading of Japan's high-growth phase in which the essence of Altvater's (1992) 'Fordist equation' is satisfied. There can be no doubt, however, that the character of Japan's internal market was very different to that prevailing in the Atlantic Fordist countries, because in comparison the productivity shareout in Japan was truncated, restricted in this case to the country's labour aristocracy. While this does indeed represent a 'substantial deviation' (Itoh, 1992: 120) from the classic Fordist account, regulationists are divided over whether this deviation undermines the integrity of the notion of Japanese Fordism. If Japan was in some senses Fordist, though, the question which is now begged is whether it experienced a Fordist crisis in the early 1970s.

The crisis in Japan: structural or not?

In the period immediately following 1973, there was a generalized deterioration in the performance of the advanced capitalist economies which regulationists have interpreted in terms of a structural crisis of Fordism. The regulationist account of the crisis emphasizes the combined effects of external shocks (the 'Nixon shock', marking the end of Bretton Woods, and the oil shocks) and internal contradictions (workers' resistance to the Taylorist labour process, progressive technological stagnancy and the saturation of consumer markets). The erosion of the hybrid Fordist regime is therefore held to have begun prior to the 1973 crisis, the implication being that even without exogenous shocks the regime would have been impossible to sustain. Following this logic, Itoh (1992, 124-5) captures the Japanese experience of the early 1970s within the general rubric of the crisis of Fordism:

> The Fordist regime of accumulation in Japan ... became untenable toward the end of the postwar long boom, as [the] basic condition [of] flexibility in the labor market was much eroded then disappeared. As a corollary, labor discipline in work places tended to loosen even in Japanese capitalism, and the working days lost by labor disputes increased. The [crisis in Japan] was basically due to labor shortages - together with the rising prices of primary products ... and the oil shock ... - [which] brought the period of Fordist prosperity to an end.

The attendant profit squeeze was exacerbated by the breakdown of the Bretton Woods system and led to an inflationary spiral. When accompanied by overaccumulation of capital and speculative stockpiling of commodities, this broke Japan's Fordist-oriented macro-economic structure.

43

Coriat (1992), however, sees no such fundamental rupture, arguing that Japan underwent a rapid *non-structural* adjustment during the period of the two oil shocks - away from a pre-crisis, capital goods-oriented and investment-based system, and towards a consumer goods-oriented and export-based system. In his account, the rapidity of this shift in economic orientation is accounted for by three factors: first, the flexible wages system, in which there was only very limited indexation, facilitated the sharp downwards adjustment of wages and rapid employment restructuring; second, the adjustment process was facilitated by state programmes in areas such as energy-saving and the restructuring of heavy industry; and perhaps most importantly, third, Japan began to exhibit 'functional flexibility' at the organisational level, as vertically-integrated industrial groups and horizontally-networked, cross-industry *'keiretsu'* developed, in the wake of the early 1970s shocks, enhanced capacities for rapid decision-making and flexible responses to changing external conditions. The crisis is consequently seen as conjunctural: Japan's development path was modified not transformed.

Tohyama (1990) also regarded the early 1970s as a period of conjunctural adjustment. While the rate of economic growth had slowed he maintains that the macro-economic structure remained in equilibrium, remaining in many ways as stable as in the phase of rapid growth. The early 1970s crisis in Japan, by this account, did not represent a crisis of Fordism:

> While its growth pattern was similar [to that of Fordism], Japanese capitalism in the period of high growth cannot be regarded as a 'pure' Fordist regime. Consequently, neither can the crisis of the early 1970s ... be referred to as a crisis of Fordism. [This crisis] differed from that of the Fordist regime in respect of both its character and its causes. ... As far as the macro-pattern of Japanese capitalism is concerned, we cannot state that a structure established during the high growth phase was dissolved by the crisis of the early 1970s. In other words, [this] crisis ... cannot be characterised as 'structural' (Tohyama, 1990, 69, 71).

This diagnosis of the early 1970s crisis as a conjunctural rather than a structural one has serious implications for the regulationist project. In the absence of a structural crisis, a transition between regimes of accumulation cannot occur. Conjunctural crises constitute *intra*-regime adjustments. Tohyama's position is tantamount to claiming that Japan has not made a transition and suffered no 'internal' crisis, but instead has exhibited a distinctive *non*-Fordist regime throughout the post-War era. This development path, which Coriat terms *'Ohnoism'*, was simply modified *within* the parameters of an established accumulation system-MSR relationship in the early 1970s crisis. Others have, however, argued that such a 'weak transition' thesis is inappropriate, given the (admittedly limited) late 1960s evidence on the Japanese profit squeeze, shifts in productivity patterns and stagnation in consumer markets.

44

After-crisis Japan: post-Fordism or not?

The capacity of the Japanese economy rapidly to recover from crisis periods - indeed to 'make the best of such extreme shocks' (Coriat, 1992: 240) - is one of its most remarkable features. The recovery from the crisis of the early 1970s was particularly strong: the existence of co-operative (not to say weak) trade unions and loosely indexed wage-productivity relationship enabled adjustments to be made with considerable rapidity, particularly concerning the introduction of microelectronics technologies and yet more flexible labour practices (Itoh, 1992). Supportive government policies, public sector demand and growing functional flexibility at the level of the production complex also played a role (Coriat, 1992), securing a strong recovery under which growth rates stabilised around 4-5 per cent and unemployment remained below 2-3 per cent, even in the immediate post-1973 period. Although Japan's growth rate slowed and stabilised during the post-1973 period, it was the 1980s and 1990s which witnessed the country consolidate and extend its position as a leading global economic power. Despite differing views about the pre-1973 situation, the majority of regulationalists agree about the post-1973 development path, which has been labelled *Toyotism*.

Toyotism has been examined by regulationists from two perspectives, as a production complex and as a system of wage relations. First, the production system is based on multiskilling and on-the-job learning, workers' 'voluntary' involvement in the labour process, significant individual incentives based on long-term employment and seniority wages, flexible organisation in which innovation and production are intricately integrated, extensive deployment of microelectronic and flexible technologies, and highly-networked and functionally-flexible production complexes (Kenney and Florida, 1988). Second, wage relations are interpreted in rather different ways by regulationists. While Dohse *et al* (1985) have insisted that the Japanese labour process (which they also characterize as *Toyotist*) represents a particularly virulent form of Taylorism, most contemporary analysts maintain that the *Toyotist* labour process is distinctly non- or post-Taylorist (Boyer, 1990; Coriat, 1992; Itoh, 1992; Uni, 1991; Yamada, 1991). Yet although mental and manual work may be unified under *Toyotism*, contrary to their separation under Taylorism, this is not to say that the Japanese system represents in any sense a looser or more humane form of labour control. Maruyama (1989), for example, argues that the integration of manual and mental labour represents a non-Taylorist labour control strategy, but a control strategy all the same. Yamada (1991) also defines the *Toyotist* wage relation in non-Taylorist terms, as one which couples life-time employment with a seniority-based wages system. Wages are determined according to seniority, but basic pay rates and the structure of bonuses are subject to collective bargaining at the firm level and within the institutionalised '*Shunto*' system (through which annual bonuses and basic wage increases negotiated with leading companies set the standard for other settlements in the industry). More recently, however, individualised payment systems, based on individual worker performance, are becoming increasingly prevalent. These developments, for Yamada, are leading to deepening inequality and to the further erosion of labour's bargaining position, intensifying as they are competitive relations between workers.

Lipietz (1992a) has sought to characterise *Toyotism* in more general terms as a hybrid of '*Kalmarism*' (following the Swedish model of firm-level negotiated involvement) amongst core enterprises, and *neo-Taylorism* in the peripheral small and medium-sized firm sector. In Japan, workers' involvement is typically negotiated at the firm level (through firm-level trade unions), producing deep segmentation in the labour market. Core workers enjoy *Kalmarian*-type privileges such as life-time employment and stable wages, though they too are forced to use competitive strategies for career progression. Peripheral workers are in most cases excessively exploited, being poorly paid and experiencing little continuity of employment. The neo-Taylorist employment practices which now dominate this sector have effectively been 'exported' from the core (where they had previously been established under hybrid Fordism). At the societal level, Lipietz associates *Toyotism* with extreme dualism and a high degree of competition between workers.

Coriat (1992) agrees that the Japanese wage relation is distinctively non-Fordist. While under Fordism wages are automatically adjusted to increases in prices and productivity, in Japan the linkage is less direct, mediated (and, importantly, regulated) through enterprise-level bargaining. This pattern of employment relations at the firm level, is termed *Ohnoism* - in deference to the pioneering Toyota production manager. *Ohnoism* describes the Japanese wage contract under *Toyotism*, being to the latter what Taylorism was to Fordism:

> With regard to Ohnoist employment relations, it is important that strategies of ... multiskilling amongst shopfloor workers are deployed in order to achieve, and to redistribute, productivity gains. It is this which distinguishes Ohnoist employment relations from Fordist ones, ... I characterise this [Ohnoist] wage relation as one based fundamentally on the discipline of 'individual incentive-oriented involvement' ... based on a particular (implicit) compromise between capital and labour. The form of this compromise is quite different to the Fordist compromise ... It is crucially important to define the Japanese wage relation as non-Fordist (Coriat, 1992, 214-15).

The productive efficiency of *Ohnoist* employment relations, Coriat stresses, is achieved at the expense of entrenched dualism in the labour market and managerial dominance in the setting of wage contracts.

In terms of the macro-economic structure of *Toyotism*, analysts agree that the post-1973 period witnessed a shift in emphasis towards an export-oriented macro-economic chain. Productivity growth in the export sector has since 1973 outstripped that experienced in the domestic consumer goods sectors. The strong export performance of Japanese corporations has provided the financial basis for a continuous process of investment in capital equipment and in microelectronic technologies, which in turn has enabled the realisation of further productivity gains (Itoh, 1992a, 1992b). This process, however, has been mainly driven by large firms, consolidating their position in the Japanese economy by intensifying the *kanban* ('just-in-time') system and further subordinating the small firms sector and its workers (Itoh, 1992; cf Friedman, 1988).

Importantly, Japan's macro-economic orientation was to shift again in the wake of the 1985 Plaza Agreement and the ensuing appreciation of the yen (Leyshon, 1994). Export markets became sluggish and production refocused on the domestic market, progressively inflating the 'bubble economy' of the late 1980s. This shift in emphasis towards the domestic market, Itoh (1992, 130) maintains, has not caused Japan to resume a Fordist pattern in its macro-economic circuit. The 'post-Fordist' nature of Japan's contemporary growth is underlined by, first, the fact that real wages have failed to keep pace with the growth in productivity (despite rising inflation), and second, the presence of highly uneven development 'with continuous economic difficulty for the majority of working people'. The domestic consumption sphere consequently became increasingly dualised during the late 1980s, as the asset-rich wealthy indulged in conspicuous consumption while real incomes and purchasing power fell amongst the working classes.

A distinctive feature of regulationist analyses of the contemporary Japanese development path is the emphasis which is placed on the implications of rising inequality. Differences between regulationists seem to occur less around the question of where Japanese development is going, and more around the issue of where it came from. Coriat (1992) insists that the foundations of the *Toyotist* model were laid down prior to 1973, that the accumulation system has always been non-Fordist and that the wage contract has always been non-Taylorist. Boyer (1990), Itoh (1992) and Yamada (1991), on the other hand, all seek to periodize Japanese development in a more traditional regulationist fashion, tracing the origins of *Toyotism* back only as far as the crisis of hybrid Fordism in the early 1970s.

Institutional foundations: a Japanese mode of social regulation or not?

In its classical formulations, regulation theory identifies two distinctive modes of social regulation, the pre-Fordist *competitive* MSR and the Fordist *monopolistic* MSR. Regulationist studies of Japan again sit rather uneasily alongside such established conceptual categories. Perhaps the most comprehensive investigation of the Japanese MSR is provided by Coriat (1992), who reached the conclusion that

> the mode of regulation of the Japanese economy is neither competitive nor monopolistic ... Japan exhibits a particular regulatory system, through which productivity gains are redistributed amongst the working class by way of codified institutional mechanisms such as the seniority-based wages system and *Shunto* [labour's spring wages offensive]. ...

47

[Moreover] decision-making processes within [industry level] *keiretsu* play an important role in regulating the distribution of profit and investment interest ... A variety of [such] institutional forms and social codes exert a controlling influence over the core of the Japanese economy, consequently the Japanese mode of regulation is non-competitive ... [Neither however can the] Japanese mode of regulation be regarded as 'monopolistic' ... because there is no 'automatic' mechanism for synchronising wage increases with productivity gains (Coriat, 1992, 229-30).

Wage regulation in Japan occurs through the 'escalator effect' of the seniority wages system and through *Shunto*, the institutionalized process of annual wage rises. In this sense, wage levels are not subject to external market forces, contrary to the strict definition of competitive regulation. Neither, however, is the Japanese model compatible with the monopolistic MSR because wages are only indirectly related to productivity (though a complex process of custom and tacit expectations) and to a certain extent remain asynchronic, while there is limited state-led income redistribution.

It is commonly accepted in regulationist accounts that Japan's distinctive labour management system, comprising long-term employment for core workers, seniority wages and company-level trade unions, plays a significant social-regulatory function. The Japanese system of employment contracts is regulated by a complex network of socially-embedded and institutionally-encoded customs and practices which is anchored at the level of the enterprise, and to a certain extent also at the level of the industrial group. Clearly less 'transparent' than the Fordist system of wage-productivity indexation, the Japanese system is characterized by unevenness across firms and sectors, short-term flexibility and the implicit assertion of managerial prerogatives (Uni, 1991). Wage settlements are not allowed to place a brake on corporate profitability, and during much of the post-War period have tended to lag productivity rises (Itoh, 1992). While this system may share some similarities with competitive regulation, an essential feature of the Japanese system is the mediating role played by the enterprise. It is at this level that many of the key social-regulatory functions are sited.

Because workers' involvement is negotiated on a firm-by-firm basis, and because the wage-contract system is also anchored at this level, it has been suggested that Japan exhibits a 'micro-corporatist' mode of social regulation. Institutional practices, rules of co-ordination and norms of strategic conduct, which are typically located at the nation-state level under western Fordism-Keynesianism, are in Japan more often sited at the enterprise level.

If we follow the idea of the intermediating nation-state [exemplified by the Keynesian welfare state's function as an intermediary between capital and labour] being defined as the key agent controlling at a strategic level the overall reproduction of capital accumulation and the labour force,

48

such a key agent in Japan can be regarded [not as the nation-state] but as *intermediating firms* ... [T]he mode of regulation in Japan is defined in terms of 'micro-scale' or 'firm-based' regulation (Coriat, 1992, 230-1, emphasis added).

Micro-corporatist regulation in Japan is not confined to the major corporations; its influence extends to peripheral workers in the small firm sector and even into the household (Maruyama, 1989). This pattern of regulation consequently plays a key strategic role in legitimating and stabilizing the dualistic *Toyotist* accumulation system, combining as it does *Kalmarian* labour practices in the core with neo-Taylorist labour practices in the periphery.

The micro-corporatist MSR, as Boyer (1990) explains, owes its institutional shape to the particular blend of competition and co-operation exhibited by the Japanese market structure. Crucial here is the dominant role played by industrial groups. These can be broadly classified into horizontally and vertically-integrated groups. The horizontally-integrated groups, or *gurupu*, based on mutual shareholding amongst member companies, consist of a set of major corporations usually drawn from various sectors of the manufacturing, trading and financial branches. As Boyer (1990) points out, a notable feature of the Japanese market structure is the particular relationships which exist between financial and industrial capital. In Japan, major corporations are usually financed within their *gurupu* by 'main banks' offering comparatively low interest rates. As a result, possible tensions between financial and industrial capital can be resolved within *gurupu* (Coriat, 1992). This 'main bank' financing system is crucial to the regulation of capital flows within the *gurupu* because it ensures that the long-term, strategic interests of the group are paramount. The investment process is both informed and secure, oriented as it is to long-term growth rather than short-term profit-taking. This was crucial in the corporations' rapid emergence from the early 1970s crisis when a premium was placed on the risk-spreading capabilities and the long-term financial orientation of the *gurupu* (Leyshon, 1994). In addition to these financial relationships, *gurupu* also exhibit complex networks of obligated trading linkages between group members, while being fiercely competitive in terms of their external (or inter-group) market relations.

The vertically-integrated industrial groups, or *keiretsu*, are typically focused sectorally around a large parent company. They tend to be hierarchically organised around three or four tiers of subcontractors, although their structure varies from sector to sector. A distinctive feature of *keiretsu* is the way in which manufacturer-supplier relationships are regulated. Contrary to the western view of subcontractors as dependent, peripheral firms, acting merely as a 'buffer' for the core sector, Aoki (1988) insists that continuous contracting allows Japanese firms to exploit 'information efficiencies'. Problem-solving and skill formation/development occur *through* the supply chain, rather than exclusively within individual firms. The *keiretsu*, then, exemplify a particular form of inter-firm relationship which combines both integration and autonomy, and which Aoki (1988, 214) terms 'quasi-integration'.

For Boyer (1990) and Coriat (1992) this highly networked, group-oriented market structure is the foundation of Japan's distinctive micro-corporatist MSR. Although there are signs that some groups are beginning to weaken, as the level of inter-group trading increases (Aoki, 1988), most commentators agree that this distinctive pattern of inter-firm regulation is central to Japan's competitive strength:

> Effectively, this structure means that the Japanese economy's input-output matrix is partitioned in a way which limits and channels direct price competition. [F]ierce inter-company price competition is limited largely to consumer markets which are expanding, though competitive pressures between large firms are always transmitted back to their suppliers - albeit often through non-price rather than price mechanisms, usually by tightening quality standards. ... This form of organization also inhibits firms from buying into a range of activities as a way of becoming conglomerates. Takeovers are rare, and most firm growth comes through internal expansion or creation of subcontractors, a situation very different from that in most western firms (Sayer and Walker, 1992, 216).

The social regulation of the market in Japan is achieved indirectly, through networks of inter-firm relations and group alliances, rather than directly, through the interventions of a centralized Keynesian state. The role of the nation-state in Japan, however, cannot be overlooked.

According to Shinoda (1989), the Japanese state plays a limited role in the co-ordination of capital-labour relations (through such means as transfer payments), but has tended to be more proactive in the co-ordination of capital-capital relations. Government policies during the 1950s and 1960s, such as long-term economic planning, the Treasury loans and investments scheme and the strategic guidance functions of MITI, were certainly influential in shaping Japan's Department I-centred pattern of macro-economic expansion during the high-growth period (Boyer, 1990; Coriat, 1992; Shinoda, 1992). More recently, MITI has been involved in fostering collaborative networks in emerging industries in fields such as R&D and market forecasting, though Itoh (1992) contends that the organisation's influence has been on the wane since the 1960s. Such forms of proactive intervention have fallen increasingly out of favour with Japanese governments in the 1980s and 1990s, which like their counterparts in the west have turned increasingly to neoliberal strategies in the face of falling growth rates and rising indebtedness:

> Aiming at [the] reconstruction of a balanced national budget without tax increases, the Japanese government began [in the early 1980s] to reduce the financial support for health and medical services, curb subsidies to private universities and schools, and to trim government subsidied programs in various areas. ... Although such a policy stance was well-suited to the post-Fordist regime of accumulation with more flexible

50

competitive strategies of capitalist firms, it certainly added to the economic difficulty of working people (Itoh, 1992, 128-29).

Many commentators now believe that these policies themselves played a part in the progressive inflation and eventual bursting of Japan's 'bubble economy' (Itoh, 1992).
The social-regulatory role of the nation-state in Japan remains, however, under-researched from a regulationist perspective. Little work, for example, has considered the important role played by the Bank of Japan in setting financial policy and in underpinning the operation of the *gurupu* banks, although a significant exception is Leyshon's (1994) recent analysis of financial regulation in Japan. While it is clear that the industrial groups are the site of significant regulatory functions in Japan, particularly concerning inter-firm relations, investment patterns and the structuring of markets, there is a need systematically to locate these functions within the regulatory framework established by the nation-state. Moreover, this evolving regulatory framework must, if the notion of micro-corporatist regulation is to be fully elaborated, be linked to historical shifts in the pattern of accumulation. Evidence on these links is currently only piecemeal - such as the role of government policies in underpinning the investment-led growth pattern of the 1960s (Boyer, 1990), the increase in 'functional flexibility' exhibited by the industrial groups in the wake of the early 1970s crisis (Coriat, 1992), and the rise of neoliberalism and its associated inequalities in the 1980s (Itoh, 1992). This falls short of the requirements of an integrative regulationist analysis. More broadly still, the Japanese experience would need to be placed within its wider geopolitical context, given the crucial function of the country's unique relationship with the US hegemon under Fordism and given the Japanese state's recent attempts to redefine its global political position.

Conclusion: regulating Japan?

Regulationist analyses of Japanese political-economic development, while representing a substantial advance on the often celebratory and typically myopic accounts of the 'Japanese miracle', remain only partially successful in their own terms. Serious difficulties remain in reconciling the inherited conceptual categories of regulation theory with the complexities and outright inconsistencies of the Japanese experience. If the theory is to realise its potential as a generalised conceptual framework for the analysis of capitalist restructuring, applicable across a range of historical and geographical contexts, then it must be able to take up, and to explain, the Japanese development path. On this score, much remains to be done, at both theoretical and empirical levels. By way of conclusion, we briefly consider three aspects of this problem here: the question of periodisation, the status of crisis and the issue of selective readings of the Japanese experience.
Within the regulation school, significant differences remain over the question of the periodisation of Japanese development. Positioned at one extreme, Kenney and Florida (1988) maintain that Japan was never Fordist, but instead took an alternative,

post-Fordist path following the Second World War, out of which emerged the contemporary *Fujitsuist* model. A mirror-image of this position is favoured by a group of writers, largely outside or on the margins of the regulation school, who maintain that Japan has always followed, and is still following, a version of the Fordist-Taylorist development path (Dohse *et al.*, 1985; Kato and Steven, 1991). Those who have followed most closely the regulationist method, however, tend to identify some form of Fordist/post-Fordist shift, but do not fully agree on either the strength or the character of the transition. On the one hand, Coriat and Tohyama propose a 'weak transition' thesis in which the underlying continuities in the Japanese development path are emphasised and in which the early 1970s period of restructuring is regarded as a conjunctural crisis associated with *intra*-regime adjustments (Table 3.1). On the other hand, Boyer, Yamada, Itoh, and Uni favour a 'strong transition' thesis wherein what is seen as a structural crisis in the early 1970s brings about a shift from a hybrid Fordist regime to the contemporary *Toyotist* development path (Table 3.2). While both these groups of transition theorists agree on the broad contours of the contemporary regime, in which a *Toyotist* accumulation is coupled with a micro-corporatist MSR, they disagree over its origins.

One source of this disagreement may be the apparently 'compressed' periodisation of the Japanese development path. Although one can argue about the precise definitions, it seems to have taken Japan less time to move from *some form* of pre-Fordist regime to *some form* of after-Fordist regime. Taylorist practices were not incorporated on a large scale until the post-War reconstruction, but having been progressively modified in line with the evolving Japanese management system, they seem to have begun to transmutate into post-Taylorist forms perhaps as early as the mid-1960s, subsequently diffusing rapidly after the early 1970s crisis. An important flashpoint in this development path, most analysts agree, was the early 1970s crisis. Some argue that this led to an acceleration of an established (non-Taylorist) trend, while others regard the crisis as a rupture between the modified Taylorism of the 1960s and the contemporary pattern of post-Taylorist flexibility. This raises the key issue of the status of crisis in regulationist accounts.

Two preliminary points need to be established concerning the treatment of crisis in regulation theory, one theoretical, the other historical. First, Jessop (1992b, 60) maintains that the label post-Fordism is a logical misnomer unless it is applied to a situation in which Fordism once existed: 'Serious analysis of post-Fordism must go beyond noting that it occurs after Fordism and show how it relates to specific developmental tendencies and crises of Fordism'. Second, Lipietz (1992b, 19) observes that the breakdown of Fordism was realised through a 'double crisis', the coincidence of a supply-side *internal* crisis of Fordism (arising from the contradictions of the labour process), and a demand-side *external* crisis (arising from the failure of the international mode of regulation). On both these readings, the Japanese case is problematic. In theoretical terms, *Toyotism* can only be conferred with post-Fordist status if it can be shown to have followed (and resolved the crises of) hybrid Fordism.

Once again the Japanese model poses problems here: if the post-Fordist future was pioneered by Japan and if Japan lacked a Fordist past, what does the concept of post-Fordiam signify when applied to Japan? (Jessop, 19923b, 353).

On Jessop's reading, the approaches of Kenney and Florida, Coriat and Tohyama all violate the theoretical foundations of the regulationist approach, denying as they do that Japan's high-growth period was Fordist. Contrarily, the Japanese experience can be used to raise questions about Jessop's conception of post-Fordism, which effectively requires that crises are resolved *in situ*. While some crises are undoubtedly resolved in such a way, spatial restructuring (particularly the geographic switching of production and local regulatory experimentation) also represent responses to, and maybe putative resolutions to, the crises of Fordism (Peck and Tickell, 1994). This suggests that the regulationist treatment of crisis, particularly in terms of its geographical constitution, needs to be refined.

In some measure, the Japanese model is also inconsistent with Lipietz's historical account of the collapse of Fordism. While there is widespread agreement that external factors were central to the 1970s crisis in Japan, the flaw in the 'strong transition' reading lies in inadequate account of the internal factors behind the crisis. Though some evidence is presented, the argument that Japan's hybrid Fordism was partly brought down by its internal contradictions is at present not as convincing as the parallel arguments advanced for the Atlantic Fordist countries. In comparison, the degree of economic and political dislocation in Japan, even in the depths of the early 1970s crisis, was not nearly so marked. Japan's rapid recovery from the crisis, moreover, also revealed a macro-economic and social-regulatory structure which was substantially intact. For the 'strong transition' thesis to be substantiated, further evidence of significant accumulation system-MSR realignments is required.

Lipietz's (1992a) assertion that Japan has demonstrated that the internal crisis of Fordism could be solved through the negotiated involvement of workers must be seen, as a result, as something of a provisional one. Japan *may indeed* have illuminated an alternative after-Fordist path, but it seems to have stumbled onto this path not having experienced a fully-fledged Fordist crisis of its own. This brings us to our third issue, that of selective readings of the Japanese experience. Here, Jessop (1992a, 16) tentatively raises the possibility that those economies which have grown most rapidly during the global crisis of Fordism and which have become models for those in crisis are especially advanced in developing Schumpeterian workfare state regimes. Among the most prominent examples might be Japan, Germany, South Korea, Taiwan, Brazil, the Third Italy, and some of the most successful regions in otherwise crisis-prone economies. Even if it would be wrong to categorize all these national and/or regional economies as literally post-Fordist (because they were never truly Fordist), their increasing role as exemplars of alternative (and apparently successful) trajectories for Fordist regimes in crisis does mean that they have a paradigmatic post-Fordist status.

Table 3.1
The 'weak transition' thesis

	High-growth phase 1955-1973	Crisis 1973-1975	Stable growth phase 1975-
Characterisation	Nascent *Toyotism*	Conjunctural	*Toyotism/Ohnoism*
Interpretation	Distinctive, non-Fordist growth pattern	Period of non-structural adjustment; following external shocks (no internal contradictions)	Maturation of distinctive Japanese development model
Accumulation system	Non-Fordist, but intensive		*Toyotist*
production system	High rate of investment in capital equipment; domestic orientation	Restructuring and rapid recovery	Flexible production, combining scope and scale economies; underpinned by labour market dualism and managerial dominance
macro-economic structure	Profit-driven rather than wages driven; Department I oriented; less developed mass market	Basic integrity of macro-economic circuit retained	Shift to export-oriented macro-economic structure; stronger Department II orientation
labour process	Early *Ohnoism*; non-Taylorist; involving multiskilling	Restructuring; enhanced flexibility	*Ohnoism*; implicit rules of managerial dominance; ostracism
Mode of social regulation	Firm-level regulation; non-competitive and non-monopolistic		Firm-level or micro-scale regulation
wage form	Non-Fordist; indirect indexation of productivity and wages; tight labour markets	Flexibility in wages and employment facilitated rapid adjustment	Individual incentive-oriented involvement; loosening of labour markets
market structure	Distinctive inter-firm, contractor-supplier and manufacturing-finance relations within industrial groups	Emerging 'functional flexibility'	'Functional flexibility'

54

Table 3.1 continued

state form	State support for Department I-oriented growth pattern; strong industrial policy; under-developed welfare state	Support provided by state adjustment programmes	Intermediating functions located at firm rather than state level
monetary form	Secure 'main bank' finance system; key regulatory role of Bank of Japan	Security of 'main bank' financing limits crisis and aids adjustment	Continuation of 'main bank' funding

Sources: after Coriat (1992) and Tohyama (1990).

Given that few of the post-Fordist 'exemplars' were ever Fordist (Baden-Württemberg and the Third Italy both have origins in pre-Fordist craft traditions, while the definition of Japan's high-growth phase remains somewhat ambiguous) questions must be raised about Jessop's theoretical requirement that a post-Fordist present presupposes a Fordist past. In general terms, further elaboration of the place of uneven development within regulation theory is needed, while more specifically, the particular status of the Japanese case in regulation theory remains less than clear.

While identifying, alongside (neo)Taylorism and *Kalmarism*, *Toyotism* as one of his three post-Fordist alternatives with respect to labour relations, Lipietz appears also reluctant to take the Japanese model *in toto* on board - either theoretically or politically. On this partial reading, Japanese labour practices are proposed as a potential resolution to the contradictions of Taylorism, while regressive elements of the Japanese model, such as societal segmentation and environmental degradation, are eschewed. Such a selective appropriation of the progressive elements of the Japanese model may have a role to play in the construction of a post-Fordist political programme - Lipietz's central goal - but it is of limited value in developing a comprehensive regulationist theorisation of Japanese capitalism. As Yamada (1991) has emphasised, such a task involves understanding how the progressive and regressive aspects of the model are intertwined. Following this logic, there are of course no guarantees that the positive aspects, such as negotiated worker involvement, can be transplanted from the Japanese model into other social-regulatory settings without either mutating in some way or breaking down altogether. Japan seems set to remain a post-Fordist exemplar, though it remains to be seen whether it will prove to be a *transferable* exemplar.

While as a rule regulationists tend to be rather cautious about indulging in post-Fordist speculation, analysts of the Japanese economy - whatever their interpretation of the after-Fordist 'transition' - continue in some ways to foster the impression that the future has arrived, and it has arrived in Japan. In the light of the country's present political-economic difficulties and the continuing uncertainty about its future geopolitical role, such positions may need to be revised. Even for Japan, talk of

Table 3.2
The 'strong transition' thesis

	High-growth phase 1955-1973	Crisis 1973-1975	Stable growth phase 1975-
Characterisation	Hybrid Fordism	Structural	*Toyotism*
Interpretation	Fordist-oriented, though more efficient production and less equitable income distribution	Combination of external shocks and internal contradictions	Establishment of new after-Fordist regime of accumulation based on principles of flexibility
Accumulation system	Intensive		Flexible-intensive
production system	Elaborated Taylorist-Fordist system; assembly line production; product differentiation	Profound restructuring; search for greater flexibility	Flexible production; extensive use of microelectronic technologies in flexible integration
macro-economic structure	Department I centred, but strong Department II sector; internal mass market	Profit squeeze; inflationary spiral broke Fordist macro-economic structure; stagnation of consumer market	Export-oriented, post-1985 domestic orientation; parallel growth of Departments I and II; fragmenting mass consumption
labour process	Modified Taylorist, with pre-Fordist management system	Culmination of internal contradictions, including opposition to Taylorism	Flexible, post-Taylorist
Mode of social regulation	Emerging micro-corporatism/limited Keynesianism		Micro-corporatism/ neoliberalism
wage form	Uneven wage distribution; loose productivity-wage indexation; tight labour markets	Erosion of labour market flexibility; wage growth exceeds productivity growth	Increasing individual meritocratic component; extreme dualism; further loosening of wage indexation

Table 3.2 continued

market structure	Combination of inter-group competition and intra-group co-operation; establishment of post-*zaibatsu* industrial groups; extension of subcontracting system	Lobbying of state by industrial groups with respect to adjustment programmes	Key regulatory roles performed by *gurupu* and *keiretsu*
state form	Under-developed welfare state; use of some Keynesian devices	Limited effectiveness of state adjustment programmes	Shift towards neoliberalism; deregulation and public expenditure cuts; emerging contradictions
monetary form	Capital investment funded by 'over-borrowing' from banks and high savings ratios	Inflationary crisis, exacerbated by breakdown of Bretton Woods system	Continuation of 'main bank' financing

Sources: after Boyer (1990), Itoh (1992), Uni (1991) and Yamada (1991).

successful after-Fordist transitions, or of durable non-Fordist regimes, seems rather premature.

Acknowledgement

This chapter is an abridged and revised version of an original article published in *Environment and Planning D: Society and Space*, 1994, 12, 639-74 (London: Pion Limited). We would like to thank Reiko Suemitsu and Yoko Miyano for their help in tracing source materials in Japan. Thanks also to John Holmes, Richard Le Heron, Bob Jessop, Andy Leyshon, Martin Kenney, Koji Matsuhashi, Andrew Sayer, Adam Tickell, Koichi Togashi and Toshio Yamada for helpful comments on an earlier draft of this chapter.

References

Aoki, M. 1988: *Information, incentives, and bargaining in the Japanese economy*. Cambridge, Cambridge University Press.

Altvater, E. 1992: 'Fordist and post-Fordist international division of labor and monetary regimes', in Storper, M. and Scott, A. J. (eds) *Pathways to industrialization and regional development*. London, Routledge, 21-45.

57

Boyer, R. 1990: *Nyuumon régulation* [An introduction to regulation theory]. Tokyo, Fujiwara-shoten.

Coriat, B. 1992: *Gyakuten no shikou: nihon kigyo no rodo to soshiki* [Turning thinking on its head: work and organisation in Japanese firms]. Tokyo, Fujiwara-shoten.

Curry, J. 1993: 'The flexibility fetish: a review essay on flexible specialisation'. *Capital and Class*, 50, 99-126.

Dohse, K., Jurgens, U. and Malsch, T. 1985: 'From 'Fordism' to 'Toyotism'? The social organization of the labor process in the Japanese automobile industry'. *Politics and Society*, 14, 115-146.

Friedman, D. 1988: *The misunderstood miracle: industrial development and political change in Japan.* Cambridge, MA, Cornell University Press.

Itoh, M. 1992: 'The Japanese model of post-Fordism', in Storper, M. and Scott, A. J. (eds) *Pathways to industrialization and regional development.* London, Routledge, 116-134.

Jessop, B. 1992a: 'Changing forms and functions of the state in an era of globalization and regionalization'. *Paper presented to EAPE conference*, Paris, November 1992.

Jessop, B. 1992b: 'Fordism and post-Fordism: a critical reformulation', in Storper, M. and Scott, A. J. (eds) *Pathways to industrialization and regional development.* London, Routledge, 46-69.

Kato, T. and Steven, R. 1991: 'Is Japanese capitalism post-Fordist?' *Papers of the Japanese Studies Centre*, 16, Melbourne, Monash University, Japanese Studies Centre.

Kenney, M. and Florida, R. 1988: 'Beyond mass production: production and the labor process in Japan'. *Politics and Society*, 16, 121-158.

Leyshon, A. 1994: 'Under pressure: finance, geoeconomic competition and the rise and fall of Japan's post-war growth economy', in Corbridge, S., Thrift, N. J. and Martin, R. (eds) *Money, Power and Space.* Oxford, Blackwell, 116-146.

Lipietz, A. 1987: *Mirages and miracles: the crises of global Fordism.* London, Verso.

Lipietz, A. 1992a: 'The regulation approach and capitalist crisis: an alternative compromise for the 1990s', in Dunford, M. and Kafkalas, G. (eds) *Cities and regions in the new Europe: the global-local interplay and spatial development strategies.* London, Belhaven Press, 309-334.

Lipietz, A. 1992b: *Towards a new economic order: postfordism, ecology and democracy.* Cambridge, Polity.

Maruyama, K. 1989: *Nihon-teki keiei: sono kozo to behaviour* [Japanese management: its structure and behaviour]. Tokyo, Nihon Hyoron-sya.

Ogawa, E. 1983: 'Nihon kigyo no seisan system [The Japanese production system]'. *Business Review*, 30(3/4), 102-119.

Peck, J. A. and Tickell, A. 1994: 'Searching for a new institutional fix: the *after-Fordist crisis and global-local disorder*', in Amin, A. (ed) *Post-Fordism: a reader*. Oxford, Blackwell, forthcoming.

Piore, M. J. and Sabel, C. 1984: *The second industrial divide: possibilities for prosperity*. New York, Basic Books.

Sayer, A. and Walker, R. 1992: *The new social economy: reworking the division of labor*. Cambridge, MA, Blackwell.

Schonberger, R. J. 1982: *Japanese manufacturing techniques*. London, Free Press.

Shinoda, T. 1989: 'Fordism no kiki to nihon-gata seisan taisei [The crisis of Fordism and the Japanese production system]'. *Ritsumeikan Sangyo Shakai Ronsyu*, 25(1), 91-125.

Shinoda, T. 1992: 'After-Fordism no paradigm tenkan [The paradigm shift in after-Fordism]'. *Ritsumeikan Sangyo Shakai Ronsyu*, 28(2), 111-186.

Tohyama, H. 1990: 'Nihon ni okeru kodo seicho to kiki [Rapid economic growth and the crisis in Japan]'. *Keizai Hyoron*, 39(4), 62-74.

Uni, H. 1991: 'Sengo nihon shihon shugi to Fordism [Post-War Japanese capitalism and Fordism]'. *Keizai Hyoron*, 40(11), 33-48.

Yamada, T. 1991: *Régulation approach* [in Japanese]. Tokyo, Fujiwara-shoten.

4 Keeping their miracles going: Questioning big firms in Korea and small firms in Taiwan

John McKay and Geoff Missen

The emergence of the industrialized, exporting economies of East Asia — notably Japan, South Korea (hereafter Korea) and Taiwan — has presented a number of challenges to analysts of industrial development. The factors underpinning their initial success have been the subject of intense debate, centred around the relative importance of market factors and the role of the state. More recently, the transition to high technology production and away from the more simple manufactures that propelled the initial phases of growth, has also generated considerable interest. A third dimension, central to both historical and contemporary debates, and which is the subject of this chapter, is the question of industrial organisation. Within the so-called 'East Asian model' are marked variations in organisational systems, especially between Korea and Taiwan.

Taiwan and Korea have followed similar development strategies in the period since the Second World War (export orientation with protected domestic production, high rates of labour use and rising real wages) and their governments have played similar roles (market governing and making industrial winners). But their organization of industrial production has been quite different. Production has been dominated by the large conglomerates (*chaebol*) and a patriarchal state in Korea, but small firms and family-type networks in Taiwan. In the past these differences made little difference to common outcomes: high growth and success in export markets. As these economies have matured and global economic forces have shifted in the 1980s, and as new social and labour movements, rising wage rates and currency appreciations since the mid-1980s have threatened their competitiveness in international markets, both economies have engaged in new rounds of restructuring. Amongst the questions raised in this exercise, two have prominence: the need to increase the level of technology and to develop new products for new markets.

Embedded in these questions is the crucial question of firm size. Some opinion in Korea argues that a retreat from the past dominance of the *chaebol* to give a larger role to smaller firms is needed. In Taiwan arguments are made for moving in the opposite direction, away from their small firms and small networks. The historical formation of the different firm-size structures has given the two countries different sets of economic advantages and disadvantages. Korea's *chaebol* have suffered high set-up and changeover costs, but achieved economies of scale, while the small firm structure in Taiwan has provided low set-up costs, and considerable product and market flexibility, but low scale-economies. While both countries have been technological learners, Korea's level of firm R&D has been higher than Taiwan where technological development has been beyond the resources of small firms and more dependent on transfer from transnational corporations (TNCs) and government science parks. As we shall see, these economic-technology dimensions to the inherited industrial structure are central to the restructuring debate taking place in both countries.

The debate necessarily goes beyond matters of scale. Associated with differences in size are different relations between capital and labour. In spite of the fact that in both countries state legislation has, until the last decade or so, stringently controlled labour, the labour regime for the creation of profits has been different in each place: in the large conglomerate system of Korea it has been a form of proletarianism; in the small firm system in Taiwan it rests on familial or small network relations. Any moves in Korea to give a larger role to the small firm, and in Taiwan to the larger firm, therefore imply changes in these labour systems and in these relations between capital, labour and the state. The question is therefore raised: does industrial restructuring now involve for these states social or political problems?

The first part of this chapter asks whether firm size has been seen as a problem in Korea and Taiwan, and suggests that the answer is no. The different industrial structures have served each country well during three decades of rapid growth. The second section explores the far more complex problem of accounting for these differences and evaluates a range of alternative theoretical frameworks. We consider explanations based upon differences in macroeconomic policies and a range of culturally determined models, but argue that basic questions of regime dynamics and survival are more fundamental. The third section briefly examines the pressures for restructuring being felt in both Korea and Taiwan since the mid-1980s. In part four we summarize the debate on firm size raging in both countries as part of the broader debate about restructuring. In Korea, for a variety of political and economic reasons, there are many who advocate a reduction in the power of the *chaebol*. One result has been attempts to limit the range of sectors in which any individual *chaebol* is involved, on the assumption that concentration of R&D expenditure is more likely to generate companies that are leaders in particular world markets. The Industrial Specialisation Plan of 1993 has been generally resisted by the big companies, who argue that they, rather than the government, should be responsible for strategic decisions of this kind. However, it is clear that the immediate future of the Korean economy will depend upon a few key industries and in two of these — automobiles and electronics — the development of an efficient and technologically innovative network of subcontractors is seen as a major priority. Thus, while the *chaebol* will certainly continue to dominate, the role of small and medium enterprises is likely to be more important, albeit in a subsidiary role. In Taiwan, again for both political and economic reasons, the alliance between the state and small capitalist enterprises will continue, but in a modified form. The product and technology mix in the present period of restructuring may mean that, instead of small firms making marginal improvements in technology for new niche markets, these companies may have to become high-tech suppliers for larger exporting companies. This will result in new networking systems with more proletarian labour relations; however, this need not mean a transformation that is socially or politically disturbing.

Was size a problem in the past?

Korea

The dominance of a small number of large firms was established from the very beginning of the transition to the modern economy during the Japanese colonial period. Most importantly, the Japanese imported a model of industrial development based upon the interaction between the three key actors in the economy: the state (and state capital), the large private corporations (*zaibatsu*), and the large banks. The implementation of this model, which some writers have termed the 'magic triangle', quickly resulted in a marked duality of the colonial economy. A small number of heavily capitalized factories in key sectors produced the vast majority of industrial products, predominantly for export to Japan. Thus, by 1939, large factories, with 200 or more workers, were little more than 1 per cent of the total number of factories but produced nearly two-thirds of total output by value. Most of the small factories were under-capitalised, used traditional technology, and produced goods for the domestic market (Ho, 1984). Much the same industrial structure appeared in Taiwan during its period of Japanese rule.

In Korea, the structure of this colonial state, with its strong and interventionist bureaucracy, had a major influence on the kind of economy that emerged in independent South Korea after 1945. A capitalist industrial class, which soon came to dominate the process of economic change in Korea, was created by the privatization of the large industrial production facilities left behind by the Japanese. Initially, these factories were taken over by the government, but were quickly privatized, the result of strong American pressure. This process started in 1954 and culminated in the sale of commercial banks in 1957. Following a period of considerable political turmoil and economic uncertainty, when there remained an intense anti-Japanese feeling that precluded the restoration of earlier trade patterns, the military coup of 1961 brought to power a strong, modernising and developmentalist state headed by President Park Chung Hee. The dynamics of this regime have, more than anything else, produced the distinctive structure of the modern Korean economy (Cheng, 1990; 1993).

It is ironic that a strongly nationalistic regime which cultivated anti-Japanese sentiment as a major force for legitimation and for national motivation should adopt both the Japanese symbolism of national renewal and similar methods of economic transformation. Certain key heavy industrial sectors were chosen for development with little or no regard for notions of comparative advantage: indeed, Amsden (1989) has characterized this policy as one of 'deliberately getting the prices wrong'. The government used a highly selective set of industrial policies to support the growth of these target industries, and in particular gave preferential loans at extremely low rates of interest through its control of the banks, nationalized in 1961 (Woo, 1991). This intensive and rapid process of industrialization used as its major vehicle the big business sector, dominated by the diversified, vertically integrated, largely family-owned *chaebol*. The rates of growth of these conglomerates were truly remarkable, especially in the era of heavy and chemical industrialization since the early 1970s. The two companies that responded most eagerly to government calls for the development of heavy industry, Hyundai and Daewoo, recorded astonishing growth rates.

However, the features of the *chaebol* which were important for rapid growth for the 1970s and 1980s are under question in the 1990s, notably the high levels of diversification and a strong degree of family ownership and control. By the early 1980s, most of the leading *chaebol* were involved in heavy and light industries and had diversified into a range of financial services. The nationalization of the banks in 1961 gave the government strong control over investment patterns. The leading *chaebol*, which, unlike the leading companies in Japan, have never been allowed to own banks, saw the development of a range of other financial institutions as a way of becoming less reliant for investment funds on the state's banks. By the mid 1980s, Samsung had one-third of its assets in financial services. The *chaebol's* growing diversity in the 1970s and 1980s was seen as good for the Korean economy, allowing flexibility in the allocation of resources and personnel, and concentrating resources for R&D. However, with increasing size and diversity came increasing economic power, a cause of growing concern.

During some three decades of economic expansion the role of the small and medium enterprises has been markedly peripheral to that of the *chaebol*. Throughout the period since 1960 SMEs have constituted more than 96 per cent of all companies, but by the mid-1970s their contribution to employment in the manufacturing sector was only 45 per cent of the total. Their contribution to output and value added in manufacturing declined even more markedly after 1960. By 1970, even before the drive to develop heavy and chemical industries, SMEs contributed only 30 per cent of output and 28 per cent of value added. Most problematic of all has been the systematic relationship between firm size and average wage in the manufacturing sector. By 1989 the average wage in large companies (with more than 500 employees) was more than twice that prevailing in companies with 5-9 employees. Since the mid-1970s, and especially during the 1980s, there has been a steady improvement on most measures (although, significantly, not in relative wage levels) in the role of the SMEs. Most marked has been the improved contribution by SMEs to Korea's export performance in some sectors, notably footwear, toys, textiles, machinery and even chemicals. In part this improvement reflects the efforts made by the government to revitalise the small business sector (Yun, 1988). A variety of institutions and loan funds have been set up to encourage investment, management skills and technological upgrading. In spite of these initiatives the Korean government regards the SME sector as weak, and providing even more assistance has been identified as one of the economic priorities of the 1990s.

Was size a problem, then, for Korea in the period of rapid growth up to the late 1980s? On the contrary, it appears that size was a major asset. For most of the period since 1961 GNP growth rates have averaged some 10 per cent, and Korea has become one of the top ten trading nations in the world. In 1961, Korea had a GNP per capita amongst the lowest in Asia, but by 1997 it is expected to join the OECD, the rich nations' club. Similarly, the distribution of income has been extremely good by comparison with most other nations passing through a phase of rapid industrialisation, even though its record did not quite match that of Taiwan. Amsden (1989) argues that a key element in maintaining a relatively equal income distribution and encouraging the emergence of a large middle class has been a recognition that, while large conglomerates have been central to the Korean model of industrialization, there was a constant need to review their monopoly power and discipline them to meet the needs of the wider society. A primary mechanism of discipline has been that provided by the export orientation of the entire economy, ensuring the constant drive for efficiency and limited price rises. International competition also forced companies to keep wages, which in real terms rose, well within the bounds of productivity increases. Amsden (1989) argues that a key feature of Korea's success has been the ability, for the entire period from 1961-87, to keep wage increases well below the rates of gain in productivity, allowing a constant upgrading of Korea's international competitiveness. Government control of investment flows was also important; indeed it was the key element according to Woo (1991). Companies were rewarded for investment in industries targeted by the government, and for many of the highly-geared *chaebol* access to these preferential loans was an essential part of their survival. Thus size was not the problem: rather the big companies were central to one of the most dramatic processes of industrial development that has ever been seen.

Taiwan

Taiwan's export-led industrialization was equally dramatic and produced high rates of growth. From the 1950s to 1980 growth rates in most years ranged between 6 and 14 per cent. At the same time, the gini-coefficient fell to less than 0.3 (TIER, 1992, Vol. VII; Chan and Clark, 1992). Taiwan climbed quickly out of poverty, from an average per capita GDP of US$200 in the fifties to above US$10,000 now (San, 1993). But unlike Korea, the predominant actors in this remarkable history have been the SMEs which became the country's exporters of a wide range of industrial products.

Operating in relatively free and very competitive markets, Taiwan's SMEs showing a remarkable capacity to adopt new products and technology as international markets changed, became the leading exporters. In the mid-1980s, manufacturing SMEs provided 47 per cent of all manufacturing sales value but they supplied 67 per cent of manufacturing exports; in 1987, the export ratio for large firms was 34 per cent, but for SMEs it was 60-70 per cent (TIER, 1992, Vols. I, VII). SMEs changed from being small household units at the time the KMT took charge of government in 1945 to small family-centred consumer goods producers in the import-substitution period of the 1950s, to export producers of textiles, food, machinery and chemicals in the export-led growth of the 1962-73 period, expanding into other and more skill-intensive industries, especially electronics, in the late 1970s and the 1980s (TIER, 1992, Vol. VII). Their contribution to total manufacturing net value more than doubled between 1966 and 1986, from 16.6 to 35 per cent. The problems small firms are supposed to have (limited ability to access credit, penetrate markets, raise technology) do not appear to have troubled Taiwan.

Contrary to comparative advantage theory that leads us to expect firms to be small at the early stages of economic growth, when labour-intensive production not dependent on scale economies predominates, and to be larger later, small firms became important *after* large firms appear in Taiwan. A few large state firms were important early in Taiwan's industrialization history and the general trend from the 1950s was for the average size of the small firm, which dominated the industrial landscape, to increase. This trend reverses in the 1970s. For example, the growing proportion of medium firms (100-499 workers) and large firms (500+) stops around 1976. Manufacturing employment tells a similar story. As the smallest firms proportionately drop in employment by a third after 1961 larger firms increase their share until 1971; thereafter the large firm's proportion drop, the medium firm's stays the same and the 10-49 and 50-99 firms increases. The SME as exporter comes into its own in the 1970s in Taiwan (McKay and Missen, 1994).

The rise of the SME as competitive and flexible exporter depended on three processes: on small firm sensitivity to and early entry into niche markets before retreating or diversifying investment into other industries, or what has been called 'guerilla capitalism' (Lam and Lee, 1992) or 'industrial nomadism' (Shieh, 1993); on a labour process involving complex subcontracting relations amongst small firms in which flexibility compensated for small scale; and on labour-intensive products and technological upgrading (rather than technological leaping) that was within the scope of small firm capital. It is, however, easy to exaggerate the role of the small firm in the Taiwan miracle story. A number of accounts crediting the small firm with the central role in Taiwan's industrialization seriously underplay the role of the large firm and of the state.

State ownership of large basic industries appeared early in the post-war era when the KMT preserved and expanded the public sector of the Japanese empire. In 1952, 52 per cent of Taiwan's manufacturing output was in state hands. This proportion declined with time (20 per cent in the 1970s, 10 per cent by the mid-1980s (Amsden, 1991; Simon, 1992) where the proportion more or less now remains). But there was no downward trend in terms of the percentage shares of public enterprises in gross fixed capital formation, which went from 31.4 to 32.4 per cent between 1951-53 and 1978-80 (Wade, 1990, 177). The state has monopolized production of the basic industries (steel, aluminium, shipbuilding, petroleum refining, petrochemicals, fertilisers, some heavy machinery) as well as utilities and drink and tobacco, and been important in integrated circuit production. In Taiwan, public enterprises (rather than the large private companies as in Korea) have been used in high-entry cost

66

industries requiring scale economies; they are also used to feed downstream firms (Wade, 1990, 179).

The state allowed large vertically integrated private enterprises to emerge in plastics, metal products and some machinery and equipment, though it restricted their growth so that domestic capital did not concentrate in conglomerate hands typical of Korea. The state also encouraged at times the investment of large foreign electronic companies, but was careful to see that foreign capital did not threaten Taiwan's economic and political autonomy. The control of large firms was, according to Wade (1990, 185) partly to restrict overexpansion or entry of ill-equipped firms (though these efficiency goals sit awkwardly with one reading of the sources prior to 1965 which point to a disastrous economy of waste and mismanagement (Gates, 1992, 177)), and partly in order to prevent undesirable wealth concentration. Large firms, both public and private, with 500 workers or more produced 56.4 per cent of Taiwan's total manufacturing output by value in 1973, a figure which exceeded that of Japan (40 per cent) and even Korea (52.7 per cent) (Amsden, 1991). The proportion was somewhat less, but still high, in 1986: 47.3 per cent (TIER, 1992, Vol. I, 30).

In terms of firm size there is considerable diversity in the Taiwan's manufacturing sector and in production and exports scale is often important. Large state and privately owned enterprises have been important in Taiwan's history of industrialization as well as SMEs. The structural contrast with Korea lies less in the relative employment and output position of LEs and SMEs and more in what each produces and exports. While in both countries SMEs produced labour-intensive goods in the early stages of industrialization, Taiwan's SMEs also became the producers of light, higher-skilled exports that came to dominate exports, with the LEs providing the inputs to the smaller firms downstream and, with some important exceptions, engaging less directly in exporting. To a large extent the reverse applied in Korea where the *chaebol*, fed at times by SMEs, have been the exporters.

The ability of the small firm to enter the markets of a wide range of product depended on the low access barriers to these particular product markets. The technology needed to enter into new products was rather easily acquired and did not require economies of scale to be employed. In these markets the small firm had a number of advantages. Its input prices and unit labour costs were low, its profit horizons were short, and often operated in a personalised system of subcontracting with other small firms in small local networks (Shieh, 1993). Accordingly entry, inventory and marketing costs were minimised. To enter international markets and the niches available in these markets as they moved, the small firm depended on marketing relations with the large international trading companies and on information networks. The small firm in Taiwan became adept at building both. The critical conditions for success of the small firm were, then, low production costs, product markets associated with low-cost entry to changing technology, and subcontracting and information networks.

So, has small size been a problem for Taiwan in the past? It appears not. The SME record of producing light industrial exports in very competitive and changing

67

product markets is testimony to an impressive economy of scope. At certain times and in certain products, large rather than small firms appeared. These larger firms were actively promoted by government, though never to conglomerate size, and it has been this involvement that has allowed Taiwan its share of an economy of scale. The large firms have been particularly associated with advancing technology. In some industries technical dynamism and low cost production was engendered in SMEs by upstream-downstream flows and feedbacks between them and the large and technically advanced suppliers (San and Kuo, 1993). The importance of the large firm sector certainly qualifies the versions of Chinese capitalism that we examine in the next section, but it should not be used to diminish the massive contribution the small firms have made to Taiwan's industrial ascendancy.

Interpreting the different industrial structures

Structural differences are not often the focus of attention in the literature and many researchers who have pointed to these differences in organization (Kim, 1993) have not attempted to develop theoretical frameworks to explain such divergence. But in so far as interpretations have been made, there are three broad sets of theories which have as their basis: differences in organization; differences in macroeconomic policies pursued in the two countries; varying cultural underpinnings to the two societies; and, contrasting regime dynamics, which we understand to mean the various strategies that are undertaken and the alliances that are formed to enhance the power and survival possibilities of ruling groups.

Theories based on contrasting macroeconomic policies emphasise that each country's industrial strategy was certainly implemented differently. Korea's 'discretionary control of industrial growth' (Cheng, 1993) was more centralized and hierarchical, with a government generous with tax benefits, tariff rebates and especially preferential credit, insistent on the social spreading of the benefits of private production, and hesitant in attracting FDI relying instead on international loans. When the push came for exports in Korea, the discretionary controls and incentives favoured the larger firms: thus low or negative real interest rates for the *chaebol* were often tied to export promotion. Taiwan's 'field manipulation of the market' was a system which relied on non-discretionary incentives such as tariffs, tariff rebates and fiscal investment incentives and on discretionary industrial policies more than on discretionary controls. In so far as discretionary decisions by the KMT existed, they hardly affected Taiwan's small firms which were left to their own profit-seeking devices within the government's incentive policies. Regulation affected the large-firm sector rather more, but even then not comprehensively (Wade, 1990, 193). One significant control on Taiwan's large private corporations was the limit placed on their entry because of state ownership of key industries.

The second group of theories argue that the different structures reflect more than policies: they involve deeper cultural differences. The strength of the Korean state's control in the economy, for example, and the government's discretionary policies which gave the *chaebol* such economic power cannot be understood unless one appreciates how deeply Confucian patrician values are embedded in Korean society. Similarly, small capitalism in Taiwan has taken root in a culture where Chinese family values and small business networks have historically always been important.

A good deal of recent literature on Taiwan illustrates this cultural orientation. In these works, values are closely attached to economic behaviour. It has been claimed, for example, that personal trust, strong at the family centre, replaces the western notion of accountability and encourages secrecy and adaptability (Lam and Lee, 1992; Orru, 1991a); that the moral strength of exchange favours amongst Chinese people (*guanxi*) underpins a number of business needs (from hiring labour and mobilising money, to subcontracting and dealing with bureaucrats); that Chinese patrilineage and inheritance customs encourage owners to establish new businesses for their sons (Hamilton and Biggart, 1988; Orru, 1991a); and that feelings of independence ('better a chicken head than an ox tail') draw workers into becoming owners, and act to transfer skills that are learned on factory floors and in government offices and research institutes into businesses (Lam and Lee, 1991; Orru, 1991a).

In such approaches the core binding mechanism which mediates relations between small businesses and groups of small companies is the concept of the network. Here the term 'network' is used to describe an organisational form that joins businesses through preferential and mutually supportive acts between people. Like hierarchical, vertically integrated businesses, networks act to reduce risks and failures that are inherent in transactions between firms, but where hierarchies rest on rules, networks rest on personal exchanges (Orru, 1991b). These values and the unique systems of networks they support tend to keep firms small, and encourage the development of further small networks between small groupings of firms (Shieh, 1993), but they are flexible enough to allow family-like networks to extend beyond families as businesses grow (Hamilton and Kao, 1990; Orru, 1991a).

A recent interpretation of these Chinese networks sees the Chinese acting as very successful 'guerilla capitalists' employing personal international connections to conduct early raids into new markets before retreating as larger, scale-economic firms enter these markets (Lam and Lee, 1991). In a similar vein, Hamilton (1992) has written of a distinctive Chinese capitalism operating throughout Asia. Both works, perhaps because of their purpose to attack the statist approach (as found in Amsden, 1989; Wade, 1990) in explaining the NICs' success, appear to elevate culture to a distinctive determinant in the organisation of capitalist production.

Culture and traditional values are of course important in any social formation of production, and it is easy enough to weave cultural attributes into the stories of production in Taiwan and Korea. In the case of Taiwan, for example, from an entrepreneurship-marketing perspective one may convincingly argue that Taiwan's industrial success rested on savings and risk characteristics typical in Chinese families; and that relations amongst firms and institutions have had a large personal component typical of Chinese networks. Personal connections have been important in disseminating market and technical knowledge internationally. Sometimes these connections are institutionalized, as in the case of the Jade-Mountain Scientific

Technology Association, an informal group of Chinese in Silicon Valley which provides technical, corporate and employment information for Chinese engineers in the US and Taiwan. Learning through investment of western firms in Taiwan has had a personal component with many employees leaving these firms to set up on their own or work for SMEs. At the national scale, what appears to have been quite crucial in the success of small firms was subcontracting between groups of small firms in which tasks and orders were put out to a variety of firms on the basis of various obligations (Shieh, 1993).

A similar argument can be constructed from the perspective of the labour-capital relations or labour systems central to profit-making. Labour relations in the family workshops and small capitalized factories, which together have formed the bulk of manufacturing establishments in Taiwan, rest on patriarchal values or 'familism' (Gates, 1992; Lauridsen, 1992a) and own-boss networking or 'micro-entrepreneurialism' (Shieh, 1993). Familism is also important in the 'filial-proletariat' system in the large and medium-size firms where temporary, low-status, low-paid employment of young women prevails (Lauridsen, 1992b). Communal paternalist relations stressing mutual responsibility and typical of family and locality may also operate in the employment of males in large and medium enterprises.

Similar claims have been made for the role of traditional values in Korea. There, it is has been alleged, Confucianism and values typical of society in the Korean countryside, from which historically much of the industrial labour has been drawn, have been instrumental in the formation of hierarchical business relations and highly disciplined work practices (O'Malley, 1988; Pye, 1988).

It is easy, however, to exaggerate the role of traditional values. A recent anthropological study of one of the leading *chaebol* (Janelli and Dawnhee, 1993) offers an example from Korea. Janelli, well-versed in the social structures of the Korean village, concludes that the influence of older, rural patterns of behaviour has been very overplayed. Rather, the culture of the conglomerate has emerged as Korean capitalism has made and remade itself.

We are particularly critical when culture becomes the determinant in organising capitalist production, as appears to be the case in Hamilton's 'Chinese capitalism' or Lam and Lee's 'guerilla capitalism'. An explanation of industrial structures must account for differences not only across places but also over time within the one place. Taiwan and Korea have each organised production in different ways at different times; and each is now in a new phase of industrial restructuring to cater for the problems that have come with economic maturity and as new competitive forces in the global economy have arisen. By itself culture is a weak explanator of such structural shifts.

In our view, more satisfactory are a third group of theories which stress that the differences between the industrial structures that developed in Korea and Taiwan had more to do with what Cheng (1993) calls regime dynamics. These dynamics may be thought of as the relational manoeuvres of leading businesses and government that take place in changing political and economic contexts and which are designed to increase political legitimacy and to reconsolidate political power. Social pressures for restructuring accompany growth and these pressures are exacerbated and complicated by changes in the global economy. Capital and the state adjust their authority patterns and legitimation strategies to these changing environments, but they do so in previously established social contexts. The industrial structures that emerged in Korea and Taiwan were as much 'situational adaptions of pre-existing organizational forms to specific political and economic conditions' (Hamilton and Biggart, 1988) as anything else.

The basic differences in policies and structures between Korea and Taiwan began with the quite different socio-political contexts that prevailed in the immediate post-war years. As we have seen, Korea's privatization of the large Japanese companies and the encouragement of the *chaebol* were nested in a strong nationalist sentiment (anti-communist as well as anti-Japanese and with long historical roots). This approach was largely precluded in Taiwan where anti-Japanese feeling was less and where, more importantly, the KMT government and its military and other supporters were, after 1949, expelled mainlanders amongst a Taiwanese majority. The problems that existed for the KMT simply did not exist for the government in Korea. Ideologically disinclined to large capitalist groups, the KMT could not risk its authority by allowing large private monopolies to develop; on the other hand it was difficult for KMT mainlanders to claim a legitimacy through state monopoly production. The answers to the legitimacy problems were, according to Wade (1990), found in the constant threat to Taiwan from the communists on the mainland, which allowed authority to be vested in a strong military state, and secondly in economic policies that allowed small Chinese businesses to operate freely, to prosper, and to absorb labour.

Categorising the socio-political differences in this way is, however, insufficient and somewhat misleading. For Gates (1992), the regime dynamics in Taiwan were more complex and periodized. The second process referred to above, legitimacy through growth and prosperity, operated only after but not before the mid 1960s. For almost 20 years after the war, the KMT adopted exclusionary policies directed more at power than growth, and during this time rates of labour absorption were low and poverty was high. Legitimacy came through the KMT allowing petty capitalism to proliferate. Through this 'unspoken alliance', traditional values were satisfied as petty capitalists busied themselves with Chinese business, and the state was protected 'against the inroads of corporate capitalism' (Gates, 1992, 179). This was a period, however, of revenue problems and inefficiencies which were only overcome with US aid, which formed nearly half of gross domestic capital formation in 1955. When this aid was cut off in the 1960s as the cold war eased, the KMT strategy changed. More or less coinciding with the policy shift to export promotion, the KMT accepted a controlled alliance with foreign capital. Hereafter, as capital is imported, the small firm sector grows, its manufacturers become exporters, and they link with larger firms by receiving inputs, by technological learning and, by supplying disciplined labour for the corporate sector from their patriarchally-run households. Out of the new regime dynamics that operated after the mid-1960s a Taiwanese brand of

71

'flexible production', of 'guerilla capitalism', of 'an economy of scope' — or whatever it might be called — is made.

Industrial capitalism is, in other words, neither culturally born nor implanted by a master state, but is made and remade in a series of periods. Change takes place principally through the transition from one period to another, and in each era new regime dynamics are established to establish or consolidate the power of particular elites. At present, new challenges are emerging in both Korea and Taiwan and pressures for restructuring are threatening the existing regime dynamics.

Challenges facing the NICs

The generation of rapid growth rates and significant trade surpluses have produced upward pressures on the currencies of both nations, with significant impacts on the competitiveness of exports. In 1986-87 the Taiwanese NT$ appreciated by more than 35 per cent against the US$, while the Korean Won appreciated 16 per cent against the US$ in 1988 alone. Both countries have also seen periods of labour unrest, as workers demanded a bigger share of each nation's success, and labour shortages have appeared in all sectors as demand for workers has outstripped population increase in these rapidly growing economies. The result has been significant increases in wages. In Korea, for the first time in more than three decades wage increases have outstripped productivity gains. In Korea there were more than 3,600 strikes in the second half of 1987 alone, resulting in annual wage increases of 21.6 per cent in the period 1988-90, compared with labour productivity increases of 5.1 per cent per annum. In Taiwan, where wage increases had for some time outpaced productivity growth, wages climbed even faster after 1986, but equally important from the point of view of total costs was the promulgation of the Labour Standards Law in 1984, which introduced a whole package of benefits, including pensions and severance payments, to the majority of Taiwan's workers. The result of these forces has, of course, been mixed. Wage increases and currency revaluations have made exports less competitive, but stronger currencies have meant that imports are cheaper and foreign investment is more attractive, while higher wages have increased the purchasing power of the domestic market. Such short-term pressures have, however, certainly forced a rapid restructuring of both economies.

From a longer-term point of view, both societies have been faced with the problem of making the difficult transition from a developing to a more mature economy. In part this is a question of technology, as currency revaluations and wage pressures force the movement to a more sophisticated industrial base. In the competitive situation of the 1990s, access to new technology from overseas is often restricted, as the advanced nations fear competition from the newcomers. Where technology can be purchased, it is expensive. The generation of home-grown technology, while improving, is difficult. Even more fundamental is the question of social change and the movement towards democracy. In both countries the population has made considerable sacrifices in the national interest and is now

72

demanding increased political freedoms as well as increased living standards. In both countries, new social movements are emerging to push particular issues, such as environmental protection. This is just one aspect of the complex interplay between democratisation and issues of economic growth, and this broad debate has significant implications for processes of restructuring. The development of new strategies to meet these challenges is central to the economic and social policy debate in both countries.

Industrial restructuring and issues of company size in Korea and Taiwan

Korea

Issues of industrial structure are central to the current debates about restructuring the Korean economy. At the most basic level, there are a series of complex relationships between issues of democracy and freedom on the one hand, and questions of economic policy on the other. Demands for democracy are not just about rights to vote in elections and the freedom of candidates from a range of parties to stand in these elections. Since the fall of the Soviet Union, the call for democracy has frequently been tied to a whole set of ideological baggage. In most versions, as these are received in Korea, the idea of democracy is closely tied up with the triumph of that particular vision of liberal democracy which is inherent in the 'end of history' debates. Thus the quite understandable demands for basic democratic freedoms and the end of various forms of authoritarian rule have become enmeshed with much more questionable assumptions about the superiority of free market mechanisms and of particular forms of deregulation and liberalization.

The role of the conglomerates

The debate about the role and power of the *chaebol* is an important component of this larger picture. Supporters of the free-market model argue that the very size and power of the conglomerates inhibits the emergence of the central mechanism of market competition. But this economic question is also tied up with issues of political power. The entry of Mr. Chung Ju-Yung, the founder of the Hyundai conglomerate, into the race for the Presidency in 1992 raised concerns about the possible over-centralization of economic and political power into the hands of the *chaebol*. The fact that most of the *chaebol* are still family owned rather than public companies gives added weight to this fear. These political fears have in turn meshed with another series of essentially economic policy questions about the most appropriate form and role of the conglomerates to meet the restructuring challenges of the 1990s.

The economic side of the debate about restructuring is dominated by the imperatives of developing new technologies and new products that will allow Korea to remain competitive in world markets. An important element here is the question of the role of large and small companies in meeting this challenge. Current plans involve a series of strategies to upgrade the design and technical efficiency of existing industries, development of home-grown technologies for new growth industries, the establishment of new production and subcontracting systems to improve the competitive position of growth sectors and offshore investments to take advantage of cheaper labour or easier market access. To the surprise of many, the design of such revitalisation strategies is allowing even supposedly 'sunset' activities such as textiles to continue as important export contributors for the 1990s. Thus, in 1992 the textile industry contributed a trade surplus of US$11.7 billion, more than any other industry and considerably ahead of electronics at US$8.1 billion. Korea is still the fourth largest textile producer in the world, with 6.6 per cent of total world exports, but even so textiles contributed 20.5 per cent of Korea's total exports compared with 25 per cent in the 1980s and more than 30 per cent in the 1970s.

However, it is also clear that Korea's strength in such industries as steel, shipbuilding, automobiles and electronics will also be vital for the next decade and beyond, and in terms of the present focus on the relationships between large and small firms, a key element of the new technologies/new products debate concerns the most appropriate structure of these key industries. While it was argued in the 1970s and 1980s that only large corporations would have the resources for effective R&D and diversified companies would be best insulated from the downturn in a particular sector, in the 1990s the dominant government view is that the very diversity of the Korean conglomerates spreads their research effort too thinly over too many fields. In late 1993 the government announced its Industrial Specialisation Plan under which by January 1994 each of the top 30 conglomerates had to nominate their 'core businesses'.

Economic policy makers hope that the Specialisation Plan will achieve several important aims. It is hoped that the more specialized *chaebol* will become world leaders within their particular industries, and this will of necessity mean that these companies will be at the forefront of global technology. The further growth of these key industries, especially electronics and automobiles, will encourage the development of more efficient systems of subcontracting that will reduce costs, increase quality and foster new technology. The industries discarded by the *chaebol* can be sold off to smaller enterprises, increasing the vitality of this sector. Finally, since most of the diversification of the conglomerates was funded by borrowings, concentrations should reduce corporate debt and consolidate the financial position of these key players in the Korean economy.

There are some early signs that these aims are being achieved. Already, several companies have announced expansion plans within their key areas. For example, Samsung, which is the world's largest producer of DRAM chips with 1992 sales of US$1,192 million or 13.6 per cent of the world market, has announced large-scale investments in the production of non-memory chips as part of a 2,000 billion Won investment program in electronics for 1994. Samsung already has 37 plants, 22 R&D centres and 272 branches throughout the world, and will set up 7 new research institutes by the year 2000. It is clear that the future development of the Korean

74

electronics industry will depend upon the organisation of a more effective subcontracting network. Korea's output and export of electronic equipment have increased rapidly since the late 1980s, but the industry still relies heavily on the import of components. One of the key policy aims of the government is to encourage more local participation in component production for both the electronics and automobile industries.

Hyundai has announced that it plans to be one of the top 10 car makers in the world by the year 2000. It will invest 3.3 trillion Won to expand domestic car production to 2 million units per year, and will devote 7 per cent of sales to R&D. These new, positive plans may have assured some commentators who, at the beginning of the government program to reform the *chaebol*, expressed concern that politics might be allowed to interfere with Korea's long-term economic interests. However, recent developments suggest that government leaders are well aware of these dangers particularly at a time of local restructuring and of recession in many of Korea's major markets.

New roles for the small firm?

One major problem in weakening the power and role of the conglomerates, and in diluting active government support for their efforts, is the weakness of the small business sector. The Korean government has looked admiringly at the success of Taiwan's small companies and has argued that Korea should attempt to replicate the flexibility and technological adroitness of Taiwan's 'guerilla capitalists'.

In spite of the power of the *chaebol*, the small business sector is very large. In 1990 small companies made up 98 per cent of all companies, employed 61.7 per cent of the total labour force and were responsible for 42.7 per cent of production and 44.3 per cent of value added. Yet there are profound weaknesses. Problems of access to finance for technology and investment in new production facilities are most frequently cited. Wage levels have increased at the same time as the emergence of a serious labour shortage. Many companies have problems in obtaining labour, especially if the jobs involved are dirty, dangerous and difficult. Higher labour costs and the progressive opening up of the Korean market to foreign imports has meant severe competition in a number of traditional areas of small business activity, such as clothing and footwear. As many companies have slid into bankruptcy, there has been a chain reaction of defaults on debts. A series of highly publicized suicides has highlighted the plight of the small business owner. Meetings of a new self-support group for small business — *Palgi-hoi*, a name which comes from the Korean proverb 'to fight seven times and recover eight times' — have also received much media attention. In spite of difficult times, new companies are constantly being created: in the first half of 1992 some 4,000 small companies disappeared, but 6,000 new ones were created.

Support for the small business sector is a key element in the new government's plan for economic reform, outlined in the draft of the Five Year Economic Plan released in early July 1993. There is already an infrastructure of government support, in the form of loans, technical assistance, and the construction of industrial estates. More is now being promised. In May 1993, a $US1.7 billion fund was established to assist small business in three key areas of upgrading: commercialisation of new technology, automation and computerisation. One central element in the implementation of this new package highlights one of the major challenges facing the Korean economy as it restructures: for small companies to receive preferential treatment, they must be in subcontracting relationships with large companies and be recommended by the *chaebol*.

It seems clear that the structure of small business in Korea is simply not like that of Taiwan. The structure of networks that has been so important in Taiwan's success is simply not present in Korea, and it would be very difficult to create such a system. To be realistic, Korea must continue to rely on the large companies, and this in turn will dictate the dominance of large scale production, relying for its international competitiveness on scale economies and the generation of new technology appropriate to new mass markets. These new markets are likely to be more diversified than in the past. The US will continue to be of major importance, especially for the automobile industry, as will Japan. But the Chinese market and others in Asia is the new hope as incomes in the region expand rapidly. In this respect Korea will not develop a form of 'guerilla capitalism' but will continue to challenge Japan head on. Success will need to be based on the development of a much more efficient subcontracting system made up of innovative small firms that can contribute to the development of new technology. Not for the first time, the Japanese model will provide the inspiration for this change.

Taiwan

If the large conglomerate is likely to remain central to the industrial structure of Korea, albeit confined to narrower sectoral ranges and more reliant on networks of subcontractors, is it also the case that the small and medium firm will remain dominant in the industrial structure of Taiwan? In numerical terms the answer is probably yes, even if the small firm's contribution to output and employment will decline somewhat. But we anticipate changes to the roles the small firm performs in this structure: a decline in its contribution to exports and a rise in the importance of medium and large firms associated with technological development.

As with Korea's *chaebol*, any assessment of the future role of the SME in Taiwan is partly political, a matter of the state's authority and legitimation strategies. To date, these strategies have involved the Taiwanese government in a dual alliance with large private concentrations of capital on the one hand and with petty Chinese capitalists on the other, the former, whether domestic or foreign, accepted but controlled, the latter, as it were, let loose. As we have seen, small flexible businesses let loose in export markets proved to be a very successful formula. The problems since the mid-1980s, however, raise the question of a continuing reliance on the small firm. We shall argue that Taiwan now faces a dilemma that is part economic and part political. The economic issue is whether a small-firm, low-

76

technology industrial structure is appropriate when higher, more expensive technology is becoming more important in the global economy. Thus, for example, the recent rush of Taiwanese small-firm capital to the PRC may resolve many of the cost-of-production or market problems faced by small firms producing in Taiwan but perpetuate a low-tech small-firm base, an involutionary process Taiwan's policy-makers may have reason to question. But this questioning is also political, for it implies altering an alliance the state has had with petty capitalists in the past.

We ask first: are there signs that a new structure is being formed out of new policy directions? We then speculate about new roles for the small firm. We stress, however, that it is not easy to draw patterns with great confidence. While it is easy enough to point to new directions from a reading of policy statements, it is not easy to predict the community and business responses to policy changes which will ultimately determine the course of restructuring. In part this is because events have moved so quickly since the end of martial law in 1987. Taiwan clearly is no longer a one-party state, with the Democratic Peoples' Party (formed in 1986) now a significant opposition party, but less clear are the relations between petty capitalists, organised labour and government, the role of the military as the community make calls for further democratisation and improved environmental standards, the strength of the independence movement, the alignments between Taiwanese and mainlanders within the KMT, and the nature of the relations between Taiwan and the PRC (Cheng and Haggard, 1992).

Recent restructuring policies and enterprise change

Current restructuring policy is enshrined in the US$300 billion Six Year National Development Plan (1991/96) but restructuring policies were being formed well before this. When President Carter severed formal US diplomatic ties with Taiwan after Deng Xiaoping's post-Mao economic reforms on the mainland in 1978, international recognition of economic success became deliberate policy in Taiwan (Wu, Yuan-Li, 1992). At the same time, better incomes, education and communications signalled political reforms. The Hsinchu Science Park was established in 1980, new labour rules came in 1984; and an Economic Reform Commission, set up in May 1985, came out with a huge report. All three predate the upward currency valuations and the wage rises after 1986 and which are often seen as the stimulus to restructuring. Since the late 1980s, however, there are signs that restructuring policy has taken a more large-scale direction.

Large, not small, is implied in three major directions of industrial policy made since 1990. These are: higher technology, new products, and key projects to help attract foreign firms to use Taiwan as their base of Asian operations. Associated with each of these three directions are questions of scale, joint ventures, and strategic joint alliances with foreign companies.

It is clear that policy-makers see new technology as crucial to Taiwan competing in new markets. The Industrial Development Bureau estimates that the value of technology-intensive products in manufacturing will increase from its present proportion of 30.6 per cent to 44.5 per cent by 2002. By itself, this trend does not mean larger scale production: Taiwan has advanced technologically in the past in spite of its small firms and Japan's SMEs are currently upgrading to very advanced levels (Missen, 1991). But for certain items in Taiwan's current technological push larger units of production and/or capital *are* involved. Taiwan's ICs tend to be mass produced and are associated with large amounts of capital and R&D, a tendency that will probably be entrenched as capital and government research institutes search for even smaller IC designs (IDIC, March 1993). The pivotal role government has assigned to high-tech investment also means producing new items, (e.g. LCD, CCD, and CIS components in the electronic industry), some of which will be mass produced.

Large amounts of capital are obviously implied in the policy move to emerging industries announced under the Six Year Development Plan, which seeks to identify and support a number of strategic industries. Telecommunications and aerospace are two such industries.[1] The high technology entry costs of these industries imply alliances or ventures with foreign companies. Thus the US company Motorola (which has been producing in Taiwan for the last eight years) has signed a letter of intent with the government to develop a global communications system with Asian operations centred on Taiwan — Taiwan's predicted investment in 1993-95 being US$4 billion. Agreement has been reached with NEC, Japan's electronic giant which handles 70 per cent of Japan's satellite launches, whereby NEC will transfer technology to Teco Electric and Machinery Company, and Teco, a leading machinery and electric conglomerate in Taiwan, will make 10 satellite parts and components. The enormity of capital to be invested in these projects suggests a quantum jump in the scale of production, but this, may not necessarily be the case. Motorola operations are likely to be large scale (as their past operations in Taiwan have been, its plant in Chungli employing 2600 workers for example); but Taiwan's SMEs are seen as entirely appropriate to an aerospace industry which, globally, employs relatively small numbers per firm and which relies on subcontracted component part suppliers.

Also part of the restructuring package are key projects. One of the most important of these is the naphtha cracker plant and associated facilities that Formosa Plastic Group (FPG) will soon build offshore in Yunlin County in West Taiwan. This petrochemical complex, Taiwan's largest-ever private project with investment of more than US$8 billion, will include a naphtha cracker, oil refinery, industrial harbour and up- and downstream petrochemical manufacturers. 1.3 million tons of petroleum and 0.9 m tons of ethylene are expected each year.

This complex symbolizes at least two changes from accumulation systems of the past. First, it marks a sizeable increase in large private capital which previously was kept in check. The fact that the project's oil refining capacity will compete keenly with the state's Chinese Petroleum Corporation, presently the only oil refinery on the island, and that the government has been instrumental in providing land and facilitating finance (over US$5 billion from 31 Taiwanese banks) for FPG, suggests that the government's legitimation strategy has changed.

Secondly, it will be attached to a 2000 hectare free-trade zone which, with associated airport and shipping facilities, will act as transhipment and storage centre for business in the wider Asian region. Such parks and free-trade zones themselves are not new; what is different is what is being sold: Taiwan's west coast as a regional operations centre in Asia, a base for luring multinational firms to Taiwan. The investment lure also involves plans for six new industrial parks, the continued upgrading and expansion of Hinschu Science Park and the Industrial Technology Research Institute (ITRI), and changes to the tax systems in the Statutes for Upgrading Industries. Part of the current restructuring policy is to formalise this investment through strategic alliances with overseas companies, mostly based in North America or Europe. Foreign investment has been important at moments in Taiwan's past, especially for technical transfer purposes, so the present investment is in one way not a break with history; what is different is, possibly, the relative size of the current investment and, certainly, the purpose of making Taiwan a regional operations centre.

New roles for the small firm?

How will the small firm fit into the new industrial structure suggested by these new policies? We anticipate three sorts of changes to the small firm role: a decline in its contribution to output and employment; a decline in its role as exporter; and an increase in its role as a supplier to larger firms. There is some evidence and some argument that all three may be happening.

First, a report of the Industrial Development and Investment Center (IDIC) claims that there are 'clear' structural changes favouring larger companies and putting smaller ones out of business. Economies of scale 'gaining the upper hand' appear across a range of industries. Second, there has been a marked drop in the export ratio of SMEs since 1987. Third, and less clearly, the relations between small and larger firms may be changing. As export markets become less important for the small firms and as government policy encourages large foreign businesses to use Taiwan as an operational centre in the Asian region, small firms may come to serve larger firms more than in the past.

What are the structural, as against any cyclical, reasons for these changes, if in fact they are general? The three conditions that we argued were crucial to the success of the SME in the international market place in the past — low production costs, product markets associated with low-cost entry to changing technology, and information networks — are now under intense pressure.

There have been two responses on the part of individual firms that appear to be related to the higher wage costs and currency appreciation of the late 1980s: a movement offshore into ASEAN, Vietnam and, more recently, mainland China; and, secondly, a shift to the domestic market. The government has encouraged both trends. The offshore movement is biased toward but not confined to small firms uncomfortable in the high-wage environment of the island (Lauridsen, 1992b), and presumably unable or unwilling to secure labour from the traditional low-priced labour markets in Taiwan (the patriarchal households) or Asian labour migrants. The government has encouraged this offshore movement of small enterprises by its capital-allowance regulation, at the same time as it has legislated to attract larger segments of foreign capital under its technology and regional policies. Paradoxically however, the attractiveness of locating businesses offshore, and particularly in the rapidly growing Chinese marketplace, may be acting to delay the technological upgrading of firms in Taiwan itself, a central focus of government policy.

Guerilla capitalism's viability is dependent on the speed of product and technological change internationally, channelled through the network systems described earlier. It is likely to be less viable when the speed of technological advance slows and the lead times and costs of developing technology rise. This appears to be happening.

Government agencies have traditionally dominated R&D expenditure in Taiwan. This is likely to continue as ITRI continues to expand its divisions (the most recent being the division for air and space industries research) and deepen technological research especially in the Electronics Research and Service Organization (ERSO), the major researcher in advanced circuitry and other complex microelectronics in Taiwan. If the SMEs prosper in the new high-tech era, then, it will be largely because government has an interest in technology transfer to the small firms from its large-scale institutes.

That interest would be partly political, motivated by a perceived need to continue with the established unspoken alliance with small capitalism and familial, patriarchal labour relations. But such a transfer must also make economic sense in a more technologically based era. The product and technology mix in the present period of restructuring may be such that instead of small firms quickly taking hold of marginal improvements in technology and produce for new niche markets, they become high-tech suppliers for larger export producers. Such a shift is likely to involve somewhat different networking relations, and more proletarian labour relations in the economy. It is also likely to involve an increase in worker training appropriate to higher technology, a significant change in a country where employers have generally invested little in their workers (Lauridsen, 1992b). These new networks and labour relations are of course speculations and it is not yet clear whether they will come to characterize Taiwan. It may be, for example, that the regime will allow the island's small producers to continue their market and investment raids in the mainland, in this sense ignoring the technological imperative, while at the same time meeting this imperative by promoting larger high-tech firms with proletarian skilled workers and subcontracting links with a few smaller firms. The point is that whatever path restructuring takes in the 1990s it will not be a path chosen by a state bent on economic maximising but one based on a broader logic of regime survival.

Conclusions

If, as our evidence suggests, the role of the small firm in Korea is becoming somewhat more important while in Taiwan it appears that larger exporting companies are emerging, does this mean that there are strong forces leading to convergence in these maturing economies? Such predictions are always difficult to make, especially in an era of globalization and liberalization, but doubly so in the case of two countries that have successfully engineered a rapid succession of economic and social transformations. The forces which lead to different industrial structures are multifaceted and complex, and similarly the processes of industrial restructuring involve the interplay of a range of economic and political variables both within the nation and at the international level.

We have reviewed the alternative theories which might account for the dominance of large conglomerates in Korea and small, family firms in Taiwan in the period since the early 1960s. While not denying the importance of cultural factors, we have argued that simple culturally-based arguments cannot by themselves explain these dramatically different structures. After evaluating the evidence we have argued that theories of regime dynamics are much more satisfactory. Such approaches seek to locate particular policy decisions about investments, products, markets and macroeconomic management within the context of coalition building at home, maintaining alliances overseas and generating growth rates that legitimate governments and enhance the survival prospects of particular elite groups. In the case of Korea the alliance between government and big business has delivered both growth and stability, while in Taiwan partnerships between the state and smaller business owners have delivered similarly attractive results for the ruling elites.

However, the evidence for a break with these earlier structures is strong. In Korea the imperative is to retain export competitiveness and hence high rates of growth. Most important is the generation and adoption of new technologies, and the development of new and more efficient production systems for these new products. In part, this technological imperative enhances the country's reliance on a few big companies that have the resources necessary for research and development, yet new production systems in the sectors targeted by Korea for future growth, especially automobiles and electronics, demand efficient and innovative networks of subcontractors on the Japanese model. The government also believes that at present the *chaebol* are involved in too many sectors and hence has moved to limit the range of each company. At the same time, political fears about the power of the conglomerates have resulted in a series of measures designed to control the *chaebol* and to encourage the growth of smaller companies. Our data show that these forces are resulting in a decentralization of the economy and a growing contribution of smaller companies to exports. The evidence suggests that this increased role in trade takes two forms: small firms are exporting more products directly; and their components are of growing importance in the exports of the large-scale product assemblers. In Taiwan, the need to develop new technologies and efficient production systems is just as strong. We have demonstrated that this is leading to a series of agreements with large, foreign corporations and to the emergence of a small number of large local companies that are assembling various export products, again building networks of subcontractors and component suppliers. These mechanisms of restructuring are further complicated by the movement offshore, and especially to China, of many smaller companies using older technologies and labour-intensive techniques. The growing interdependence of the Taiwanese economy with that of the mainland is also helping to diminish the military threat from the mainland, something which has always been used by the regime to encourage stability and national effort.

But will these forces for convergence be sufficiently strong to make these very different economies and societies more like each other, and each of them more like Japan? The first issue is whether these forces will survive given the continued imperative for regime survival. In Korea the products and the markets which have been chosen to propel the economy over the next decade demand large-scale production and massive investment in certain key technologies. The growing importance of the Chinese market will encourage the intensification of systems of mass production, albeit using networks of component manufacturers. The dependence on the *chaebol* will surely limit the extent to which the government can threaten the viability of these large companies. Also, the state-large capital alliance cannot be seriously undermined in the absence of a viable alternative coalition. In the case of Taiwan, it is far from clear whether there will be a continued reliance on niche markets, especially in the United States and Europe, or whether there will be some attempt by the emerging larger companies to penetrate a range of mass markets. However, as in Korea, there do seem to be limits to the disruption that is possible of the existing coalitions. Thus, in both countries the continued logic of regime survival will place strict limits on the range of policy options that are available. The forces for convergence are making some impact on the industrial structures of the two countries, but the logic of regime survival as well as the undoubted cultural differences seem certain to ensure that Korea and Taiwan will retain their distinctively different structural characteristics.

Note

1. Eight other capital and technology intensive industries are named in the plan: information, consumer electronics, semiconductors, precision machinery and automation, advanced materials, specialty chemicals, medical and health care, and pollution control.

References

Amsden, A. 1989: *Asia's Next Giant: South Korea and Late Industrialization.* Oxford, Oxford University Press.

Amsden, A. 1991: 'Big business and urban congestion in Taiwan: the origins of small enterprise and regionally decentralized industry (respectively)', *World Development*, 19, 9, 1121-1135.

Chan, S. and Clark, C. 1992: 'Changing perspectives on the evolving Pacific Basin: international structure and domestic processes', in Clark, C. and Chan, S. (eds) *The Evolving Pacific Basin in the Global Political Economy.* Boulder, Lynne Rienner, 1-26.

Cheng, Tun-Jen 1990: 'Political regimes and development strategies: South Korea and Taiwan', in Gereffi, G. and Wyman, D. (eds) *Manufacturing Miracles: Paths of Industrialisation in Latin America and East Asia.* Princeton, NJ, Princeton University Press, 139-178.

Cheng, Tun-Jen 1993: 'Distinctions between the Taiwanese and Korean approaches to economic development'. *Journal of East Asian Affairs*, 7, 1, 116-136.

Cheng, Tun-Jen and Haggard, S. (eds) 1992: *Political Change in Taiwan.* Boulder and London: Lynne Rienner Publishers.

Gates, H. 1992: 'Small fortunes: class and society in Taiwan', in Simon, D. and Kau, M. (eds) *Taiwan: Beyond the Economic Miracle.* Armonk, NY: M.E. Sharpe, 169-186.

Hamilton, G. 1992: 'Overseas Chinese capitalism'. Institute of Government Affairs, University of California, Davis, Working Paper No. 42.

Hamilton, G. and Biggart, N. 1988: 'Market, culture and authority: a comparative analysis of management and organization in the Far East'. *American Journal of Sociology*, 94, S52-S94.

Hamilton, G. and Kao, Cheng-Shu 1990: 'The institutional foundations of Chinese business: the family firm in Taiwan'. *Comparative Social Research*, 12, 95-112.

Ho, Samuel Pao-San 1984: 'Colonialism and development: Korea, Taiwan and Kwantung', in Myers, R. H. and Peattie, M. R. (eds) *The Japanese Colonial Empire, 1895-1945.* Princeton, NJ: Princeton University Press, 347-398.

Industrial Development and Investment Centre (IDIC). Various issues. *Taiwan Industrial Panorama*, Taipei.

Janelli, R. L. and Dawnhee, Kim 1993: *Making Capitalism: The Social and Cultural Construction of a South Korean Conglomerate.* Stanford: Stanford University Press.

Kim, Hyuk-Rae 1993: 'Divergent organisational paths of industrialisation in East Asia'. *Asian Perspective*, 17, 1, 105-135.

Kuo, Wen-Jeng 1992: 'The marketing of small and medium-sized enterprises in Taiwan', in seminar on the Development of Small and Medium Enterprises in R.O. C. Taiwan Institute of Economic Research, 4-17 May, Taipei: TIER,

International Economic Cooperation Development Funds and Ministry of Economic Affairs, ROC.

Lam, Kin-Kong and Lee, I. 1992: 'Guerrilla capitalism and the limits of statist theory. Comparing the Chinese NICs', in Clarke, C. and Chan, S. (eds) *The Evolving Pacific Basin in the Global Economy: Domestic and International Linkages*. Boulder, Lynne Rienner, 107-124.

Lauridsen, L. 1992a: 'Labour and democracy in Taiwan? Continuity and change of labour regimes and political regime in Taiwan'. Department of Geography, Socio-Economic Analysis and Computer Science, Roskilde University, Denmark, Research Report No. 87.

Lauridsen, L. 1992b: 'New technologies, flexibilization and changing capital-labour relations — the East Asian NICs, with special reference to Taiwan and South Korea'. Department of Geography, Socio-Economic Analysis and Computer Science, Roskilde University, Denmark, Research Report No. 88.

McKay, J. and Missen, G. 1994: 'The problem of being big in Korea and small in Taiwan: restructuring firm and institutional networks'. Development Studies Centre, Monash University, Monash-Melbourne Joint Project on Comparative Australian-Asian Development, Working Paper No. 94-1.

Missen, G. 1991: 'Industrialization and restructuring in Northeast Asia: the state and small firms'. Development Studies Centre, Monash University, Monash-Melbourne Joint Project on Comparative Australian-Asian Development, Working Paper No. 91-7.

O'Malley, W. J. 1988: 'Culture and industrialisation', in Hughes, H. (ed) *Achieving Industrialization in Asia*. Cambridge, Cambridge University Press, 327-343.

Orru, M. 1991a: 'The institutional logic of small firm economies in Italy and Taiwan'. *Studies in Comparative International Development*, 26, 1, 3-28.

Orru, M. 1991b: 'Practical and theoretical aspects of Japanese business networks', in Hamilton, G. (ed) *Business Networks and Economic Development in East and Southeast Asia*. Hong Kong, Centre of Asian Studies, University of Hong Kong.

Pye, L. 1988: 'The new Asian capitalism: a political portrait', in Berger, P. L. and Hsiao, H. M. (eds) *In Search of an East Asian Development Model*. New Brunswick, Transaction Books, 81-98.

San, Gee 1993: 'Taiwan's economy and trade'. *Taiwan's Economic Success: Trade, Finance and Foreign Exchange Conference*. Monash University (Victoria, Australia) 25 May (mimeo).

San, Gee and Kuo, Weng-Jen 1993: 'Technological dynamism behind Taiwan's successful export performance: an examination of the electronics and textile industries'. Report for *UNCTAD Research Report on Technological Dynamism and R&D in Exports of Manufacturers of Developing Countries*, May 1993 (mimeo).

Shieh, G. S. 1993: *"Boss Island": The Subcontracting Network and Micro-Entrepreneurship in Taiwan's Development*. New York, Peter Lang.

Simon, D. F. 1992: 'Taiwan's strategy for creating competitive advantage: the role of the state in managing foreign technology', in Wang, N. T. (ed) *Taiwan's Enterprises in Global Perspective*. Armonk NY, M. E. Sharpe, 97-122.

Taiwan Institute of Economic Research (TIER) 1992: *The Development of Small and Medium Firms in Taiwan*, various vols., Taipei (in Chinese).

Wade, R. 1990: *Governing the Market: Economic Theory and the Role of Government in East Asian Industrialisation*. Princeton: Princeton University Press.

Woo, Jung-En 1991: *Race to the Swift: State and Finance in Korean Industrialisation*. New York, Columbia University Press.

Wu, Yuan-Li 1992: 'Shaping Taiwan's future', in Wang, N. T. (ed) *Taiwan's Enterprises in Global Perspective*. Armonk NY, M. E. Sharpe, 81-96.

Yun, Yeo-Gyeong 1988: 'Promoting small and medium industries: the Korean experience'. *Asian Development Review*, 6, 2, 96-109.

5 Japanese structures: Integrating state and corporate strategies

Paul Parker

Japan offers lessons beyond the end of history. Williams (1994) joined Johnson (1982), Dore (1986), Wade (1991) and others to argue that the Anglo-American model of economic development is not the only viable model for the late 20th century and beyond. Fukuyama's (1989) question as to whether history had come to an end with the collapse of the former Soviet Union has been interpreted to imply that there is no alternative to Anglo-American style free-market capitalism as the way to organize economic life. That conclusion ignores other political economies which have proven successful in the promotion of international trade and economic growth. In particular, the dynamic development processes which are accelerating Asian Pacific economies often exhibit differences from the apparently polarized separation of government and business in the Anglo-American tradition.

Japan and its East Asian neighbours have created the most dynamic region in the global economy and are expected to continue their rapid rate of growth (Drysdale, 1988). However, to better understand the processes underlying the economic success of this region, researchers need to abandon the assumption that economic models based on the experience of North Atlantic economies provide universal answers which work equally well in all national settings. It is equally important to avoid the opposite position that the achievements of Japan or other East Asian countries are the product of unique national factors. If the development path is strictly a function of a unique national character, then it is not transferable unless the underlying culture is transferred as well. This chapter explores an explanation between the extremes of economic universalism and unique nationalism.

Initial efforts to develop a 'new' economic geography at the global scale (Dicken 1992; Johnston, 1989; Knox and Agnew, 1989) have paid limited attention to institutions which facilitate globalization processes. Grant (1993) responded with an institutional analysis of Japanese and US trade policies to start to fill the gap between macro and micro level analyses. The approach adopted for institutional analysis was based on the structural framework to international political economy proposed by Strange (1988, 1991). This chapter uses the same structural framework for the analysis of institutions and the strategies adopted by key actors in the Japanese economy. The strength of these structures varies from country to country, but national structures are interconnected at the global level. As a result, one can use the framework to better understand domestic structures, their interconnections and the

87

role of each country in constructing and controlling structures at the global level. In the end, global forces as well as unique combinations of domestic institutions are expected to influence development in Japan and are argued to offer insights for those seeking to extract generalizations from the Japanese experience to consider the implications for other countries.

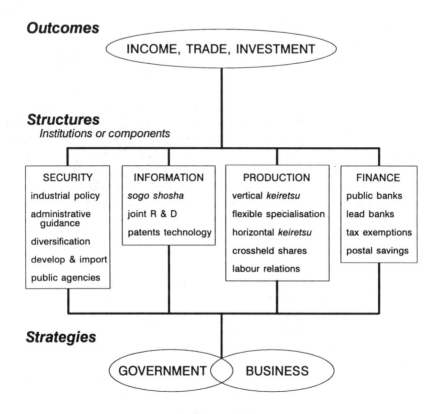

Figure 5.1
Japanese strategies, structures and outcomes

Sources: adapted from Strange (1988, 1991).

The Japanese context for this study is provided by Peck and Miyamachi (Chapter 3) who systematically reviewed the contribution of regulationist analyses of the Japanese development experience. They considered the form which the production structure has taken in recent periods and presented alternative arguments as to the type of crises experienced by Japanese industry and the extent of restructuring undertaken to restore profitable operations. To extend their analysis further, they called for a more detailed analysis of the social institutions of Japanese capitalism. This chapter seeks to contribute to this analytical process by going beyond the macro-level relations in society to identify how particular structures are built with national institutions which reinforce each other to create highly competitive international structures.

Rather than debate the relative position of the US or Japan in the global economy (Taylor, 1985; Wallerstein, 1991) the chapter examines some of the institutions which comprise the Japanese structures. Many studies have focused on the relations surrounding the production structure, labour relations and how Japanese production differs from American production (Friedman, 1988; Kenney and Florida, 1988) . The chapter moreover seeks to balance the emphasis of most research on the production structure with equal recognition being given to the security, financial and knowledge structures. Subsequent chapters (Alvstam, Chapter 6 and Humphrys, Chapter 7) examine the outcomes of the operation of Japanese structures, as indicated by foreign direct investment and trade patterns and internal spatial arrangements.

Trade and investment patterns are important to measure the global impact of the relationships identified and hypothesised by macro-level analysts. However, to better understand the process which leads to these outcomes one needs to examine the set of institutions which translate macro-level social relations into micro-level investment or trade decisions (Figure 5.1). These institutions form the substantial structures that shape and control Japanese production, finance, security and knowledge structures. Key attributes of each of these four structures and their interrelationships are outlined. Particular attention is paid to the integration of state and business objectives within each structure. It is argued that state and corporate leaders in Japan have adopted cooperative strategies, not simply because of a group focused culture, but because both groups benefit from the structures which emerge to enhance Japan's position in the global economy.

State-corporate separation or integration?

Aono (1993, 32) asserts that the concentration of Japanese corporate head offices in Tokyo is primarily attributable to the close relationship between large companies and government bodies. This relationship between state and private actors requires further investigation. The traditional academic divide of international relations as the study of state-state negotiations and international business management as the study of firm-firm relations needs to be replaced with both of these types of relations being studied along with state-firm relations (Strange, 1991). Geographers have included state-firm relations as part of their study of location decisions and the changing geography of production and consumption, but the efforts of researchers dealing with all three sets of relations could be combined to build a better understanding of international political economy. The investigation of state-firm relations invites the study of cases where state-firm relations may differ from those generally assumed in the Anglo-American tradition. Japan provides a particularly useful case study because of its achievements in international political economy over the post-1945

89

period and the assertion that its state-firm relations differ from those found in North Atlantic states, especially the US.

Johnson (1982, 1988) challenged the western model of two separate spheres for politics and economics when he argued that the Japanese experience was based on a developmental state which took an active role in the stimulation and support of selected economic activity. Rather than being competing interests, public and private interests joined to pursue the shared objectives of economic growth and increased economic welfare. This approach has been termed neomercantilist by Nester (1991). In this model the government and corporations share objectives and act to accumulate national wealth. In its extreme this approach depicts a heirarchically integrated 'Japan Inc' with lead government agencies performing head office functions and firms passively following orders. A more detailed examination of the interaction between government and business is expected to reveal both groups taking action to implement strategies which are mutually beneficial.

Different societies have different sets of values, so the study of the different institutional forms which result in these societies may yield a better understanding of international political economy (Strange, 1991, 23). The framework of four 'unifying structures' can thus be used to articulate differences in structural arrangements and the basis for divergent outcomes in terms of the income, trade or investment patterns generated by respective societies.

The importance of structural analysis is demonstrated by trade issues. Trade is often used as an indicator of economic power and the balance of trade is the indicator which is often identified in the media. Great concerns have been raised over the size of the Japanese trade surplus which grew to US$122 billion in 1993. Bilateral imbalances, such as that between the US and Japan (US$51 billion) and the even larger surplus (US$56 billion) which Japan accumulated with its East Asian partners (MOF cited in Shinmura 1994) generate intensive political dialogue. Despite the attention it receives, trade balance is simply a relative measure and fails to identify the structural underpinnings of the trade process. In the US-Japan case, this issue was partially recognised in the Structural Impediments Initiative which implies that attention is being paid to structural issues. However, the associated series of policy discussions often resulted in negotiators for each side proposing that the other side change attributes, such as savings or investment rates, to match those of the other country without paying attention to the structures which produce those patterns (JETRO, 1993). More fundamentally, trade outcomes are the product of structural power, the ability to construct structures which facilitate trade flows. These trade outcomes are not simply the neutral products of inherent comparative advantage as suggested by neoclassical trade theory. Instead, Japanese trade achievements have been built on the basis of a shared state and corporate belief in their ability to create dynamic comparative advantage through the construction of globally competitive production and trade systems. The assertion that GATT agreements represent a liberal consensus on the means by which global trade is conducted, is a gross oversimplification of the realities of trade (Strange, 1988, 182).

Trade is also shaped by security concerns as secure international supplies are sought to meet the needs of domestic industry and consumers. Finance is of critical importance, not only to invest in the production system, but also to facilitate exchange and overcome the risks of trade. Finance and technology are critical to creating trade opportunities, yet access to these resources is unevenly distributed. The knowledge and information structures are central to the evaluation of trade opportunities and the management of timely and efficient trade flows. In short, to understand a relative measure of economic power like the balance of trade, one needs to look at the four primary structures and the creation of structural power which enables that outcome to be achieved.

The Japanese security structure

The security structure is the framework used to provide security for society. In modern times, the state has been the central institution in the security structure (Strange, 1988, 45). However, the means by which a state ensures security for its population is not restricted to the capability of its military. In some cases military expenditure has been considered to have a negative effect on the well being of people. The security issue needs a broader interpretation and is better seen as the broad range of initiatives undertaken by a government to promote the security of its population. Japan provides a striking example of a country which had invested heavily in military capability, but after losing World War II redirected its efforts to economic initiatives to secure a better economic future for its population. In this way, the security structure encompasses the institutions established by the state to promote the well-being of its population.

Given the post-war context of a defeated military and shortages of food and consumer goods for the population, the Japanese government, business leaders and general public reached a consensus on setting economic prosperity as the most important objective to pursue. The resulting coalition of conservative politicians, business leaders and ministry officials appears in retrospect to have formed as a cooperative arrangement with all parties benefiting from the collective actions taken. However, this outcome was not a forgone conclusion at the time of the poverty, labour unrest, social dislocation and uncertainty of the immediate post World War II period (Buckley, 1990). Change was required and priorities needed to be set. One of the important factors was the role of government in promoting industry and stimulating economic growth. A wide range of industrial policies were developed as government and industry interacted on a frequent and multidimensional basis.

The rapid growth of Japanese firms was supported directly by industrial policy, but the indirect support of education reform and welfare policies to redistribute wealth was also important (Shimizu, 1989). Before considering industrial policy, the general policy formation process should be noted. Despite a high turnover rate in government ministers, a consistency in most policy directions is maintained through the use of permanent policy committees which have a broad membership and monitor developments in their particular area. When the need arises for new legislation it is usually proposed by the ministry rather than a political party, but its content draws heavily from the discussions of the associated policy committee. This policy formation arrangement reflects a formal consultative process which precedes political debate in the Diet. In this way, the interests of various groups are taken into account.

The role of government in Japanese economic development has been debated extensively. Some argue that government was directing the economy with lead agencies like MITI acting as an effective head office to direct the economy. This 'Japan Inc.' interpretation depicts firms as passive agents playing out their prescribed role in the centrally derived plan for the future. Others regard government as having minimal impact: the success of Japan is attributed primarily to economic factors, especially the free ride offered by US military protection, low cost access to proven technologies and access to large consumer markets. However, even those who argue that the role of government has been exaggerated, concede the important role of some government agencies:

> MITI "plays an important role co-ordinating business activity... MITI does not have strong legal powers but through fragmented powers to issue permits and licenses, and through persuasion, it has influential power... The Economic Planning Agency under the authority of the Prime Minister's Office set up long range plans... These long-range plans gave a stimulus to business, became guidelines for business long-range planning, and encouraged management in long-term thinking." (Kono, 1984, 10-11)

The role of government in general and MITI's administrative guidance (*gyosei shido*) in particular, changed form over time. In the 1950s MITI was responsible for the distribution of scarce funds. The coal, steel, electric power and shipping industries were assigned a high priority for investment in new equipment. During the 1960s MITI allocated funds for the rationalization and modernization of heavy industry and chemical industry. Export promotion and import restriction were the primary policies for the automobile and household electrical appliance industries (Shimizu, 1989, 45). Domestic industries were protected not only by trade restrictions such as tariffs and quotas, but also through restrictions on foreign investment by the use of foreign exchange controls and foreign investment restrictions. More generally, Japanese laws and directives were written in a general language which enabled the bureaucracy to interpret the intent of government according to the circumstances.

By the 1970s the need for the distribution of government funds, export promotion and import protection was reduced. Most large firms were successfully competing internationally and MITI support for export promotion was restricted to SMEs (Higashi and Lauter, 1990, 19). In most cases, import quotas were removed, tariffs lowered and restrictions on foreign investment eased. Instead, of proposing micro-level decisions for firms, MITI would present a vision of Japan's future industrial structure and promote growth through competition to achieve these goals.

These visions or scenarios for the future were not the independent product of government, but instead reflect the views of industry/government committees which reviewed each industry. During this period, MITI continued its role as a facilitator in the structural adjustment of declining industries (Shimizu, 1989, 46). Some public support was available, but most of the cost of restructuring was born by industry.

The guiding role of MITI provides a contrast to the role of government in industrial development in the US and UK. Other contrasts can also be provided. The Supreme Allied Command introduced many laws based on American models during their period of power in Japan. However, the effect was not to create regulations which operated the same as in the US. For example, an Anti-Monopoly law was based on US antitrust law. However, many changes were made to make this law compatible with Japanese practice. By the 1950s, changes were made to the rules on interlocking directorates and the limits on bank ownership of corporate stocks were increased (Higashi and Lauter, 1990, 18). Similarly, MITI sponsored special industry laws to exempt particular types of joint economic behaviour from the antitrust laws. In particular, many cartels were exempted from the provisions of the law. The number of authorised cartels rose from 53 in 1953 to 1,079 in 1966 before declining to 886 in 1970 and 422 in 1986 (Higashi and Lauter, 1990).

By the 1980s the main directions in government economic policy were liberalization and internationalization. This period of deregulation, especially the removal of financial controls, has been interpreted as 'Japan Disincorporated' to reflect the decline in the role previously held by government (Hollerman, 1988). Despite the general trend of deregulation, MITI programs continued to target particular industries where change was desired. The energy security of Japan was a major issue following the oil crises of the 1970s. MITI responded with two major initiatives: the Sunshine project to develop non-oil sources of energy and the Moonshine project to promote energy conservation and demand reduction. Direct Japanese investment in overseas energy projects by Japanese companies was facilitated. The policies used to respond to the energy crises reflect earlier policy initiatives where the Japanese government responded to the scarcity of resources in Japan by adopting policies to promote the development of international projects which would provide raw materials for Japanese industry. This 'develop and import' policy illustrated Japan's resource diplomacy whereby the government took initiatives to promote access to secure supplies of raw materials (Ozawa, 1979; 1980).

While many writers highlight the role of MITI and other government ministries in the coordinated attempt to achieve economic security for the Japanese people, others point to the failures or conflicts which MITI has encountered with firms. For example, MITI initially objected to car export plans, but then supported these plans from 1962 onwards. It also proposed mergers among car firms and opposed new entrants - in an attempt to create a dominant firm. Three small mergers occurred, but new entrants appeared so from 1969 MITI decided to leave the firms to succeed on their own (Higashi and Lauter, 1990, 20). Similarly, television, stereo equipment and cameras were not high on MITI's list of industries deserving support. Their subsequent success indicates that MITI direction was not a prerequisite for success.

The implication is that many Japanese firms were able to become internationally competitive without direct government support. If government did not direct industry decisions at the micro level, but instead promoted alternate periods of cooperation and competition depending on the situation in each industry (Sasaki, 1990), how did firms interact to create the production structure? Several of the institutions used and strategies adopted to construct the production structure are examined next.

The Japanese production structure

The production structure in Japan differs from that in the Anglo-American model because a different set of strategies have been adopted to construct the structure. A substantial business literature has developed to identify differences in the strategic priorities of Japanese firms in comparison to western counterparts (Aoki, 1988; Kono, 1984; Sasaki, 1990; Shimizu, 1989). Abegglen and Stalk (1985) highlight the priorities of successful large Japanese firms (*kaisha*) as first, a growth bias to grow faster than their industry (increase market share or diversify to faster growing industries), second to monitor the actions of competitors (be better than competitors or be different through product differentiation), third to create and exploit competitive advantage through R&D initiatives for product development and the improvement of existing production processes. A more detailed set of policies are then developed to achieve these general objectives. Many analysts have highlighted the long term and growth orientation of Japanese firms. Okamoto (1984) argued that the growth oriented strategy is a synthesis of the firm's product market orientation and its labour market orientation. Shimizu (1989) argued that the emphasis was placed on new product development with this being a function of the creativity of the employees.

The strategy of focusing on new products is reflected in the high value placed on manufacturing units within Japanese firms (Shimizu, 1989). Sales and finance units were less valued as reflected in the history of many corporations when the marketing and finance units were loosely integrated with production. In many cases, trading companies (information structure) or affiliated banks (financial structure) may have played a leading role in these functions (Suzuki, 1991, 10).

Distinct production strategies were reinforced with a distinct production structure. Kenney and Florida (1988) argued that the stereotypic Fordist model of production based on the mass production and consumption of standardized goods was replaced with a stylised Japanese model based on structured flexibility. Friedman (1988) was of the view that an emphasis on flexibility and small production units was more important than either bureaucratic regulation or market regulation to explain Japan's economic success. Production plants were designed to produce variations of standard goods to meet the needs of market niches. Japanese corporate structures typically differ from the single vertically integrated Fordist plant. The vertical relations between large firms and their suppliers are neither the complete vertical integration of units within a Fordist firm, nor are they pure contracts as expected in transactions between independent firms. The resulting 'quasi-integration' has been described as a Toyotist approach and depicted as offering a new form of production based on flexible specialization (Dohse *et al.*, 1985; Friedman, 1988; Piore and Sabel, 1984). Debates over the classification of Japanese firms and their associated form of production structure and their relations with labour and the state continue (Peck and Miyamachi, Chapter 3). However, most analysts agree that it differs from the Anglo-American tradition.

Within firms, labour relations are also argued to differ from Anglo-American models. The three treasures of lifelong employment, seniority based wages and enterprise based unions stand in contrast to the productivity based wages and trade based unions of Anglo-American firms. However, the stability and employment security associated with these labour relations is restricted to large Japanese firms (Aoki, 1988). SMEs offer less security of employment and lower wage rates. In addition, some firms responded to the recession of the early 1990s by moving away from lifetime employment and towards productivity based wages.

Many analysts have pointed to the distinctive corporate structures of Japan as a key ingredient to economic success. Corporate groups or *keiretsu* are usually divided into two types: vertical *keiretsu* and horizontal *keiretsu*. Vertical keiretsu are centered on a particular large firm and consist of its multiple layers of contractors and subcontractors. Each group may consist of three or four layers of hierarchically organised and integrated subcontractors, as in the cases of Toyota, Nissan, Matsushita and Hitachi (Sasaki, 1990).

Horizontal keiretsu include twenty or more major firms. They have a major bank and *sogo shosha* (general trading company) as central members of the group and include manufacturers and insurance and trust companies (Akira, 1993). Cross-shareholding among major firms, major loans from the affiliated bank, interlocking directorates, personnel exchanges, joint investment in projects, Presidents clubs and intra-group trade all act to strengthen relations within the group (Terry, 1990b). Three of these groups (Mitsui, Mitsubishi and Sumitomo) are based on pre-war *zaibatsu* structures which had dominant holding companies that were family owned. Following the war the *zaibatsu* were dismembered by the Supreme Allied Command, but they reformed in the looser horizontal *keiretsu* format in the 1950s (Johnson, 1982). The other three major horizontal *keiretsu* (Fuyo, Sanwa and Daiichi Kangyo) are centered on their respective banks, but also include a *sogo shosha* and many *kaisha* or large firms from major industries. These six horizontal *keiretsu* form a network of many of the largest manufacturing and financial firms in Japan.

Keiretsu have been identified as a one of the Structural Impediments targeted in US-Japan trade disputes because they are argued to restrict foreign access to Japanese markets (Lawrence, 1990; Terry, 1990a). Sheard (1992) argued that they create increased stability and act as an effective insurance mechanism to protect member firms from sudden market changes. The practice of cross shareholding prevents mergers and takeovers because one-quarter of the shares are usually held by affiliated firms while additional shares are held by financial institution investors. With many shares held by parties which are unlikely to sell suddenly, firms are able to concentrate on long term strategies of maximising sales and marketshare rather than concentrate on short term profits as in American firms (Aoki 1988)[1].

Keiretsu are also argued to restrict trade because of a preference to trade with affiliated firms. Hoshi (1990) estimated that *keiretsu* members are three times more likely to trade with group members than with independent firms. However, the total value of intra-group sales typically accounts for less than 10 per cent of total sales for the group (Akira, 1993). Regardless of the impact *keiretsu* have on market operations, it is clear that they form a distinctive form of production structure which differs markedly from earlier Anglo-American corporate structures. *Keiretsu* style structures have been reproduced in other East Asian countries, South Korea and Taiwan in particular and are argued by some to represent the new model of corporate relations for western firms in the 1990s (McMillan, 1992).

Japanese production structures have expanded internationally through direct foreign investment, but the process accelerated rapidly when the level of annual investment rose to US$40 billion in the late 1980s (Edgington, 1992; Rugman, 1990). This level has since declined, but the global orientation of production remains. The extension of the Japanese production structure overseas was necessary to ensure access to markets, lower wage costs and extend Japanese management techniques overseas.

The relationship between production firms and banks is also important. Within each *keiretsu*, the major bank provides not only investment capital in the form of shares purchased, but also loan finance for investment by individual firms. It also acts as the lead bank for other private banks to join in the financing of new projects. These links between the production and finance structure are explored in more detail next.

The Japanese financial structure

The financial structure is broadly defined by Strange to mean the system by which credit is created, allocated and used (Strange, 1991, 35). Links between the financial and production structure are very strong. Credit can be used for investment in new productive capacity by allocating it either to those owning established means of production or to those proposing new ventures in new industries. Credit was especially important to finance growth in Japanese firms as their debt:equity ratio was typically much higher than in western firms. In the 1960s and 1970s the debt:equity ratio averaged 5:1 to reflect the high level of borrowing to support investment. By the mid-1980s this ratio had fallen to 3.5:1 for all firms and 2:1 for manufacturing firms (Sasaki, 1990, 26).

The financial structure is also closely linked to the security structure through the strong influence of government in the creation and allocation of credit. One example of an institution which promotes savings which can be used for subsequent loans is the postal savings system. The system was established in 1875 and managed by the Postal Savings Bureau of the Ministry of Posts and Telecommunications. The system provided a substantial part of the capital needed by industry and despite the proliferation of many competing institutions, still accounted for 30 percent of all personal savings in the 1980s or over US$500 billion per annum. The high level of personal savings (20 per cent of income) maintained by Japanese people is supported by tax incentives such as no tax being collected on income from small savings accounts, postal savings accounts and central government bonds (Higashi and Lauter, 1990, 24).

Government sources of funds were particularly important in the early phase of post war development. In addition to the regulatory and institutional arrangements (e.g. postal bank) which facilitated a high savings rate and its conversion to loan capital, the government created special public sector banks to promote particular types of projects. The Japan Development Bank is a prime example. In 1953 it provided 83 billion yen to industry and this accounted for 22 per cent of the industrial capital raised (Endo Shokichi 1966 cited in Johnson, 1982, 212). By 1961 Japan Development Bank loans of 86 billion yen represented only 5 per cent of the industrial capital raised, but other government banks (185 billion yen) and special government accounts (99 billion yen) increased the share of industrial capital raised from public financial organs to 20 per cent of the total.

The government not only provided one-third of the new industrial capital in the early 1950s, it also used taxation and depreciation policies to stimulate private investment in particular industries. Accelerated depreciation rates (2-3 years) were introduced for key industries to create tax benefits for those who invested in the designated industries. In the 1960s the government stimulated heavy investment in plant and equipment with a sixfold expansion of the Ministry of Finance's Fiscal Investment and Loans Programme (Higashi and Lauter, 1990; Shimizu, 1989, 43). These funds were typically allocated through the Japan Development Bank as low interest loans to firms creating new capacity in emerging industries. Some of these funds were also used to support R&D to add to the knowledge base for subsequent application to production. Investment was also promoted by the low interest rate policy of government initiated by the Ikeda administration of 1965 (Higashi and Lauter, 1990), Projects which received government funds usually attracted substantial private sector funds as well. Over time, the private sector became an increasingly important source of funds, but the allocation of these funds remained a function of both private and public decisions.

Links between banks and manufacturing firms were particularly strong within *keiretsu*. Most post-war firms were financed primarily by banks within the same *keiretsu* which provided 60-80 per cent of the firm's total loans (Suzuki, 1991, 328; Sasaki, 1990, 13). The importance of the affiliated bank as a lead banker continues with them providing the largest share of loans for new investment, but typically many other banks join with smaller shares of the total financing package for major projects. The banks also provided some of the capital raised internally within firms by purchasing shares directly. This practice was well established within keiretsu and became more prevalent during the 1980s when business partners were asked to buy shares as part of the equity-financing boom (Nishimura, 1994).

Despite the strategy of Japanese firms to reinvest more of their profit into capital for future production than US counterparts, these internal sources of funds could not meet the investment needs of manufacturing firms. In the late 1980s the major manufacturing firms were able to raise approximately 45-55 per cent of their capital internally through reserve funds, depreciation expenses and increases of capital stocks (Bank of Japan cited in JETRO, 1993, 102). However, the other half of their funds was borrowed. Some borrowings were raised in the form of corporate bonds, but most of the remainder were short and long term loans. Banks continue to play a central role in creating this capital for new investment.

This pattern proved particularly effective in the mid-1980s when Japanese firms responded to *endaka*, or the high yen, with renewed investment to lower production costs with the latest and most efficient technology. In 1987 Japanese industry set a new record by investing the equivalent to 19.5 per cent of Japan's GNP in new plant and equipment (Williams, 1994, 56). In 1990 Japanese investment exceeded 25 per cent of GNP, a record for any OECD country[2]. This system of high savings and investment levels is achieved through strong linkages among government ministries, banks and manufacturing firms. The knowledge/information structure is also closely linked to the first three structures and is examined next.

The Japanese knowledge/information structure

The knowledge/information structure serves to extend Japanese structures globally in several ways. The structure can be divided into three levels: beliefs, knowledge/information and channels of communication. As in the case of the financial structure, power in the information structure is important in both the positive and negative direction (Strange, 1988, 115). The decision to withhold or restrict information may be just as important as the decision to withhold or restrict financial credit or loans. To construct an effective international trading system both finance and knowledge are required.

The shared beliefs or assumptions of Japanese actors are often argued to contribute to national success. The emphasis on group interests over individual interests, the adaptation of new ideas within the context of old ideas and the cultural homogeneity of Japan are often cited as contributors to Japanese economic success (Sasaki, 1990). More generally, Morishima (1982) supported Weber's argument that a distinct set of beliefs results in a distinct type of economy. In the case of Japan, Morishima explained how many ideas had evolved from an initial form in China to a different form in Japan. The evolution of a distinct society and economy was thus to be expected.

At the general level of shared beliefs or ideas, the extensive links among government, business and conservative politicians described earlier and the emphasis on reaching consensual decisions results in shared beliefs among a wide range of actors. This shared set of beliefs provides a strong foundation for the implementation of shared decisions. Indeed, it has been argued that although the consensus approach takes longer to reach a decision, it is faster in implementing the agreed actions because of the widespread support.

Sasaki (1990) highlighted four dimensions to the coordination of economic activities and group structures within Japan. Each type of coordination involves institutional arrangements which facilitate the exchange of information and promote shared beliefs or goals. Vertical and horizontal coordination among affiliated firms is achieved within *keiretsu* through several of the institutional arrangements identified in the section on production structures. The mechanisms extend beyond equity and executive links to include the reallocation of significant numbers of workers to firms in growing sectors from affiliated firms in declining sectors (Sasaki, 1990, 90). Coordination within an industry is achieved across firms and corporate groups through hundreds of approved cartels and industry associations. Government agencies, such as MITI, interact with industry to influence the expansion of capacity and, especially in recent years, the negotiation of capacity reductions as part of industry-wide restructuring. Finally, overall coordination across groups is achieved through industry councils which act as advisory bodies to government and promote visions or scenarios of the future size of various sectors within the economy (Sasaki, 1990). The result is a pool of shared ideas and information to combine public and private efforts in the direction of a significant share of the economy. Despite these extensive institutional networks to share basic beliefs, attitudes and information, individuals and firms may respond to the available information with innovative individual responses. The influence of shared beliefs and group efforts is thus extensive, but not universal and by no means uniform in their impacts.

Beyond the sharing of common beliefs and information, one can examine the creation and use of new information. Technology represents a solid form of knowledge which is created through investment in R&D. Large Japanese manufacturing firms typically spend 40 per cent more of their sales revenue on R&D than their American counterparts (Abegglen and Stalk, 1985, 12). Japanese firms continually assess their technology relative to that in other countries. Regardless of the assessment, further research is required. When the Japanese technology is considered superior, it is a source of national pride and efforts are made to maintain the position. If the technology is inferior, then efforts are increased to improve the technology further (Abegglen and Stalk, 1985, 12). Almost all manufacturing industries allocated an increased share of sales to research and development efforts in the 1980s with the percentage of sales from all industries allocated to research increasing from 1.6 per cent in 1981 to 2.8 per cent in 1990 (JETRO, 1993, 50).

Private investment in R&D is supported by government initiatives. MITI often assumes a high profile role in the promotion of R&D projects on advanced technology where the designation of a 'national project' brings together researchers from competing firms to work cooperatively on general technologies which can later be applied in the participating manufacturing firms on a competitive basis. An example of this industry-wide approach to R&D was the super large scale integrated circuit project. Overall, the role of government is to facilitate the establishment of the project with private firms paying most (over 90 per cent) of the cost (Shimizu, 1989, 46).

Intense efforts to devise new variations and applications of technology result in Japan leading the world in the annual registration of patents. Differences exist in the Japanese patenting system not only in the number of patents generated, but also in the distribution of the resulting information. While new patents in Japan, the US and many other countries are not disclosed for 18 months, access to the information after this period varies dramatically (EAIT, IST, 1991). Patent information is typically only available at the patent office in the US or Canada while in Japan the information is published in journals to make interested parties aware of recent developments in the field. This emphasis on the publication and dissemination of information is not restricted to patents. Japan is also the source of over 20,000 periodicals providing information on an extensive range of topics.

In addition to the generation of information in Japan, firms also scan the globe for sources of information on technology and market opportunities. The import of technology has been an important means for Japanese firms to quickly acquire the most advanced method of producing a particular good. The average annual number of cases of technical imports rose from 250 in the 1950s to 1000 in the 1960s and 2000 in the 1970s and early 1980s. A total of US$17 billion was paid for these technology imports, but this cost reflected only a fraction of the R&D costs associated with developing the technology in the first place. The import of technology was of critical importance to many firms, but government also had a direct hand in the final arrangements as MITI representatives typically participated in negotiations and suggested that royalty payments, length of contract and export restrictions not be too high (Abbeglen and Stalk, 1985, 127). The import of technology provided the base for Japanese firms to improve upon. Not surprisingly, the import of technology has been followed by an increase in the export of technology. The value of technology sales rose from 1 per cent of the payments for technology imports in the 1950s to 9 per cent in the 1960s, 18 per cent in the 1970s and 30 percent in the 1980s (Abegglen and Stalk, 1985, 126; Sasaki, 1990, 28).

The group-directed quest for knowledge was asserted by Vogel (1979) to be the single most important factor to explain Japan's economic success. One of the most efficient and effective means to gain international information was the specialization of tasks which firms undertook from the Meiji Restoration onwards. Rather than having individual manufacturing firms each attempt to negotiate trade deals with foreign firms, *sogo shosha* acted as intermediaries. *Sogo shosha* established trade offices overseas to both procure the raw materials and technology required by Japanese industry and to sell the products manufactured by Japanese industry (Yoshino and Lifson, 1986). Each of the major horizontal *keiretsu* have an affiliated trading company. The six largest *sogo shosha* are among the ten largest firms in the world as measured by total sales. By the 1980s some argued that *sogo shosha* were no longer required as Japanese firms had grown sufficiently large to undertake their own international marketing. However, they still accounted for one-half of Japan's trade in the late 1980s. Their role remains significant, even though it is not dominant.

Sogo shosha provide a similar distribution and wholesale role within Japan where they act as frequent suppliers to manufacturing firms and the small specialized stores which comprise much of Japan's retail sector.

The knowledge/information structure constructed by Japanese actors extends internationally and increasingly includes diverse networks among other countries. The specialised trade information services which *sogo shosha* established to conduct global trade for Japanese firms extend beyond direct Japanese trade links. To maximise their global trade opportunities, *sogo shosha* found the fastest growing segment of their activity in the 1980s to be trade between third countries where Japan is neither the importer nor the exporter. Indeed, *sogo shosha* demonstrate how specific institutions developed to meet the developmental objectives of Japan are being extended in many other countries to promote increased trade there. *Sogo shosha* typically have over 100 offices in over 80 countries world wide and consider themselves to be global corporations (Yoshino and Lifson, 1986). Certainly, their information network is global in function and form. The trade information services of private *sogo shosha* are complemented with the activities of JETRO, the government's trade promotion agency. At all three levels: beliefs, information and communication, institutions have been developed to achieve shared private and public goals. Basic shared beliefs are established to facilitate group oriented consensus, new information is created and disseminated from domestic sources, as demonstrated in the case of patent journals, and from international sources, as in the case of *sogo shosha* providing trade information services. Institutional interaction is faciliated by the concentration of government, public agencies, manufacturers' head offices, banks, *sogo shosha* and R&D institutions in Tokyo[3]. The result is an extensive network of linkages among the four structures to provide a structural base of interconnected institutions to achieve the outcomes desired by government and corporate actors.

Conclusion

To understand Japanese development processes better, we need to explore the institutional structures built to facilitate the social relations identified in macro level studies and provide the context for micro level decisions as reflected in trade and investment patterns. It has been argued in this chapter that institutions are built to promote partnerships and shared strategies within each of the four primary structures. In each case a strong domestic base was built which provided the foundation for international expansion and the creation of a global set of structures which is highly interconnected. The complex web of shared public and private interactions creates a model of development which contrasts with the bipolar regulatory model of Anglo-American political economy.

The developmental state model demonstrated by Japan offers an alternative to the Anglo-American regulatory model for the promotion of economic development. Many analysts argue that the developmental role of the Japanese state has declined as Japanese firms have established competitive positions in the global economy. However, the structures built to achieve public and private strategies served not only to facilitate growth in the earlier stages of development, but also continue to provide a base for future initiatives. The result is a series of structures which offer collective security through flexible production, ready access to credit and extensive trade and technical knowledge for the pursuit of shared goals. These extensive interconnected structures are not the only means of conducting economic activities in Japan: many actors also pursue individual initiatives. The argument is not that government agencies, such as MITI or the Ministry of Finance (MoF), directed the micro level actions of private firms, but that institutional initiatives were undertaken to achieve shared goals and create opportunities for actors to benefit both individually and collectively. This model of shared strategies and partnerships between state and private interests offers insights for development options and strategies to meet societal needs and objectives in a manner distinct from the Anglo-American model.

Notes

1. The pattern of stable crossholding of shares continues, but its importance varies among firms and over time. The recession of the early 1990s acted as a trigger for some corporate investors to sell their bank shares and by the end of the 1992 fiscal year the percentage of cross held shares declined to 39.9 percent of all shares issued by the companies listed on Japan's stock exchanges (Daiwa cited in Nishimura, 1994). This decline in the percentage of cross-held shares from the stable level of 41-44 percent in the late 1970s and 1980s remains well above the earlier level of 29-33 percent in the late 1950s and early 1960s. The sales of bank shares in the 1990s reflect greater flexibility in financial markets resulting from deregulation in the 1980s. Other cross shareholdings, like those among horizontal *keiretsu* members, are considered secure and are not expected to be sold (Nishimura, 1994).

2. High investment levels were achieved with the guidance of government through the MoF and its constituent bureaux. For example, the Banking Bureau has an official obligation to protect the interests of depositors, however, Williams (1994, 66) asserts that its primary mission was to ensure that the nations savings were 'manipulated in ways that aided the rebuilding of ... strategic industries'. Long term investments in heavy industry, power generation and coal were priority concerns from the late 1940s until the 1960s. This period of support was much longer than that required for the post-war emergency period or to support infant industries. The policy was one of sustained investment support. A second dimension to the MoF's support of Japanese industry was its effective protection from foreign capital. Foreign investment was restricted through foreign exchange regulations and only relaxed after many Japanese firms had proven their ability to compete internationally (Williams, 1994).

3.   Tokyo represents the focal point for economic decisions in Japan. It is the location of government and national ministries as well as the headquarters of the majority of the largest businesses.   The Tokyo metropolitan area encompasses Tokyo prefecture plus three neighbouring prefectures (Chiba, Kanagawa and Saitama) to account for approximately 25 per cent of Japan's population and manufacturing output. However, it accounted for 39 per cent of commercial sales, 49 per cent of private manufacturing R&D institutes and 55 per cent of all bank loans in the late 1980s (Aono, 1993, 34). Similarly, 57 per cent of the firms listed on the First Section of the Tokyo Stock Exchange have their headquarters in Tokyo, especially in the three wards of central Tokyo. The concentration among the 186 member firms of the six largest *keiretsu* was even higher at 70 per cent (Aono, 1993, 34).   The overwhelming majority (86 per cent) of foreign owned subsidiaries established in Japan are also located in Tokyo (Aono, 1993, 35; Terasaka, 1993, 41). In short, government, manufacturing firm headquarters, financial institutions, research institutes and subsidiaries of foreign firms are all concentrated in Tokyo. Some Japanese analysts argue that this concentration is a simple economic function of agglomeration economies and benefits created by specialised high order services. Others argue that the concentration reflects a growing spatial division of labour by monopolistic capital. Proximity does not cause integration, but it creates increased opportunities to establish institutions which promote the coordination of actions among various actors.

References

Abegglen, J. and Stalk, G. Jr 1985: *Kaisha: The Japanese Corporation*. New York, Basic Books Inc.

Akira, G. 1993: 'Corporate Groups Japanese Style: A Historical Overview'. *Journal of Japanese Trade and Industry*, 6, 8-11.

Aoki, M. 1988: *Information, incentives, and bargaining in the Japanese economy*. Cambridge, Cambridge University Press.

Aono, T. 1993: 'Research into the Location of Business Core Functions in Japan', in Sargent, J. and Wiltshire, R. (eds) *Geographical Studies and Japan*. Japan Library, Sandgate, Kent, 32-38.

Buckley, R. 1990: *Japan Today* (2nd edition) Cambridge, Cambridge University Press.

Dicken, P. 1992: *Global Shift: The Internationalization of Economic Activity* (2nd edition). New York, Guildford Press.

Dohse, K., Jurgens, U. and Malsch, T. 1985: 'From 'Fordism' to 'Toyotism'? The Social Organization of the Labour Process in the Japanese Automobile Industry'. *Politics and Society*. 14, 115-146.

Dore, R. 1986: *Flexible Rigidities: Industrial Policy and Structural Adjustment in the Japanese Economy, 1970-1980.* London, Athlone Press.

Drysdale, P. 1988: *International Economic Pluralism: Economic Policy in East Asia and the Pacific.* Sydney, Allen and Unwin.

Edgington, D. 1992: *Japanese Direct Investment in Canada: Recent Trends and Prospects.* B. C. Geographical Series #49. Vancouver, Department of Geography, University of British Columbia.

EAIT, IST 1991: *Protecting Intellectual Property: An Introduction to Japan.* Ottawa.

Friedman, D. 1988: *The Misunderstood Miracle: Industrial Development and Political Change in Japan.* Ithaca NY, Cornell University Press.

Fukuyama, F. 1989: 'The End of History?' *The National Interest.* Summer, 3-18.

Grant, R. 1993: 'Trading blocs or trading blows? The macroeconomic geography of US and Japanese trade policies'. *Environment and Planning A,* 25, 273-291.

Higashi, C. and Lauter, G. P. 1990: *The internationalization of the Japanese Economy* (2nd edition). Boston, Kluwer Academic Publishers.

Hollerman, L. 1988: *Japan, Disincorporated: The Economic Liberalization Process.* Stanford CA, Hoover Institution Press.

Hoshi, T. 1990: 'The Role of Banks in Reducing the Costs of Financial Distress in Japan'. Working Paper No. 3435. Cambridge MA, National Bureau of Economic Research Inc.

JETRO 1993: Business Facts and Figures. Tokyo, JETRO.

Johnson, C. 1982: *MITI and the Japanese Miracle: The Growth of Industrial Policy 1925-75.* Stanford, Stanford University Press.

Johnson, C. 1988: 'The Japanese political economy: a crisis in theory'. *Ethics and International Affairs,* 3, 79-98.

Johnston, R. 1989: 'Extending the Research Agenda'. *Economic Geography,* 65, 338-348.

Kenney, M. and Florida, R. 1988: 'Beyond Mass Production: Production and the Labour Process in Japan'. *Politics and Society,* 16, 121-158.

Knox, P. and Agnew, J. 1989: *The Geography of the World-Economy.* New York, Edward Arnold.

Kono, T. 1984: *Strategy and Structure of Japanese Enterprises.* London, Macmillan Press.

Lawrence, R. 1990: 'Efficient or Exclusionist? The Import Behaviour of Japanese Corporate Groups'. *Brookings Papers on Economic Activity,* 1, 311-330.

McMillan, C. 1992: 'Japan's Contribution to Management Development'. *Business and the Contemporary World,* 4(2), 21-33.

Morishima, M. 1982: *Why has Japan succeeded?: Western technology and Japanese ethos.* Cambridge, Cambridge University Press.

Nester, W. 1991: *Japanese Industrial Targeting: The Neomercantilist Path to Economic Superpower.* Hong Kong, Macmillan.

Nishimura, H. 1994: 'Recession forces firms to dump shares of allies'. *The Nikkei Weekly,* 32(1618), 1 and 12.

Okamoto, Y. 1984: 'The Grand Strategy of Japanese Business', in Sato, K. and Hoshino, Y. (eds) *The Anatomy of Japanese Business*. Armonk NY, M.E. Sharpe Inc., 277-318.

Ozawa, T. 1979: *Multinationalism Japanese Style: The Political Economy of Outward Dependence*. Princeton NJ, Princeton University Press.

Ozawa, T. 1980: 'Japan's New Resource Diplomacy: Government-backed Group Investment'. *Journal of World Trade Law*, 14, 3-13.

Piore, M. and Sahel, C. 1984: *The Second Industrial Divide: Possibilities for Prosperity*. New York, Basic Books Inc.

Rugman, A. 1990: *Japanese Direct Investment in Canada*. Ottawa The Canada-Japan Trade Council.

Sasaki, N. 1990: *Management and Industrial Structure in Japan* (2nd edition). Oxford, Pergamon Press.

Sheard, P. 1992: *International Adjustment and the Japanese Firm*. St. Leonards NSW, Allen and Unwin.

Shimizu, R. 1989: *The Japanese Business Success Factors*. Tokyo, Chikura Shobo.

Shinmura, T. 1994: 'Trade surplus with Asia tops imbalance with US'. *The Nikkei Weekly*, 32 (1617), 1 and 27.

Strange, S. 1988: *States and Markets*. London, Pinter Publishers

Strange, S. 1991: 'An Eclectic Approach'. *International Political Economy Yearbook*, 6, 33-50.

Suzuki, Y. 1991: *Japanese Management Structures, 1920-80*. London, Macmillan.

Taylor, P. 1985: *Political Geography: World-economy, nation-state and locality*. New York, Longman.

Terasaka, A. 1993: 'The Transformation of Regional Systems in an Information-Oriented Society', in Sargent, J. and Wiltshire, R. (eds) *Geographical Studies and Japan*. Japan Library, Sandgate, Kent, 39-42.

Terry, E. 1990a: 'Japan's New Capitalism: The Land of the Rising Cartels'. *The Globe and Mail*, 22 September, Section B, 1.

Terry, E. 1990b: 'Japan's New Capitalism: The Ties that Bind'. *The Globe and Mail*, 24 September, Section B, 4.

Vogel, E. 1979: *Japan as number one: Lessons for America*. Cambridge MA, Harvard University Press.

Wade, R. 1991: *Governing the Market: Economic Theory and the Role of Government in East Asia Industrialisation*. Princeton NJ, Princeton University Press.

Wallerstein, I. 1991: *Geopolitics and Geoculture*. New York, Cambridge University Press.

Williams, D. 1994: *Japan: beyond the end of history*. London, Routledge.

Yoshino, M. and Lifson, T. 1986: *The Invisible Link: Japan's sogo shosha and the organization of trade*. MIT Press.

6 Integration through trade and direct investment: Asian Pacific patterns

Claes Alvstam

This chapter describes the process of economic integration between the economies in East and Southeast Asia from a spatial point of view. The approach followed shows how the external economic relations of a single country play a role in determining the organization of industrial space within the country in itself, as well as between separate countries. The spatial pattern of foreign trade and foreign direct investment (FDI) is an integral part of any framework for a deeper understanding of the forces behind industrial change. The findings of the chapter are mainly applicable in an East and Southeast Asian context, rather than to the more mature and intense, mutually interdependent economic interaction that takes place between the states of Western Europe.

Beginning with Japan, a number of economies in Pacific Asia have since the mid-1950s gone through a process of industrial growth and transformation. This change has in general been characterized by a far more accelerated pace than was the case in the old industrial countries. This process is often linked with a strategy of state-managed export-oriented growth within a market economy context (World Bank, 1987, 1993). In most cases, the industrialization strategy in countries treading in Japan footsteps has followed a pattern featuring striking similarities, despite obvious differences in what Porter would classify in terms of domestic factor endowments, structure and rivalry, existence of related and supporting industries, extent of direct government influence and size of home market demand (Porter, 1990). The second generation of economies to get involved in this process included (South) Korea, Taiwan, Hong Kong and Singapore, followed by a third group consisting of Malaysia and Thailand, the Philippines, parts of Indonesia and the Special Economic Zones in the Chinese provinces of Guangdong and Fujian. Finally, a fourth group comprising Vietnam and additional Chinese provinces, particularly along the coast, e.g. Jiangsu and Zhejiang. This process of industrialization has until recently been mainly externally driven, in the respect that it has been coupled to the corporate strategy formulated within a number of mostly American and Japanese enterprises. In the second generation of corporate dominance, however, Taiwanese, Hong Kong, and Korean companies have also pushed forward their positions as determinants in the organization of industrial space in many countries throughout the region. The theoretical framework of such a process can be linked with recent research within the field of critical international political economy, particularly, *Rival States, Rival Firms* topford *et al.*, 1991), as well as with the geographically oriented new international economics, primarily expressed in *Geography and Trade* (Krugman, 1991). The empirical examples used to illustrate this evolution are drawn from the island of Taiwan. The Taiwanese example symbolizes the dynamics of the change, as it represents an intermediate level in the trade hierarchy within the region, behind Japan, Singapore and Hong Kong, roughly equal with Korea, and well ahead of the ASEAN countries, except Singapore.

Point of departure

During the entire post-war period and up to the middle of the 1970s, the extraordinary development of internationalization, specialization and the continuous processes of division of labour between the Western European economies has been one of the most significant features in the growth of world trade. Simultaneously, there was a long-term decline in the importance of North America in the world trade system from an all-time high in the late 1940s. Since the mid-1970s, the American share of world trade has continued to tumble, the rate of growth in intra-European trade has been slower, while trade with and within the Asia Pacific region has been growing much more rapidly than in other areas. In parallel, the relative importance of manufacturing production reached its peak in the old industrial countries between the early 1960s and the late 1970s, while the share of service production in their GDPs have risen significantly. Consequently, the growth of value added in intra-European and North Atlantic trade, is more to be derived from a growing content of research, knowledge, and service factors, rather than a volume growth in pure physical terms.

Even though a number of similar patterns between past economic integration in Western Europe and the recent process in East and Southeast Asia can be found, the differences are equally obvious. First, the notion of American dominance in Asia Pacific trade, was and is at a much higher level than it ever has been during the process of European economic integration. This pattern has persisted also through the phase of a more intense intra-regional trade during the 1980s (Table 6.1). The US took the role as the key trade partner for countries in Northeast Asia already during the inter-war period, while it replaced the European dominance in Southeast Asia during the first decade after the Second World War.

Secondly, there are larger differences in levels of economic development and resource endowments between the single states, including the apparent dominance of one single state, Japan, which alone still accounts for some 40 per cent of the total export value in the entire East and Southeast Asia. Thirdly, the Asian Pacific economic interaction, unlike the cases of the European and American trading blocs, so far has not been the result of political decisions to promote intraregional trade through official, supranational agreements. On the contrary, the function and purpose of international economic interaction in Asia Pacific, has developed *in spite* of political obstacles to trade (Schive, 1993, 31). Despite 25 years of formal economic

108

cooperation within the ASEAN bloc, very few barriers between the member states have been removed until recently. The share of intra-trade within ASEAN is roughly at the same level today as it was in the late 1960s (Table 6.2).

The political and ideological barriers between the PRC and Taiwan, and Korea are other obstacles to intra-regional trade. The proposed creation of various constellations of economic blocs with higher ambitions, like AFTA, APEC and EAEC, reflects current political visions of economic integration within the Pacific Rim. The multilateral trade talks within the GATT since the late 1940s, and the finally successful conclusion of the Uruguay Round in 1993, have played a much greater role in liberalizing trade between East and Southeast Asian countries than various intra-regional arrangements. One important theoretical consideration in the present discussion on formation of intra-regional trade blocs within the Asian Pacific Rim, is whether the East and Southeast Asian production and trade system of tomorrow will converge with the corresponding system of economic integration in Europe, or whether the two integration 'strategies' will develop along quite different routes in the future.

To a certain extent, the absence of an early economic integration between the states of East and Southeast Asia is thus to be understood in terms of European, American and Japanese dominance as key trade partners to these countries at different times. This feature has persisted in aggregate terms through the process of industrialization, even though it has altered considerably in character. The constituents of the economic interaction between a single East or Southeast Asian country on one hand, and America or Japan on the other, is completely different in the early 1990s, compared with the situation in the 1950s and 1960s, or even in the late 1970s. This is evident within the commodity composition of exports from East and Southeast Asian countries to the US and Japan, in which the pace of progress of upgrading in technological advancement, capital intensity and value added has been striking. Thus, the diminishing technological gap in trade between the NIEs in the Pacific Rim on one hand, and the US and Japan on the other, is the key factor in understanding the process of economic integration within the region.

Some methodological considerations

International economic interaction is defined here as the aggregate of transfers in commodities, services, and capital. While physical trade has been well documented through internationally recognized and uniform customs routines for at least the last century, trade in producer services is a much more elusive concept. The usual approximation while measuring service trade is to estimate the differences between the current account statistics, representing an *ex post* evaluation of all flows in goods and services, and the trade statistics as reported by the customs authorities, and representing physical flows only. It is well established, that this measurement grossly underestimates the value of the service trade. The underrating has three sources: the degree of service content, that is built-in the physical trade, which is valued in gross rather than net terms; limitations in the data collection; and the invisibility of the services in themselves, as they are consumed in the moment of

Table 6.1

The role of the US as a consignee of exports from East and Southeast Asia (share of total export value in separate countries, selected years 1981-1993, in percentages)

	1981	1985	1987	1989	1991	1992	1993e
PRC	7	8	8	8	9	10	18
Taiwan	36	48	44	36	29	29	28
Hong Kong	36	31	28	25	23	23	23
Indonesia	18	22	20	16	12	15	15
Japan	26	38	37	34	29	28	29
South Korea	27	36	39	32	25	21	16
Malaysia	13	13	17	19	17	19	19
Philippines	31	36	36	38	36	39	41
Singapore	13	21	24	23	20	17	16
Thailand	13	20	19.	22	21	21	23

Sources: UN, International Trade Statistics Yearbook; IMF, Direction of Trade Statistics; Monthly Statistics of Exports, The Republic of China, Taiwan District.

Table 6.2

Share of intra-trade within ASEAN, 1968-1993 (percentage of total export and import values)

1968	1973	1978	1983	1988	1992	1993e
15.0	14.3	16.3	23.7	18.2	17.8	18.1

Source: Own adaptions and estimations based on IMF, Direction of Trade Statistics.

production, making them far more volatile and difficult to comprehend, particularly in terms of establishing their movement over state boundaries. This chapter mainly emphasizes the manufacturing sector.

International capital flows are even more complicated to record, and there is still confusion over how to measure them appropriately from a geographical viewpoint. Usually, a distinction is made between portfolio investments and foreign direct investment in production, the latter being the concept investigated in this chapter. The flows of foreign direct investment vary largely in size, depending on different methods of measurement (Alvstam, 1993). This notion is particularly relevant in

East and Southeast Asia, where one can find astonishingly varied descriptions of the same phenomenon[1]. After adapting various methods of measuring FDI flows in empirical studies of East and Southeast Asian countries, my conclusion is that all measures are useful, acting as reference points for each other (Alvstam, 1993, 65). Nevertheless, the accuracy of measurement in capital flows is far less than is the case in commodity or service flows. The deregulation of international capital flows in many countries, as well as the revolution of telecommunication that has facilitated capital transfers, have further obstructed the possibility to a proper valuation of these flows. Empirical observations of foreign direct investment flows must therefore be interpreted cautiously.

The nation-state is the usual territorial unit for the measurement of international economic interaction. An issue that should be given high priority in research on the organization of industrial space is the proper understanding of spatial economic interaction, within and across state boundaries, at short and long-distances. Normally no distinction is made between 'arm's-length trade', that is trade between independent actors and trade between dependent parties, usually intra-corporate transfers. Conventional neoclassical trade theory has indeed very little to say about the dynamics of intra-firm trade, The interrelationship between the theory of corporate decisions and theories of organisational change on one hand, and changes in the international trade pattern on the other, remains still an underdeveloped field within economic geography as well as in international economics. In this context, the use of the nation-states as the unit of analysis in the modelling of integration through trade and investment represents the statistical shortcomings of measurement of spatial economic interaction as well as the identification of intra-firm trade.

Another important methodological problem is the conversion of exchange rates between different economies. The exchange rate of a freely convertible national currency should in theory reflect differences in interest rates in the short term perspective, changes in the current account balance in the middle term, and relative level of competition in the long term view. In reality, the exchange rate policy in several East and Southeast Asian countries is more a result of much broader considerations, particularly the negotiations between the G7 countries. The Japanese Yen went through one of the most radical changes in modern international economy during the nearly 100 per cent appreciation towards the US$ between Summer 1985 and the end of 1987. Other Asian currencies, which traditionally were more or less pegged to the US$ until 1985, did in most cases also go through a period of revaluations during the first two years after the Plaza Agreement, and have thereafter either become linked to various 'baskets' of currencies of the countries' own choice, (e.g. in Malaysia and Thailand), or been subject to so-called managed floating, (e.g. in PRC, Taiwan, Korea, Indonesia and Singapore), or, been independently floating, (the Philippines) or, remained relatively fixed to the US$, (Hong Kong). In short, the volatility in the conversion rates is usually larger than is reflected by long term changes in industrial competition levels. Resulting changes in the industrial structure as well as the organisation of industrial space are difficult to forecast and to build into a general model. Relative effective exchange rates between separate economies are reflected by a number of factors apart from changes in economic competitiveness. The short term effects of changes in conversion rates between single currencies are often considerable. This fact is well illustrated by the latest appreciations of the Yen towards the US$ and several currencies in other East and Southeast Asia during 1993-1994. In order to cope with this methodological problem, an *ex post* attitude is taken here towards the changes of relative conversion rates.

Theoretical framework

An analysis of the process of economic integration can be based on three different perspectives. First, an institutional and structuralist is discernible, as developed within theories of critical international political economy (Strange, 1988; Stopford *et al.*, 1991). Secondly, 'old' as well as 'new' spatially-oriented theories of international trade and international investment abound. These have arisen from several sources, within international economics (Krugman, 1991), classical studies of the geography of international trade (Grotewold, 1979; Hanink, 1989; Johnston, 1976; Johnston, 1989; McConnell, 1986), management-oriented research of multinational operations of the manufacturing firm (Dunning, 1988; Pitelis and Sugden, 1991) and about the competitive advantage of nations (Porter, 1990). Thirdly, a network perspective is present in industrial geography (Conti, 1993). It is assumed that the growing interdependence among states and transnational corporations means that the rivalry between states, as well as the rivalry between firms has become far more intense than previously was the case. Consequently, the mutual interaction between states and transnational firms has been much more complex, and difficult to foresee. Stopford *et al.* (1991) single out six general propositions that also form the theoretical starting point of this study. States are now competing more for the means to create wealth within their territory than for power over more territory. The emergence of new forms of global competition among firms also affects how states compete for wealth. As a result firms harness the power of new technology to create systems of activity linked directly across borders, increasingly concentrating on those territories offering the greatest potential for recovering their investments. Small, poor countries face increased barriers to entry in industries most subject to global forces of competition. States no longer merely negotiate among themselves, they must also negotiate with foreign firms. TNCs themselves have to become more state-like as they make different kinds of corporate alliances, to enhance their combined capacities to compete with others for world market shares. The number of possible policy options for governments and for firms has multiplied, which in its turn has greatly complicated the problems for both of managing multiple agendas. The shifts have in total increased the volatility of change. Development thus becomes a function of nations' abilities to link and control their economic affairs in cooperation with others. While Stopford *et al.*, (1991, 1-2) conclude that these propositions suggest reasons *why* industrial and economic policy most become more outward-looking they also stress that *how* these policies are implemented becomes a far more critical determinant of success.⌐

⌐It is furthermore assumed, that international trade does not take place between equal parties. On the contrary, trade flows are the substantial results of an unequal relationship that is taken advantage of by authorities, private firms or other actors, who are in control of production and trade. Such an unequal relationship is always under pressure for change and preservation. It is assumed that a country simultaneously can be subordinated and superior to other countries in the same time⌐ and in the same commodity group. In the case of completely developed mutual interaction between two states, these differences are too complex to being caught in one single aggregate. To overcome these conceptual problems the idea of a 'trade hierarchy', an approximate ranking between states at different levels of economic development is useful. A high rank in the trade hierarchy is defined as:

· increasing share of exports of manufactured goods in the total exports;
· an increasing share of exports of technically advanced manufacturing, in the total export of manufactured goods;
· an increasing degree of commodity diversification in the total exports of manufactured goods;
· a declining degree of concentration regarding countries of destination in the total exports of manufactured goods;
· an increasing share of services in international economic interaction;
· an increasing degree of diversification in the service trade;
· a long-term equilibrium between inward and outward FDI;
· a shift from labour-oriented towards market-oriented FDI

A high rank in the trade hierarchy is not necessarily accompanied by a high trade-intensity. In neither the US nor Japan does foreign economic interaction play any dominant role in the formation of the national economy. However, with these exceptional cases, where the domestic market accounts for the greater part of the total demand, there is generally a high positive correlation between an increasing trade-intensity in the national economy and a higher rank in the trade hierarchy.

The growing share of manufactures in the total export value has been the most visible sign of a successful industrialization of a national economy. This change is not in itself a sufficient condition for a higher rank in the trade hierarchy. It seems that a far more important indicator of the process of industrial transformation is the exports within the engineering sector (mainly Section 7 in the SITC system), in which products with a high intensity of R&D technical sophistication and a high added value are classified. In order to distinguish between externally managed lay-off production, usually located to export-processing zones, two more indicators are added, namely the degree of commodity concentration in exports, and the degree of geographical concentration of the export consignments. A declining degree of commodity concentration in exports of manufactured goods indicates that the national economy is moving from a dependence of single products within the machinery and equipment sector and towards a more complete coverage of products within various

113

branches and at different technological levels. Likewise, an increasing diversification regarding partner countries in exports indicate a higher national level of competition, a more intense participation in the international division of labour and a decreasing dependence towards single foreign corporations.

On the other hand, a trade surplus in the bilateral balance with another country must not necessarily be accompanied by a higher rank in the trade hierarchy. The trade surplus may well indicate that the exporter is subordinate in terms of the technological level of its industry, delivering mainly pure raw materials and semi-processed manufactures, in exchange for consumer products. Also, a shrinking trade surplus may be a result of a country. As promotion in the trade-hierarchy, as the stagnation in exports may be caused by a phasing out of inefficient production through FDI directed to countries at a lower level in the hierarchy.

The increased portion of service trade in the total trade of goods and services indicates the growing role of services. However, such a higher ratio must be accompanied by a larger degree of diversification in the service trade, in order to avoid inclusion of countries with an exceptional high dependence on certain kinds of service exports, (e.g. tourism). In addition, economies like Hong Kong and Singapore with a traditionally large proportion of services in their exports, have to be treated as special cases as well.

The criteria concerning a move towards a more balanced FDI pattern and a shift towards market-oriented FDI emanates from the observation that all countries in East and Southeast Asia, recorded an initial extreme surplus of inward FDI, concentrated in a few sectors in the economy, reflecting a subordinate country's role as a recipient of foreign capital. In Japan the transformation in the direction of a more balanced ratio between outward and inward FDI started in the early 1960s, while in Korea the corresponding process took place in the 1970s, and in Taiwan in the 1980s. It is further assumed that the role of intra- as well as extra-regional FDI in the total foreign economic interaction will grow considerably in East and Southeast Asia during the next 10 years, as all countries in the region still lag far behind Europe and North America in terms of overseas production capacity relative to total capacity in their industries. Still, less than 10 per cent of the production capacity controlled by Japanese firms, is located outside Japan, compared to the US, where the share is about 33 per cent, and Sweden, more than 50 per cent. The assumption of an outward/inward FDI ratio approaching 1.00 is based on the fact that countries with an excessive degree of outward FDI will sooner or later go through a phase of specialization and increased participation in a general division of production of goods and services, at the same time opening boundaries for foreign competition. The previously high proportion of outward FDI, directed towards resources and cheap labour, is gradually balanced by FDI, aiming at strengthening the domestic companies' position in foreign markets. Most European and American FDI are made in countries where the wage costs are roughly equal to the level in the home countries. In the last few years however Japan has moved to more labour- and resource-oriented FDI, after a couple of years in the late 1980s, when the market-oriented FDI directed towards North America grew at a considerable rate. This pattern can once again be explained by the relative unimportance that foreign production plays in the Japanese economy and a phase of relocation of labour-intensive industries, which up to now have stayed in Japan in spite of considerably higher production costs than in neighbouring countries. The largest growth of outward FDI from Japan during the 1990s has been directed towards East and Southeast Asia in general, and Mainland China in particular.

The general growth of both outward and inward FDI in East and Southeast Asian countries will reactivate the old debate regarding the substitutability between trade and investment. Vernon (1966) and Wells (1973) used the product-life cycle model to show the effects of FDI on exports. Kojima (1978) concluded that there are two polar models of FDI. These models were argued to be typical for the Japanese and American economies respectively. The American, anti-trade oriented model was characterized by a pattern, where FDI resulted in a decrease of comparative advantage, while the Japanese, trade complementary model used FDI to enhance the comparative advantage among countries, resulting in an increase in international economic interaction. In this sense Japanese investments abroad have usually taken place in industries in which the foreign country has had a comparative advantage relative to Japan. As a result, the growth and development of Japanese industries has followed the so-called 'catching-up product cycle' (Akamatsu, 1961) that is suitable for standardized products, instead of Vernon's innovative-product cycle. The theoretical standpoint taken in this chapter is that the trade-oriented strategy is still dominant in East and Southeast Asia and that countries, which recently have gone through a transformation from a surplus of inward FDI to a surplus of outward FDI, (Taiwan) have in broad terms repeated the Japanese strategy. To borrow the flying geese analogy for the evolutionary process of product development, suggested by Akamatsu, only in this region can there be found a team of neatly flying geese, whose pecking order closely reflects the different stages of development (Schive, 1993, 32).

By using a network perspective to understand the process of FDI, new dimensions of the pattern of the internationalization of the firm can be revealed. The neoclassical approach has to a large extent been unable to explain those forces behind exports and FDI that can be traced back to the manufacturing company and its spatial behaviour in itself. Particularly relevant are the notions of the continuous increase in complexity, as well as the move from single vertical relations to a combination of multiple vertical and horizontal relations (Conti, 1993). The network perspective does also put the true actors behind economic integration in focus, those decision-makers in single companies or organizations, who react to various internal and external signals from governments, competitors and partners.

The dynamics of intra-regional economic interaction

An in-depth analysis of the evolution of the intra-regional merchandise trade pattern within East and Southeast Asia (Alvstam, forthcoming) confirms the general observations above. Between 1985 and 1992 the share of intraregional imports increased from 40.5 percent to 49.5 percent of the total imports to the East and Southeast Asian countries (Figure 6.1). The most rapid growth took place in the three Chinas[2], while the Southeast Asian countries showed less marked increases. The assumed Japanese dominance as a country of origin could not be verified. The share of Japan in the imports of goods to most countries has stagnated. Instead, the main part of the growth of intra-regional trade was a result of a rapid growth of imports within the quadrangle PRC, Taiwan, Hong Kong and South Korea. Japan's role as the leading actor in the total foreign trade in the Pacific Rim has continued to decline. In 1985 Japan alone accounted for more than 40 per cent of the total imports to the region, compared to 30 per cent 7 years later. The total imports to the three Chinas, including their official triangular intra-trade, increase from 29 per cent in 1985 to 34 per cent in 1992.

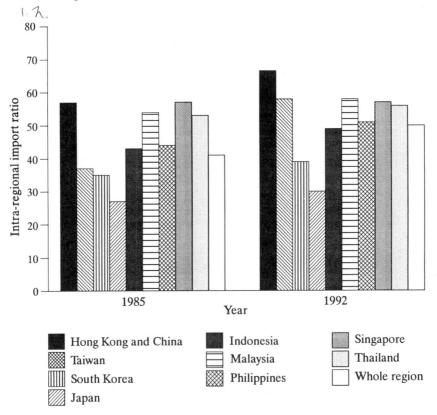

Figure 6.1
Intra-regional import ratio in single countries, 1985 and 1992

Source: Own calculations, based on IMF, Direction of Trade Statistics, National Taiwanese statistics.

116

Another important change is the declining degree of concentration, away from a few important bilateral flows. Despite the more significant role played by the largest single trade-flow, the imports to the PRC from Hong Kong in 1992, compared to 1985, there has been a clear tendency in direction of geographical dispersion of foreign trade to a larger number of flows. The 15 most important single trade-flows accounted for 70 per cent of the total intra-regional foreign rade in 1985, compared to 66 per cent in 1992. Imports to Japan dropped from 38 per cent to 32 per cent during the period. It is evident that the medium-ranked bilateral flows originating in the three Chinas and South Korea have gained most in importance, while the intra-regional exports from Brunei, Indonesia, Malaysia, The Philippines and have lost their previous positions (Table 6.3).

Table 6.3
Percentage change of position in intra-regional exports between 1985 and 1992

PRC	HKG	IND	JAP	ROK	MAL	PIL	SIN	THA	ROC	BRU
+36	+56	-45	-15	+48	-23	-39	+10	+52	+35	-71

Source: Own adaptions and estimations based on IMF, Direction of Trade Statistics, and Taiwanese data.

These aggregate figures do not however, take into account the dramatic changes in commodity composition of exports that have taken place in particularly the exports from single countries in East and Southeast Asia. Since the 1950s, the ratio of exports to production (X/P) within the manufacturing sector has soared, beginning with Singapore and Hong Kong, continuing during the 1960s and 1970s with Taiwan and Korea, followed by Malaysia, The Philippines, Indonesia and Thailand during the 1970s and 1980s (Figure 6.2). Due to its vast domestic market, the same ratio for Japan has grown to a much less extent, while in Mainland China the export of manufactured goods been insignificant compared to its total industrial production. Comparing the situation between the late 1970s and the early 1990s, the most important shift is to be found in Southeast Asia. In none of these cases has the ratio of imports to the total consumption of raw materials (M/C) grown more than moderately during the last 15 years. In addition, the imports of raw materials are to a relatively low degree originating from East and Southeast Asia itself. The important areas of origin are instead Australia, the Persian Gulf and North America. The only major exceptions are the oil import flows from Indonesia and Brunei. The relative position of a country, considering the dynamics of the X/P and M/C ratios, is of significance in deciding the potentials for future growth in trade and FDI. It is obvious that the most dramatic change of position during the coming 10 years will occur in China. It is moreover apparent that the shift of positions for the Southeast Asian countries between the late 1970s and the early 1990s have not primarily taken place in increasing the X/P ratio in manufacturing for intra-regional consignees.

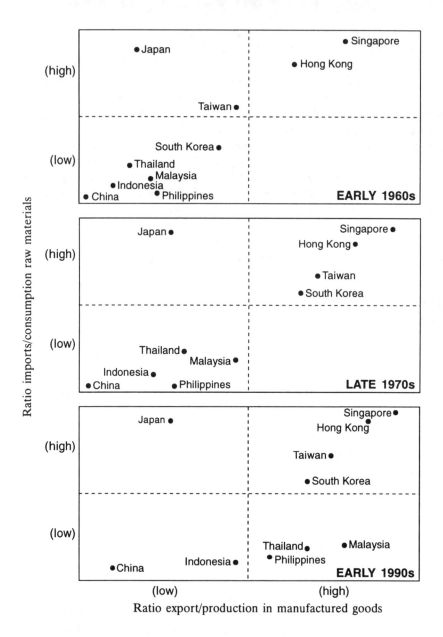

Figure 6.2
Comparison of Export/Production ratios in manufacturing and Import/Consumption ratios of raw materials in single countries in East and Southeast Asia, 1960s-1990s.

Source: Own revision, based on UN International trade statistics, complementary with national data.

118

Instead, the largest growth of manufacturing exports have been recorded to the US. Taiwan and Korea, in contrast, have shown minor changes in their positions. In these routines, there has been a rapid upgrading of exports within the manufacturing sector, combined with an even faster growth of intra-regional exports and intra-regional FDI. If it is assumed that the same pattern as in Taiwan and Korea will occur in the Southeast Asian countries, a quick growth of intra-regional exports of manufactured goods is to be excepted there as well.

The transformation of the trade pattern is matched against changes in the FDI flows, a comparison that has certain methodological restraints, as was indicated above. The results can be summarized in a simplified model, representing growth in the geographical distribution of the outward FDI between two periods (Figure 6.3). The mode is not displaying the total stock of investment and takes no account of differences in size of investment between single home countries. The geographical pattern of approved FDI is closely linked to the pattern of foreign trade. The time-lag between expansion of exports and growth of outward FDI is smaller than in European and American experiences, probably because of the more intense expansion of economic integration in East and Southeast Asia during a limited period of time. The initial Japanese intra-regional FDI were mainly oriented towards the raw material sectors, but already in Stage I it is possible to trace a growth of labour-intensive FDI in manufacturing production, mainly directed to Hong Kong and Singapore. During Stage II, the outward FDI from Japan stagnated in most directions, except for a continuous expansion of layoff production in the NICs. Later, in Stage III, the Japanese investment in labour-intensive production shifted in the direction of Southeast Asia, and at the same period there was an expansion of Korean investment, as well as the introduction of investment at a larger scale from Hong Kong to Mainland China, mainly to the newly introduced Special Economic Zones in Guangdong and Fujian. The characteristic feature of the last 10 years has been the outstanding growth of inward FDI to China and Vietnam, as well as the tremendous growth of outward Taiwanese investments, which took off after 1987. During Stage IV, new home countries of FDI have started to emerge as well, like Thailand and Vietnam.

The case of Taiwan

The model developed to describe the continuous transformation of the spatial pattern of international trade and investment in East and Southeast Asia has been explored further using Taiwanese data. Taiwan represents a case of evolution similar to Japan. Taiwan does also have the advantage of having moved through this process earlier than all Southeast Asian countries, excluding Singapore, and it represents in the mid-1990s a situation characterized by a combination of a relatively high import dependence within raw materials, and a high dependence on exports of manufactured goods. At the same time, the trade dependence, which grew rapidly in the 1960s and 1970s, reached its peak in the early 1980s, when it stagnated and declined (Figure

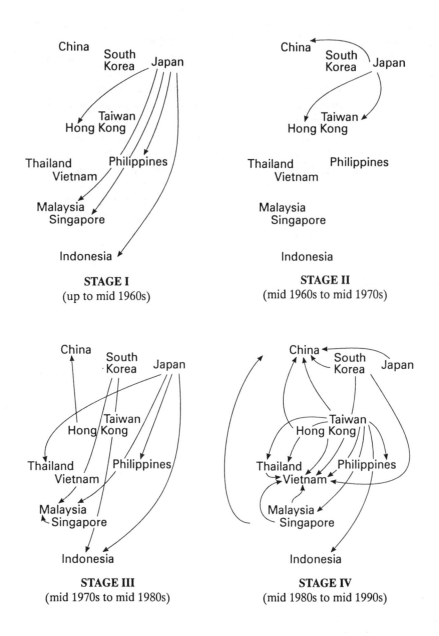

Figure 6.3
Geographical shifts in the intra-regional investment pattern in East and Southeast Asia - a simplified model.

Source: Own revision based on official national investment statistics.

120

6.4), reflecting a substitution between export growth and growth of FDI. Particularly after 1987, the outward FDI from Taiwan has faced an exponential growth, an effect of the deregulation of the previously very restrictive rules for capital exports.

The transformation of the commodity pattern in exports has gone through two main phases (Figure 6.5). The first occurred during the 1960s, when the exports of raw materials in the agricultural sector (SITC 0+1) tumbled, at the same time as exports of semi-manufactured goods, particularly within the textile sector (SITC 6+8), grew rapidly. The second phase, the 1970s and 1980s, saw the share of machinery and equipment (SITC 7) soar, while the more labour-intensive, low-technology products stagnated. Within SITC 7, there has been a continuous process of upgrading. During the entire period the commodity composition of imports has in general terms been stable, merely reflecting changes in oil prices (Figure 6.6). Behind these figures is an upgrading trend in imports in terms of technology content, as well as an increasing share of capital goods at the cost of goods for final consumption.

In aggregate terms, the Japanese share of Taiwanese exports tumbled rapidly during the 1950s and 1960s, while the American share rose. The US lost its position as the leading country of origin for Taiwanese imports, replaced by Japan. The declining role of Japan as recipient of Taiwanese exports is almost wholly explained by the decline of agricultural exports. The US, however, was the main destination for products in the first industrial revolution in Taiwan, with a majority of low-technology, labour-intensive consumer products. A certain amount of these export flows were directly related to the inward FDI to Taiwan of US firms in the 1950s and 1960s and was an expression of the growth of intra-firm trade between the two economies. The Japanese FDI in Taiwan did not result in exports to Japan. Rather, products were shipped to the US market, supporting further growth of Taiwanese exports to the US.

This pattern partly changed in the 1970s. The American share of Taiwanese exports remained at a high level throughout the 1970s and 1980s, while the Japanese share kept stable at a much lower level. Beneath the surface, however, the composition of exports to the two countries underwent dramatic changes. An important difference between the two markets has been that the US has received a far higher share of consumer products, while the increase of exports to Japan has mainly taken place in the field of parts and components within the machinery and equipment sector. There has furthermore been a growth of intra-firm exports from Taiwan to Japan during the last two decades. Variances in the US share during the 1980s reflect the volatility of exchange rates.

After 1970, Japan's position as the leading source country for Taiwanese imports went through a long period of decline, reaching its lowest level in the early 1980s. This process is a good illustration of the import substitution strategy in Taiwanese industrial policy, where imports of Japanese capital and consumption goods were gradually replaced by domestic production, to some extent controlled by Japanese firms with own production in Taiwan. Since the middle of the 1980s, however, the share of Japan in Taiwanese imports started to grow again, propelled by a rapid upgrading of the domestic production, particularly in the field of electrical and

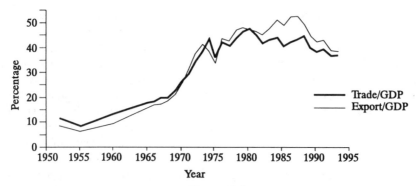

Figure 6.4
Export dependence and total trade dependence, Taiwan 1952-1993.

Sources: Council for Economic Planning and Development, Taiwan Statistical Data Book 1993; *Industry of Free China*, 81(6), June 1994.

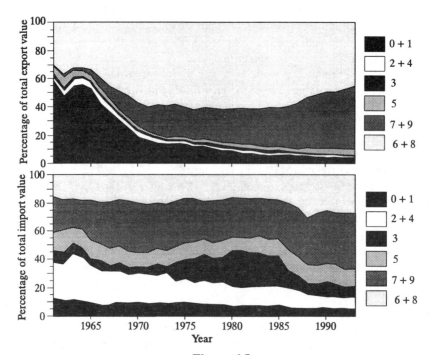

Figure 6.5
Taiwan's exports by SITC section 1961-1993.
Figure 6.6
Taiwan's imports by SITC sections 1961-1993.

electronical industries. As was the case in the late 1960s, the input products used for domestic industrial upgrading, were imported from Japan. The peak occurred in 1986-87. Since then a new phase of import-substitution has taken place, coupled to a large-scale increase of outward resource and labour related FDI to neighbouring countries in the region (Figure 6.7), and a rapid growth of exports of intra-firm related parts and components, particularly to Southeast Asia. The share of Japan in Taiwanese foreign trade has been consolidated during the last years at about 30 per cent of Taiwanese imports, and 11-12 per cent of its exports. The exports to ASEAN and South Korea, on the other hand, grew from 6 per cent to 12 per cent of the total value between 1986 and 1990, and remained at that level during the consecutive years (Figure 6.8). The growth of FDI to ASEAN went thus in parallell with the growth of exports. After 1990 the investments in ASEAN began to generate a return flow of imports to Taiwan from these countries. This pattern can be identified through the rapidly declining Export/Import ratios with separate ASEAN countries, particularly Thailand (Figure 6.9). It seems that the major share of the Taiwanese import growth, which took place within the electronic sector, has been of intra-firm type.

Taiwan's subordination to Japan, in its bilateral trade and investment, has remained so far, despite signs of changes during recent years. The relatively poorly developed bilateral economic relations with South Korea since the middle of the 1980s has changed in favour of South Korea, whose trade surplus with Taiwan has expanded to reach about the same relative level as that between Taiwan and Japan (Figure 6.9). Furthermore, this surplus is isolated to capital and technology intensive sectors within the chemical and electronical industries. In all likelihood Taiwan's outstanding performance in industrial upgrading will be reflected by a better position in the trade hierarchy with Japan and Korea. In particular potential exists for further division of labour and specialization in the bilateral economic relations between the two competitive economies of Taiwan and South Korea.

The most rapid transformation of Taiwan's external economic relations, though, has taken place with the Chinese Mainland (Figure 6.10). Since the trade across the Taiwan strait through Hong Kong was officially recognized, there has been a formidable growth in trade and investment, particularly from Taiwan. The exports officially destined to the PRC amounted to 9 per cent of the total Taiwanese export value in 1993. Moreover, the exports to Hong Kong have grown at a considerable pace since 1987. A large part of the increase from 7 per cent of the total Taiwanese export value in 1987 to almost 22 per cent in 1993, is probably re-exports to the PRC. The FDI from Taiwan grew from around US$100 million in 1987 to at least US$7,000 million in 1993.

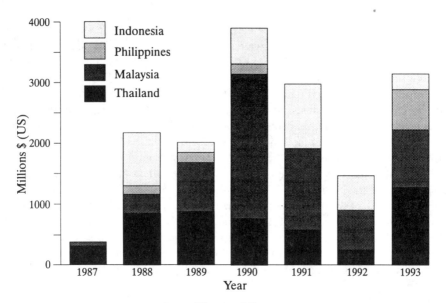

Figure 6.7
Taiwan's investment in ASEAN countries 1987-1993 (US$ million).

Note: Approved investment, as recorded in the host countries.
Source: Investment Commission, Ministry of Economic Affairs, quoted by Schive (1994, 52).

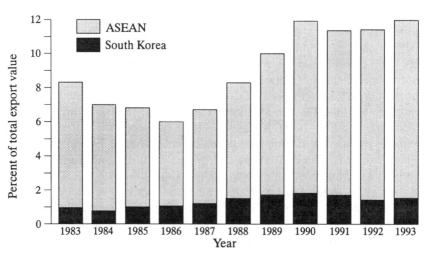

Figure 6.8
Exports from Taiwan to South Korea and Asean 1983-1993 (percentage of total export values).

Sources: Directorate General of Customs, Monthly Statistics of Exports, The Republic of China, Taiwan District, various issues.

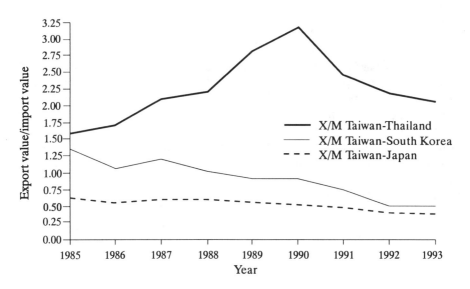

Figure 6.9
Taiwan's export/import ratio with Japan, South Korea and Thailand 1985-1993 (measured by values).

Source: Investment Commission, Ministry of Economic Affairs, quoted by Schive (1994, 52).

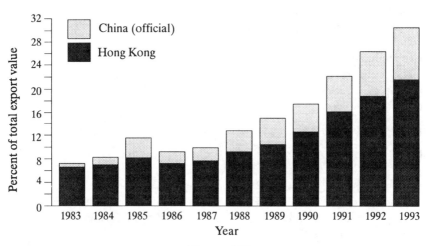

Figure 6.10
Exports from Taiwan to Hong Kong and Mainland China 1983-1993
(percentage of total export values).

Source: Industry of Free China, 81(6), June 1994.

125

Conclusion

Since the mid-1980s, intra-regional trade and investment growth within East and Southeast Asia has accelerated. This process has many similarities with the previous growth of intra-European economic integration during the 1950s and 1960s, but is also characterized by even larger differences, mainly due to larger variations in economic size and development level than was the case in Europe and a much more rapid transformation. The main feature of intra-regional economic integration is the growing role of the PRC as well as the diminishing gap in the trade hierarchy between the different economies, the continous upgrading in technological advancement in the physical trade and the growing significance of service trade. The current trends in the FDI pattern can thus be summarized as follows: 1) the introduction of new home countries, and diminishing difference in volumes between the established home countries of FDI and the declining stance of Japanese total outward intra-regional FDI; 2) the gradually appearance of a more balanced FDI flows in several bilateral relations as a result of growing Taiwanese, South Korean and Singaporean investment in Japan, and Malaysian investment in Taiwan and Singapore; 3) a gradual shift of investment from labour-intensive sectors to market-oriented FDI in technologically advanced industries; 4) a rapid growth of labour-intensive investment to Chinese inland provinces and; 5) a continuous increase of investment in the service sectors.

Is it possible to urge in general terms, that despite differences in economic structure the economies in East and Southeast Asia follow a similar route in their industrial transformation? Before an answer to this question can be given, it is necessary to investigate the determining factors behind these results. In particular the decision-makers behind changes in industrial organization and location of commodity and service production in the involved economies, as well as the emergence of a common industrial network in the region, should be the subject of future studies in the geography of industry and international economic interaction in the Asian Pacific Rim.

Notes

1. During the period 1987-1992 Taiwanese authorities approved 138 cases of FDI to Thailand, at a total value of US$388 million, while Thai authorities during the same period gave approval of 1,081 cases of FDI from Taiwan, at a total value of US$3,632 million (Schive, 1994, 52).

2. For methodological reasons, the PRC and Hong Kong are grouped in Figure 6.1. A detailed study of the geographical origin and destination of the foreign trade of the PRC (Alvstam, forthcoming) shows large inaccuracies concerning which flows should be accounted for under the heading of the PRC and Hong Kong

respectively, due to the particular role of Hong Kong in the foreign trade flows to and from the Mainland.

References

Akamatsu, K. 1961: 'A Theory of Unbalanced Growth in the World Economy'. *Weltwirtschaftliches Archiv*, 86(2), 205-208.

Alvstam, C. 1993: 'The Impact of Foreign Direct Investment on the Geographical Pattern of Foreign Trade Flows in Pacific Asia - with special reference to Taiwan', in Dixon, C. and Drakakis-Smith, D. (eds) *The Growth Economies of East Asia*. London, Routledge.

Alvstam, C. (forthcoming): International Economic Interaction in East and Southeast Asia. Working Paper, Centre of East and Southeast Asian Studies, Göteborg University.

Conti, S. 1993: 'The Network Perspective in Industrial Geography'. *Geografiska Annaler*, 75B(3), 115-130.

Council for Economic Planning and Development, Taiwan Statistical Data Book, 1993.

Directorate General of Customs, Monthly Statistics of Exports, The Republic of China, Taiwan District, various issues. *Industry of Free China*, 81(6), June 1994.

Dunning, J. H. 1988: *Explaining International Production*. London, Unwin Hyman.

Grotewold, A. 1979: *The Regional Theory of World Trade*. Grove City PA, Ptolemy Press.

Hanink, D. M. 1989: 'Trade Theories, Scale and Structure'. *Economic Geography*, 65(4), 267-270.

Johnston, R. J. 1976: *The World Trade System: Some Enquiries into its Spatial Structure*. London, Bell.

Johnston, R. J. 1989: 'Extending the Research Agenda'. *Economic Geography*, 65(4), 338-347.

Kojima, K. 1978: *Direct Foreign Investment*. London, Croom Helm.

Krugman, P. 1991: *Geography and Trade*. Leuven, Leuven University Press; Cambridge MA, M.I.T. Press.

McConnell, J. E. 1986: 'Geography of International Trade'. *Progress in Human Geography*, 1, 471-483.

Pitelis, C. and Sugden, R. (eds) 1991: *The Transnational Firm*. London, Routledge.

Porter, M. E. 1990: *The Competitive Advantage of Nations*. London, Macmillan.

Schive, C. 1993: 'The Emerging Role of Taiwan in the Rising Asian-Pacific Regionalism'. *Industry of Free China*, LXXIX, 5. Executive Yuan, Taipei, Council for Economic Planning and Development.

Schive, C. 1994: 'Regional Operations Center and the ROC Economy in the 1990s'. *Industry of Free China*, LXXXI, 2, 43-53.

Stopford, J. M., Strange, S. and Henley, J. S. 1991: *Rival States, Rival Firms - Competition for World Market Shares.* Cambridge, C.U.P.

Strange, S. 1988: *States and Markets.* London, Pinter Publishers.

Vernon, R. 1966: 'International Investment and International Trade in the Product Cycle'. *Quarterly Journal of Economics*, 80, 190-207.

Wells, L. T. 1973: *The Product Cycle and International Trade.* Cambridge Mass., Harvard University Press.

World Bank 1987: *The World Development Report 1987.* New York, Oxford University Press.

World Bank 1993: *The East Asian Miracle: Economic Growth and Public Policy.* New York, Oxford University Press.

7   Japanese integration and the geography of industry in Japan

Graham Humphrys

It is difficult to exaggerate the impact of Japan on global industrial patterns as it grew to be an economic superpower in the second half of the twentieth century. It changed the map of the world economy by becoming a third centre of advanced economic development, a change that was all the greater because Japan is Asian with a history and cultural heritage very different from the that of the two earlier centres in western Europe and North America. It restructured world trade too, as it exported consumer goods to every corner of the world and became an important market for every country which is dependent upon the export of raw materials. It contributed to industrial restructuring in other advanced economies, first by successfully competing in their home markets and later by its choice of locations within them for its factories as it expanded production abroad. At the same time Japan contributed to the dramatic economic growth achieved by other East Asian countries after 1970 by investing in their industries and providing them with an important market. Equally obvious has been the way Japan has influenced the organization of manufacturing throughout the world, leading the way in developing a lean production approach, in demonstrating how new technologies could be used to achieve flexibility and economies of scope and in showing that Fordist relationships in production could be replaced by an alternative which could be more successful. A variety of factors contributed to the remarkable achievements of modern Japan, but prominent among these and a diagnostic characteristic, is the degree of integration which the Japanese system exhibits. It is this which provides the focus of this chapter in an examination of the part played by integration in shaping the structure and spatial patterns of Japanese manufacturing and the role of the state in the development which took place. The chapter begins with a review of the spatial and institutional substrate and its evolution in the post Meiji period, before looking at the contemporary organization and spatial patterns of manufacturing, which provides the basis for assessing the challenges facing Japan in the 1990s.

The societal and institutional substrate

The nature of Japanese society derives at least partly from a moral basis which differs from that of western industrialized countries (Fruin, 1992; Morishima, 1984).

Whereas in the latter egoism underlies the prevailing economic morality, Japanese society is based on a morality deriving from Confucianism. In this, caring is a duty and not derived from inherent self interest, and honesty in business affairs is expected. Social interest rather than self interest is the basis for economic existence and achievement, so that there is a profoundly cooperative outlook on social order, institutional purpose and individual effort. This philosophy also includes an acceptance of a natural order of things, with a hierarchy which is part of the world and not imposed on it. The Confucianist morality can be seen in the way that people are keen to do their jobs conscientiously, having the knowledge and skill to do them well and are trusted to carry them out without supervision (Dore, 1986). It is also apparent in the way that all relationships are based upon mutual obligations and responsibilities, which the partners involved accept and respect irrespective of personal feelings. One important expression of this heritage is the way that the Japanese system involves a lot of relational contracting rather than spot contracting. What this means is that firms entering into contracts also establish a relationship which is expected to be long standing and with two way exchanges of information and help of mutual benefit. If needed this would extend to providing support if one partner got into difficulty. An important ingredient is a basis of trust between the two. These relational structures which are apparent throughout the Japanese system, result in an emphasis on quality and service which is an important underpinning of Japanese economic success.

A particular feature of Japanese society is the strength of commitment to the group. The antecedents of this lie in the traditional kinship structure of Japanese families. Instead of a strict notion of genealogical relations, family members are those who contribute to the economic welfare of the household. This attitude was fostered by the widespread practice of adoption. The bonds which hold together family and household groups are thus not confined to blood relationships and marriage ties. A common feature of such households which has been transferred to other groups including the firm, is the striving of individuals to become homogeneous members of the group, and the way in which members are protected regardless of their position. Those belonging to a group see it as close, intimate and protective, while outside groups are seen as comparatively alien, potentially unkind and probably hostile (Bucks, 1981). Japanese groups are exclusive, with the ultimate group of exclusivity being the nation-family. Most Japanese believe that they are different from all other nations, a feeling which is encouraged by a formidable language barrier, and a cultural gulf between Japanese and outsiders, especially westerners. Within the group, most individual relations are hierarchical, that is with those above and below, but with decision making by consensus. The normal process is one whereby leaders obtain all the views of subordinates and constituents before announcing a final decision. The objective of such a process is to retain within-group harmony. Inside groups there is mutual reliance horizontally and a patron-client relationship in a vertical chain. The middle level in such an arrangement is in a critical position, since it accommodates different views from the lower half and transmits them to the upper half and then relays ideas on implementation of policy from top to bottom (Bucks, 1981).

These societal characteristics provided the basis for the emergence of the integration which is a distinctive feature of the modern industrial system of Japan and which helps in an understanding of the influence of the state on the patterns which can be observed. This is not to suggest that the societal substrate determined the particular features, or that there was a simple constancy in their influence. What is suggested is that these influences were always there, and that while they were modified over time they did help mould the Japanese system. The significance of the societal characteristics for the integration which is a particular feature of the mode of social regulation of post-Fordist Japan, becomes readily apparent when the evolution of the Japanese industrial structure is examined.

Interacting with and being interpreted by the societal substrate, the geography of Japan also played a part in the way the industrial system evolved. Dominant elements in the physical geography of Japan are the surrounding seas and the rugged mountains which make up most of the land. Lowlands suitable for agriculture and settlement comprise less than 10 per cent of the whole and occur in small pockets separated one from the other by difficult terrain. This has always made land transport difficult, while weather conditions and exposed coasts made water transport hazardous except around the protected Inland Sea. The pre-industrial economic effect was to encourage separated local markets which were interlinked but relatively protected from competition with each other, while in the industrial period it encouraged discrete labour markets. In occupying this land the Japanese spread from south to north, with the northernmost main island of Hokkaido not settled until after 1870. Offshore and with a relatively harsh environment to overcome, the Japanese maintained a homogeneity of language and culture as they spread north. Japanese farmers were remarkably successful in developing their rice based agriculture in what is a land poorly endowed with natural resources, but they also developed a frugality which is still apparent in modern Japanese society. At the time of the Meiji Restoration in 1868, Japan was still very much a rural society, though as early as 1750 about 22 per cent of the population of 30 million was urban, which is unusually high for an agricultural society. Tokyo was probably the largest city in the world in the 18th century with a million people, and Osaka and Kyoto had in excess of half a million.

1868 -1880

Following the Meiji restoration in 1868, the government stance shifted from a traditional concern with regulation, to one obsessed with modernising the economy through industrial development. The merchant houses which had previously accumulated most capital, did not have sufficient funds for the needed investment in railways and modern factories, nor did they have expertise or experience of such large scale projects and were unwilling to take the risk. Government alone could afford the costs involved. It took the lead in stimulating domestic industry to compete with foreign products and to increase the military strength of Japan. The initiatives included railway building and showcase factories to produce iron and steel, textiles, cement and glass, few of which were a commercial success. It also used local associations to disseminate western technology, modern management methods, commercial law and practical education (Fruin, 1992). The State having demonstrated the possibilities, private sector investment began in earnest in the 1880s. The privatization of most of the state enterprises at this time provided the basis for the formation of the first *zaibatsu*. In these, family ownership was dominant with the owners directly involved in control of factory operations. The main impact of the early developments on the geography of the country was the start of a railway system which facilitated movement of raw materials to production sites and the distribution of imported goods.

1880 - 1920

This phase lasted until about 1920. Two critical developments of this period laid foundations which were to influence the post-1954 patterns. The first was the nature of state involvement with economic development. Government, business and the people shared a common intent to become modern and western as well as Japanese. There was implicit recognition that the state championed domestic business institutions and in return the progress and well being of Japanese enterprise system promoted the national welfare (Fruin, 1992). The government adopted policies to help achieve these aims but the private companies were mainly influenced by the bureaucrats who implemented them. The improved and expanded system of university and technical education played an important part in this. Tokyo Imperial University was very influential in these years, with its graduates acquiring a common ethos and many of them going into government service. However, the majority of university and technical college graduates went into industry. A common practice developed of bureaucrats taking up careers in industry when they retired from the civil service. This helped to maintain a communality of interest between business and government.

The second development of vital importance later, was the emergence of the two business traditions of large scale conglomerates or combines known as *zaibatsu*, and the independent smaller urban and local enterprises. *Zaibatsu* began to appear in the late nineteenth century with family based businesses at their centres exercising control through a holding company. Typically the holding company was at the apex of the *zaibatsu* and operated as a major shareholder in the most important production and trading companies belonging to the group. Each *zaibatsu* had a nucleus of financially related enterprises as well as specialized sales, marketing and distribution companies to service the manufacturing firms. *Zaibatsu* and western corporations were very different in that the former grew for the most part through unrelated diversification, whereas the latter tended to grow by vertical integration in particular

132

industries. The small size of the domestic market for most products also helped to make economies of scope more important than economies of scale. Fruin (1992, 91) claims that

> Economies of scope, that is cost reductions which accrue through joint production and distribution, were pivotal in bringing *zaibatsu* groups together. Briefly stated, economies of scope are possible when the costs of producing or distributing two or more products together are lower than the costs of doing so separately.

By 1912 secondary industry was still contributing less than 22 per cent of GNP with 45 per cent of industrial output caming from textile spinning and 20 per cent each from food production and heavy industries (Murata, 1980). Even after the major expansion during the First World War when domestic output was boosted by military demands and by the interruption of supplies from Europe, there were still only 22,400 factories employing ten or more people in Japan. Given these conditions it is not surprising that the *zaibatsu* essentially concentrated on economies of scope while most western enterprises were concerned with economies of scale.

Production and distribution were nearly always separated in Japan. There were various reasons for this, including previously well developed wholesale and retail networks, which were reinforced when the government built railways which mostly followed previously existing roads (Fruin, 1992). The earliest industries of importance were almost all domestic raw material based, with cotton and silk textile manufacture especially important. The need for the then basics of industrial development - coal and steel production - was met initially by government action to import the necessary technology, provide the necessary transport infrastructure and invest in their development. The heavy industries located in northern Kyushu, western Honshu and Hokkaido, where the raw materials they needed were found. Textile manufacture concentrated near the major urban areas especially Osaka, but was also important in the rural areas where small factories used local raw materials.

Independent smaller urban and rural enterprises existed in far greater numbers than the *zaibatsu* and contributed over 70 per cent of national output. They entered the market for western goods mainly after 1880. In the urban areas they were mostly single product firms making simple products but with professional management and open financing structures. In the rural areas an earlier tradition of farm families diversifying by taking on activities other than farming was maintained. This rural industy was less open in ownership and control. It stayed competitive mainly because it served local markets and usually made products using local natural resources.

1920 - 1954

The 1920-54 period saw the development of the distinctiveness of the Japanese industrial system. At the heart of this was the rise to dominance of the focal factory where managerial and production responsibilities were combined, production and distribution were coordinated on a territorial basis and with a vertical near integrated network of supplier firms which cooperated in striving for success.

The *zaibatsu* now evolved into large modern corporations in which ownership and management now became separated. By the 1920s they had become pyramidal organizations containing hundreds of companies engaged in a wide variety of economic activities. The member companies were integrated through interlocking shareholdings and directorships and through personal ties. There were also close links between the *zaibatsu* banks and government financial institutions. New *zaibatsu* appeared in this period which were different in some ways from the old. They were mostly concentrated on the new industries which made much more sophisticated products such as electrical machinery and synthetic chemicals, which appeared as a result of the second industrial revolution. Unlike the older *zaibatsu*, they did not include banks and commercial elements within their structure so that financial ties between the member companies, were much weaker. They raised their finance more from government subsidies and independent city banks which encouraged them to have strong business-government ties at the local and Prefectural level.

The connections between the member companies of the *zaibatsu* were based on interlocking shareholdings and directorships rather than on production integration and individual member firms were essentially specialised product companies. No widely diversified Japanese companies appeared until the end of the period. Within this structure, control and production decisions became concentrated at the factory level, with production sites acquiring the entire range of corporate functions - assets, means and labour power. Thus regional manufacturing centres became established which had both managerial and production responsibilities.

This distinctive Japanese system was created as a response to the complexities of markets, technologies and organizations which the corporations and companies faced at the time. With considerable technological and economic uncertainty, the *zaibatsu* benefited from the common practice of segmenting activities by setting up separate legally independent entities because this minimised the corporate liability. The lack of resources and the difficulties faced in adopting and adapting the needed western technologies and transferring them into local knowledge, forced companies to narrow their core competencies to specific products and processes. Limited availability of capital encouraged them to outsource component manufacture, a trend which was facilitated by the ready availability of skilled and semi skilled workers in the labour market following cutbacks after the First World War. The smaller subcontractors normally relied heavily upon orders from one purchaser. By outsourcing in this way, the core factory companies were able to take advantage of the lower wages, technical strengths and underemployed workers through sub-contracting. This led to a distinction between employees with well paid, relatively secure jobs with seniority based pay working in the core companies, and the less well paid majority of workers in SMEs where tenure, wages and livelihood were uncertain.

The limited resource availability and the uncertain conditions, also encouraged a further form of integration. The member companies of the *zaibatsu* were linked by

134

the holding company owning shares in other members and vice versa. But it was also common for core factory companies and their subcontractors to hold limited shareholdings in each other. Obtaining finance in this way from a small number of reliable and friendly firms, was infinitely more attractive than public offerings and underwriting. With large blocks of shares effectively off the stock market, these linkages also limited the possibilities for takeovers with their associated disturbing effects (Ito, 1992). For the purchasing firm, these kinds of links obviated the problem of seeking information to choose between alternative suppliers and ensured security of supply. It also avoided such difficulties as management control and sup-optimal scale which would have arisen if it chose to manufacture components itself.

All these relationships extended well beyond the formal links to include informal mutual obligations and responsibilities and relational contracting (Francks, 1992). The result was a pattern of focal factories with interfirm networks of suppliers and subcontractors in vertical near-integration relationships which were characteristically Japanese. This structure exhibited the relational contracting, mutual obligations and group coherence of the cultural substrate. Almost everyone involved was striving for quality, looking for ways of furthering success and trusting each other. What this integrated system also did was to maintain the numbers and importance of small firms to a much greater extent than in other advanced economies. The focal factories at the heart of the system organised local resources and coordinated production and distribution systems on a territorial basis, in a way that was crucial to Japanese industrial development. Similar patterns of organised production by separate firms was familiar in the rural areas and craft industries, where the coordination of small separate producers was provided by merchants and wholesalers who often supplied materials and bought the products.

There were substantial geographical shifts during this period. The textile and food industries which had provided over 60 per cent of industrial output in 1922, provided only 35 per cent in 1937, their place had been taken by the chemicals, metals and machinery industries which in 1937 provided over 64 per cent of industrial output (Murata, 1980). While the textile and food industries were widespread in the rural areas, the more advanced industries were now expanding rapidly in the larger urban areas of southern Honshu in particular. This was boosted after 1937 by the demands for equipment and material for the war effort which were met largely through industrial expansion in the Tokyo-Kitakyushu belt. It was there that the market was concentrated, the infrastructure was best developed and where the seat of government which was a major purchaser, was located. In the late 1940s, wartime destruction had left Japanese economy and industry devastated. Recovery did not seriously begin until the outbreak of the Korean War in 1950. Japan became a major supply and resort and recreation base for the war, generating demands and supplying the capital which initiated the subsequent dramatic industrial growth.

The contemporary pattern

When the *zaibatsu* were disbanded at the behest of the Allied Occupation forces after the end of the Second World War, the pattern they had established soon reappeared in the form of *keiretsu* which were more loosely organised networks of legally independent enterprises of various kinds (Gerlach, 1992). These *keiretsu* are less commercial in character than the pre-war *zaibatsu* and are often tied together by financial links through city or private banks rather than internal banks as had been the *zaibatsu*. These new corporations also enlarged their activities so that they had at least one member company in each business and the individual companies are larger too (Fruin, 1992). Much more significant changes also occurred which transformed the Japanese system into its contemporary shape. Three were especially important - new systems of industrial relations, changes in manufacturing operations and changes in management organisation. In all three the cultural substrate can be discerned in the persistent importance of interrelationships and the degree of integration which they developed.

The most dramatic change with the most far reaching effects, was the reformation of the labour relations of the work place. From the mid 1950s industry-wide unions gave way to enterprise or company unions which became the norm. With their advent the workers came to accept the managerial hierarchy and the managers recognised the authority of labour in such matters as production layout, work control, and worker compensation. In large firms of more than 500 workers, all employees except Department heads and above belong to the company union, which effectively means over 90 per cent of the workforce are union members. Thus company unions became universal and inclusive. Labour management conflict is avoided because everyone involved would be adversely affected, and employees would lose everything if the company fails. The acceptance of this situation was eased by the long post war boom in the economy so that everyone was benefiting from continuous growth. A critical feature was the way in which the work content in Japanese production was specialized, but the work skills of the labour force were generalised. In such a system it is cost efficient to educate and upgrade worker skills in such things as job control, shop layout, multiple machine competency and general communications systems, rather than to invest in complex hardware intensive manufacturing where worker skills are minimised (Fruin, 1992) Because workers have high levels of education and ability in Japan and are well motivated, flexible manufacturing systems have come to characterise the Japanese system. These contrast with the much less flexible hardware dependent systems developed in the West under Fordism. In Japanese companies employees are motivated to learn by goal setting, problem definition and action and reward for performance. These skilled, committed and flexible workers with accumulated experience, were recognised as a very valuable asset and Japanese companies aimed to retain them by providing guaranteed lifetime employment and income levels based on education and seniority. This integration of unionism and employment security, was developed in the context of a long and strong tradition of corporate paternalism in which companies deliberately incorporated family

136

symbolism, language and customs into their practices to engender group loyalties. Group harmony is seen as a valuable aim.

The major change which took place in manufacturing operations was a shift from labour intensive small batch production of the inter-war years, to the scale economies of larger batch production in the 1950s using capital intensive techniques, and then to product differentiation scope economies from the 1970s. At the centre of this change were the focal factories which had originated as a solution to the problems of how to transfer technology from the west in conditions of limited resources and small localized markets. In the post-1945 period the characteristics which they had acquired, were adapted to meet new and different conditions. These included extremely high rates of growth of demand, rapidly shifting, maturing and segmenting product markets, and dramatic improvements in engineering and manufacturing structure and techniques. The focal factories continued to be localized integrated production units, which included within them research, product design and design engineering, product and production planning and manufacture and sales coordination. They came to manufacture a number of products in varying amounts, chosen to take advantage of the human and physical resources they had accumulated over time and providing opportunities for further advances and/or innovations in products and the processes and organisation of production. In embodying responsibilities such as these and in emphasizing learning, creativity and resource transformation, they contrast with the labour intensive production sites, employing standardized, narrowly specialized work routines for high volume manufacture of a limited range of products developed in the Fordist regimes of western nations. Because they link directly with other companies in interfirm networks the focal factories strengthen the operational and strategic interdependence and integration of the whole system. In adapting to the new circumstances of the post war world, they consciously organized themselves for functional integration and product/process innovation rather than simply mass production. As models of adaptable flexibility they emerged as ideally suited to manufacturing evolution in the post-Fordist world.

The third major change was the modification of the organizational structures which had been established in the earlier periods. Within *keiretsu*, the constituent companies have become more independent as financial links based on equity and debt have lessened. Important features of these links are illustrated in Tables 7.1 and 7.2. Institutional holdings other than pension funds, are much larger in Japan and share interlocking is typical. Dore (1986) suggests that this means that shareholdings 'are dominated by corporate owners more interested in long term growth and the stability of their trading partners and customers than in dividend revenues'. The difference can be expressed as the inter-locking shareholders being exercisers of voice or influence, while the short term investor, more common in western economies, are threateners of exit (Hirschman, 1971 as quoted in Dore, 1986, 71). The 'mutual-obligating-cementing cross holdings' helps the expansion of new firms in new industries, as owners take the long term view and are more willing to accept low return over an extended period to get to low-cost high-returns in the long run.

At the same time, other kinds of interrelationships which bind companies together were strengthened. Two typical organisational patterns emerged each with many variations. One is where a core firm manufactures some parts and assembles the final product from these and other parts supplied by an outer tier of companies. Some of these will be sub-contractors while others belong to the same *keiretsu*. The outer tier of companies will have similar links to their suppliers and so on down the chain. Functional leadership and strategic direction is provided by the core firm but it does not control the whole system. What it does do is encourage, allow and require in some cases, the contribution of the other participants. The production system is thus intricate and coordinated, with a great deal of relational contacting and integration, based on mutual trust and obligation much more than on financial ties.

Table 7.1
Share interlocking ratios in Mitsubishi Group 1987
(percentage of ownee's total shares)

Ownee[1]	Owner[1] 1	2	3	4	5	6	7	8	Group Total[2]
1	-	1.93	5.92	4.53	1.80	1.50	3.16	1.08	24.69
2	3.12	-	5.43	1.97	3.14	1.75	3.02	1.87	28.98
3	Mutual company, stocks not publicly offered								
4	4.90	3.99	4.55	-	2.36	0.41	1.89	0.94	23.31
5	4.77	4.81	5.47	5.95	-	1.45	3.19	0.85	31.75
6	3.18	5.57	4.05	1.21	0.98	-	1.56	0.52	17.65
7	3.94	6.17	3.25	2.27	1.73	0.97	-	0.76	20.76
8	4.21	7.09	4.22	3.53	0.67	0.66	1.20	-	25.06
Average	3.74	5.02	4.99	2.90	1.96	0.68	2.76	0.85	27.80

Notes: 1   Key to numbering of firms: 1 Mitsubishi Bank; 2 Mitsubishi Trust; 3 Meiji Life; 4 Tokyo Marine and Fire; 5 Mitsubishi Trade; 6 Mitsubishi Electric; 7 Mitsubishi Heavy Industries; 8 Mitsubishi Real Estate
   2   Includes other companies in the group
Source: Ito (1992)

The other typical organization pattern is one where production is less dependent upon outside companies and more dependent on associated companies of the *keiretsu*. In this there is a core production company again, but the interconnected supplier firms are linked to it through interfirm shareholding, a limited rotation of senior level personnel, movement of personnel to affiliates and subsidiaries, and a coordination of business activities. In this more matrix structure, many planning and control functions are carried out for the group as a whole, by corporate management and technology boards. Below this level, divisions and affiliate companies have operational independence but may choose to operate interdependently.In both types of organization the relationships are very frequently two way and may be reinforced by informal personal relations. Many of the part manufacturing suppliers will be undertaking their own research and have bright ideas for improving products and will pass on these suggestions to their partners and vice versa. There is a high expectation of mutual cooperation and reciprocity in all the relationships and not simply through the financial ties.

A third way in which firms interrelate and cooperate which is different from the other two, is seen in industry associations to which different companies in the same industry belong. These are well organised, often having good research sections and permanent officials who wield some authority. They play an important role in those industries in which the state sponsors joint R&D projects while in other industries they delicately balance conspiracy and competition. They are also a channel by which MITI can influence change. These associations reflect a strong sense of membership of an industry, with individual members accepting the constraints and comforts of group membership. The latter is a feature evident throughout Japanese life, fitting in very well with the concept of collectively bargained involvement described earlier (Dore, 1986; Fruin, 1992).

Table 7.2
Distribution of equity ownership: United Kingdom and Japan

	UK 1981	Japan 1982
Persons and charities	30	28
Stockbroking companies	-	2
Unit Trusts	4	1
Investment Trusts	7	
Other Financial Companies		
Banks	0	38
Insurance Companies	21	
Industrial and Commercial companies	5	26
Pension Funds	27	-
Foreigners	4	5
Public Sector	3	-
	100	100

Source: Dore (1986)

State involvement in the managing of the economy as an element of a Mode of Social Regulation, also exhibits a very Japanese form (see also Peck and Miyamachi, Chapter 3). There is considerable debate about the role that the State played in the economic success of modern Japan. That it was influential is very evident, but whether it merely changed the pace of development and made minor adjustments to the direction being taken, or whether it was instrumental in deciding either or both, is not obvious. What are relatively easy to identify are the elements of macro-economic policy which played a part in what happened. Throughout the modern period, governments have accepted and maintained economic advancement as a paramount aim and have seen industrialisation and industrial growth as the means to that end. From this have stemmed various government actions meant to achieve desirable results. The establishment of showcase industries in the 1870s, the provision of grants and subsidies to help fledgling industries or to stimulate innovation, import controls to protect domestic industry, use of government purchases to increase a market and major investment in roads, railways and other infrastructure which have affected locational choices, are all examples of how industry has been helped directly and indirectly by government. Policies to influence regional development and stimulate industrial dispersion, such as the technopoles initiative of the 1960s, have also influenced change at the meso level. There have also been blunders and errors of judgment which have resulted in serious economic difficulties or costly mistakes. The disastrous Pacific War and the pursuit of oil refining and petrochemical industry expansion up to the 1973 oil crisis are good examples. Evidence can be found to support the two alternative views either that the State played the determinant role, or that its overall effect was merely as a helpful partner of the private sector. Whichever position is adopted it is hard to identify major shifts of direction that are directly attributable to action by the state alone.

Much more attractive is the thesis proposed by Johnson (1982). He argued that in Japan government action is not ideologically determined as is found in the Anglo-American tradition where the role of the state is to enforce the rules and administer, or as is true in the state centralist systems of the former communist bloc. Instead he suggests, the government has takes a pragmatic approach, with the framework of vague general laws interpreted and implemented by government bureaucrats. With this approach the action taken may be different in each case which arises, and may be achieved through informal as well as formal channels. This interpretation fits the Japanese experience much better. The state seems to have been involved in a whole process of learning what is best by trial and error, which is how the private sector in Japan also proceeded. In this approach the state is seen as one of a number of different participants and contributors to the process rather than the dominant partner. The government can be seen to provide the directions and even mould the influencing context and decide on policies, but it is the private sector which will actually produce the results and so interaction with business is a necessary element to achieve progress. What is suggested is that government action has taken on a very Japanese form, with characteristics which can be seen to have antecedents in the cultural substrate. Certainly in the Confucianist heritage bureaucrats had a duty and responsibility for the welfare of the people they served. The method of approach of achieving consensus and influencing change by this means rather than directing it or coercion, is also a feature. Here again the theme of integration is very much in evidence. The bureaucracy and the ruling party are strongly integrated, partly as a consequence of the Liberal Democratic party being continuously in power from 1955 to 1993. The bureaucracy have high intellectual quality, with the politicians largely ratifying policy rather than shaping it. The policy to be ratified, emerges from open and public debates between the main organised interests. The latter include the Ministry of Finance, the Bank of Japan and representatives of commercial, industrial, financial interests. Some of the most able bureaucrats with suitable personalities, have moved into the Liberal Democratic Party. Once there they have a better chance of becoming ministers than politicians who move from the local to the national level. For example, most of the Prime Ministers of Japan in the post-1954 period have come from this source. The practice of early retirement from the bureaucracy and then entering another job, sometimes into a leading position in a business corporation, also contributes to a bureaucratic industrial complex within which the achievement of consensus is much easier (Dore, 1986).

What has been described is a Mode of Social Regulation in which considerable interlocking occurs throughout a four dimensional matrix of connections between enterprises, labour, government and bureaucracy. The cement of the matrix is a Confucianist based philosophy of caring as a duty and a legacy of family-clan structures and relationships. These features of the economic sphere appear to have been shaped by the socio-economic heritage of Japan, (Hendry, 1987) although they are not direct linear descendants of it (Ito, 1992).

But how is this integration reflected in the geography of the Japanese industrial system?

Contemporary geographical patterning

The industrial pattern in Japan is distinctive amongst the advanced industrial nations in the degree of clustering and geographical concentration that can be observed. This is strongly influenced by the vertical near-integration which is characteristic of Japanese industrial organisation, with close two way relations between component suppliers and final assemblers. On the production side this relationship embraces design and specification of components, quality of product, quantity of components needed and timing of deliveries, and on the financial side it includes reciprocal investments. In both of these it normally involves relational contracting. In addition, the financial interlocking which is common has meant that sources of finance, at least until the recent past, were quite often regionally based. Together these mean that in many key industries there is a propensity for spatial proximity. Where these complex relationships require continual close face-to-face interaction, the need for spatial proximity is further influenced by the limitations of the transport system in Japan, which has to cope with a difficult topography (Association of Japanese Geographers, 1980). The large population of Japan which provides the market for consumer goods, is concentrated on very small areas of lowland which are separated by steep mountains (Kornhauser, 1982). For personnel, movement between the major conurbations is relatively easy where they are linked by Shinkansen or where frequent air services are available, but beyond these, travel by ordinary rail services

141

and by road is slow (Witherick and Carr, 1993). Transport of materials and components can also be very slow, especially in the more densely peopled parts of the Tokyo-Kitakyushu belt where the road system is frequently choked with traffic and the ordinary railway service slow and sometimes complex. Water transport is usually easier where it is available. Given these characteristics and constraints it is readily understandable why most of the expansion of manufacturing has been highly concentrated within the Tokyo-Kitakyushu belt, and why the greater majority of the population are also located there (Teikoku-Shoin, 1989). Older industries, especially those originally based on domestic raw materials, can be found elsewhere, but only recently are there signs of significant amounts of new manufacturing choosing to locate outside this belt; when it does, it is not surprising that it is tending to choose to be in or near larger cities with good transport links and where suitable labour is available.

While the Japanese system has developed distinctive characteristics of its own, it has also experienced and participated in worldwide trends in industrial development. Two of these in particular are important in contributing to an understanding of the geographical patterns which can be observed. The first is the continuing increase in output per person in manufacturing. Until 1990 increases in industrial output were sufficient to offset the effect of such productivity increases so that in the 1980s the size of the manufacturing labour force in Japan was maintained though not increased. The second trend is the increasing emphasis in advanced industrial nations on the production of higher value added goods, and a reduction of dependence on processing industries (Hamilton and Linge, 1981). This has been in response to the success of developing countries with lower labour costs, in targeting the latter as part of their strategies for achieving economic advance. This structural shift means that even in a successful industrial country such as Japan, there are declining industries which often have a different regional distribution from industries which are expanding.

An obvious feature of manufacturing in Japan is the propensity for individual industries to be concentrated in a small number of the 47 Prefectures, and for the industrial structure of many Prefectures to be dominated by a small number of industries. The pattern tends to be complicated because of the industrial restructuring of Japan which has occurred since mid century. The older, mainly processing, industries which have been experiencing continual decline, still survive as large employers in some Prefectures. The newer, mainly consumer oriented industries, are those which are more concentrated in inner Japan, but as they have continued to expand, these have chosen to locate some of the expansion in more peripheral Prefectures. The contemporary pattern is thus a snapshot of a still evolving dynamic situation which reflects both recent and historic decisions.

The national pattern

The degree of spatial concentration of total manufacturing employment in Japan in 1988 can be seen in Figure 7.1. Three distinct industrial zones are readily recognised. At the national level, manufacturing is heavily concentrated in the seven Prefectures which have 45 per cent of the Japanese manufacturing labour force and which together form Inner Japan. Nearly 6 million Japanese manufacturing workers, almost 60 per cent of the total, live in the 3 conurbations centred on Tokyo, Nagoya and Osaka. The Prefecture of Tokyo has 25 per cent of all manufacturing workers. This is more than either Kyushu or Hokkaido, which are two of the other main islands of Japan, and only slightly fewer than the whole of the Tohoku District, which comprises six large Prefectures in northern Honshu.

Middle Japan is defined as those Prefectures which had between one and four per cent of the national manufacturing labour force each in 1988. Not surprisingly, most of the Prefectures which have more than two per cent of the national manufacturing labour force each, are contiguous with inner Japan.

Outer Japan is defined as those Prefectures with less than one per cent of national manufacturing employment each in 1988, plus Hokkaido. It can be seen to equate largely with the peripheral parts of the Japanese archipelago and are mostly located in western and northern Honshu together with the greater part of both of the islands of Kyushu and Shikoku. Despite having more than two per cent of national manufacturing employment, Hokkaido is also included in this grouping. This is because it is far larger in area than any of the other Prefectures of Japan and in all other respects it is very much part of outer Japan.

Individual industries

The geographical concentration of individual industries in Japan, even when identified at the coarse level of the 22 Orders of the Standard Industrial Classification and mapped at the Prefecture level, is well illustrated by looking at four representative industries.

The Textile industry was an early basis of industrialization in Japan. As a raw material processing industry it declined by 31 per cent or some 250,000 workers between 1980 and 1988. Thirty per cent of the employment was located in just three Prefectures - Mie (centred on Nagoya), Osaka and Kyoto, as shown in Figure 7.2. Two other Prefectures, Fukui and Niigata, shared nearly 10 per cent between them, so that just 5 Prefectures accounted for 40 per cent of the textile labour force in 1988.

The Fabricated Metals industry is an intermediate industry concerned with forming primary metal into a more useful form. This industry was even more geographically concentrated (Figure 7.2), with the 3 major conurbations of Inner Japan - Tokyo, Nagoya and Osaka, having over 30 per cent of the employment in the industry in 1988.

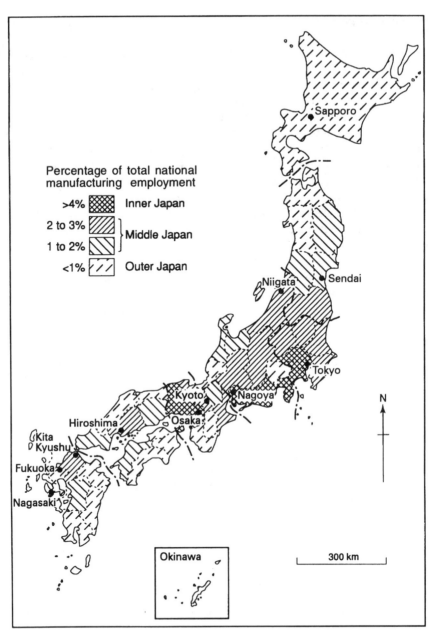

Figure 7.1
**The distribution of employment in all manufacturing industries of Japan in
1988 by Prefecture.**

Source: Japan Statistics Bureau, 1992.

144

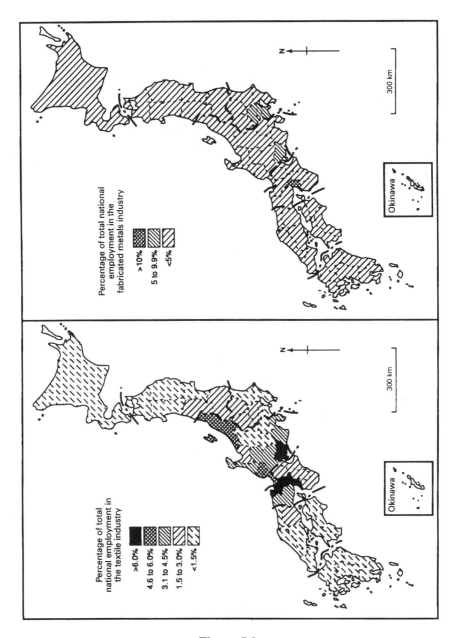

Figure 7.2
The distribution of employment in selected industries in Japan in 1988 by Prefecture.

Source: Japan Statistics Bureau, 1992.

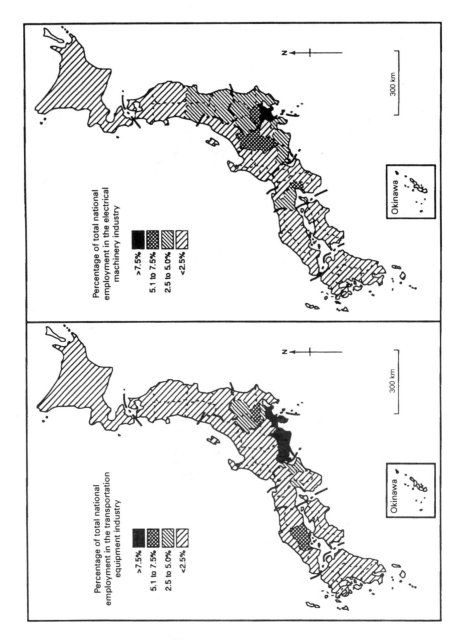

Figure 7.2 continued
The distribution of employment in selected industries in Japan in 1988 by Prefecture.

Source: Japan Statistics Bureau, 1992.

146

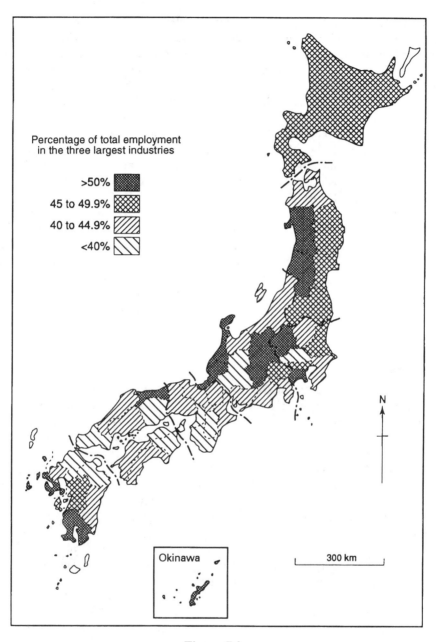

Figure 7.3
Percentage of employment in the three largest industries in each Prefecture in 1988.

Source: Japan Statistics Bureau, 1992.

Even Transportation Equipment, which includes motor vehicle manufacture, the most important engine of growth in the Japanese economy in the 1960s and 1970s, was little more dispersed (Figure 7.3). The 3 Prefectures extending from the south side of Tokyo along the coast to Nagoya, together employed 44 per cent of total employment in the industry. A further 12 per cent was found in the 2 Prefectures of Hiroshima and Saitama, so that over 50 per cent of employment in the industry was clustered in 5 Prefectures.

The Electrical Machinery industry was the largest and fastest growing industry in Japan in the 1980s, expanding by over 40 per cent. Five Prefectures between them employed nearly thirty per cent of the industry. Figure 7.3 shows how highly concentrated the industry was in the Tokyo area and extending north into the southern Tohoku District.

What these maps bring out is the high degree of geographical concentration in Inner Japan, with Middle Japan having some concentration of older industries such as textiles and benefiting from the expansion of the growth industries of the 1980s.

The other indication of geographical concentration is the extent to which individual Prefectures are dominated by a narrow range of industries. Figure 7.4 shows that 10 Prefectures had over 50 per cent of their manufacturing employment in just 3 industries, while another 6 had over 49 per cent.

Local clustering

Information about the way industries cluster within localities is much less readily available, nevertheless what evidence there is provides further support for the suggestion that Japan exhibits a geography of spatial concentration, specialisation and clustering of manufacturing. The automobile industry in the late 1970s is illustrative. Yazawa (1980) documents the localised pattern of subcontractors of Toyo Kogyo who make Mazda cars, within Hiroshima Prefecture, showing only the then newest subcontractors spreading to adjacent Prefectures. Toyota were even more concentrated at that time, as is indicated by the following description (Takeuchi, 1980, 161) which also emphasises the dominant role played by Toyota in this local area.

> At present out of approximately 2 billion yen worth of industrial production by Toyota City (1975), 95% is provided by Toyota and its sub-contractors and these factories employ approximately 90% of the total industrial workers in the city. Toyota contributes 55% of the tax income of the city and has enormous influence in municipal politics and economy and in all phases of the citizens lives. Many parts factories of the Toyota Group are located in Kariya City, adjacent to Toyota City and account for almost the entire industrial production of Kariya City. It is not true, however, that the assembly works of Toyota find all their

necessary parts in the local area. 35% of its sub-contractors are in southern suburbs of Nagoya.

Murata and Takeuchi (1987) reported the even more remarkable concentration of microelectronics-based industry, with the Tokyo metropolitan region accounting for between 70 per cent and 90 per cent of the factories assembling and finishing products such as industrial robots, computers, medical equipment, aircraft and space equipment.

Conclusions

What has been argued in this chapter is that the Mode of Social Regulation developed in Japan derives its distinctiveness in part from a particular cultural and societal inheritance. An especially important element which has persisted is a cohesiveness based on interrelationships which go well beyond the simple economic and which are evident in the informal as well as the formal integration found throughout Japanese industry. It is particularly obvious in the vertical near-integration of much manufacturing, the relational contracting and work relations. The influence of the inheritance is no more than that. It has not been constant but has been modified and adapted to suit the historical circumstances of particular times. Its expression in the economic life of Japan after 1954, created a manufacturing system which was particularly well adapted to achieving success in meeting domestic and world demand and which has proved to be particularly well adapted for success in the post-Fordist conditions which have appeared in the world since the mid-1970s. Not surprisingly it also finds expression in the geography of Japanese manufacturing which is localised and concentrated in the way described. In the mid-1990s global conditions are changing once again and Japan is changing too. The question arises as to whether the economic success achieved in the recent past can be sustained. What this chapter has demonstrated is that the economic system which has become established also has another characteristic which will help in this. The mixture of large corporations and smaller businesses interrelated and bonded as described, appears to have great flexibility and a high propensity to change. In an uncertain world these two augur well for continuing economic success.

References

Association of Japanese Geographers 1980: *Geography of Japan.* Tokyo, Teikoku-Shoin.

Bucks, A. W. 1981: *Japan; A postindustrial power.* London, Westview Press.

Dore, R. 1986: *Flexible Rigidities: Industrial policy and structural adjustment in Japan.* London, Athlone Press.

Francks, P. 1992: *Japanese Economic Development: Theory and Practice*. London, Routledge.

Fruin, W. M. 1992: *The Japanese Enterprise System*. Oxford, Clarendon Press.

Gerlach, M. L. 1992: 'Twilight of the Keiretsu? A critical assessment'. *Journal of Japanese Studies*, 18, 79-118.

Hamilton, F. E. I. and Linge, G. J. R. 1981: *International industrial systems*. London, Wiley.

Hendry, J. 1987: *Understanding Japanese Society*, London, Croom Helm.

Ito, T. 1992: *The Japanese Economy*, Cambridge, Mass., MIT Press.

Japan Statistics Bureau 1992: *Japan Statistical Yearbook 1991*. Tokyo, Management and Coordination Agency.

Johnson, C. 1982: *MITI and the Japanese Miracle*. Stanford, Stanford University Press.

Kornhauser, D. H. 1982: *Japan*. London, Longman.

Morishima, M. 1984: *Why has Japan Succeeded? Western technology and the Japanese ethos*. London, Cambridge University Press.

Murata, K. (ed) 1980: *An industrial Geography of Japan*. London, Bell and Hyman.

Murata, K. and Takeuchi, A. 1987: The regional division of labour: Machinery manufacturing, microelectronics and R & D in Japan, in Hamilton, F. E. I. (ed) *Industrial Change in Advanced Economies*. London, Croom Helm, 213-239.

Takeuchi, A. 1980: Motor Vehicles, in Murata, K. (ed) *An industrial Geography of Japan*. London, Bell and Hyman, 152-162.

Teikoku-Shoin Co., Ltd 1989: *Atlas Japan*, Teikoku-Shoin.

Witherick, M. and Carr, M. 1993: *The changing face of Japan*. London, Hodder and Stoughton.

Yazawa, T. (ed) 1980: 'Collection of the Guide Books for the Excursions, Appendix'. *24th International Geographical Congress Proceedings*. Tokyo, The Organising Committee for the 1980 International Geographical Congress, Japan.

8   State, investment and territory: Regional economic zones and emerging industrial landscapes

Leo van Grunsven, Shuang-Yann Wong and Won Bae Kim

As Dicken (1992) has observed, the most significant development in the post-World War II economy has been the increasing globalization of economic activities. While the genesis of this process can be traced to changes in the operation of international capital, its further development has received a significant boost from national and/or regional governments, eager to increase the pace of industrialization. Southeast and East Asia is one region where economic development has been significantly impacted by globalization. Since the 1960s Southeast Asia and East Asia have experienced a dramatic growth of export-oriented manufacturing activities. Favorable national policies fostered the investment of North-American, European and Japanese industrial enterprises, as well as the growth of large local manufacturing organizations. Gradually, the West Pacific Rim region became incorporated in the New International Division of Labour.

The pattern of incorporation has evolved substantially over the past decade, and with this the industrial landscape. Until the 1980s the growth of export-oriented manufacturing activities focused on the Asian NIEs and a number of EPZs in the ASEAN countries (notably Malaysia). The geographical unevenness of 'early' export-oriented manufacturing growth is emphasized by the fact that, also, in Taiwan and South Korea, this growth focused on selected sub-national spaces (emerging industrial regions). In the 1980s export-oriented manufacturing emerged in more locations in other parts of the region. From the early 1980s complex structural and geographical adjustments and shifts have been, and are, occurring within the region. Partly, these shifts reflect a re-orientation of globalization processes. They also derive from a new element in the industrial dynamics, namely regionalization, which can be 'defined' as a spread from the early nuclei of export-oriented manufacturing. New 'industrial spaces' have been and still are in the making. In addition, the collective actions of states and firms, in policies and investment behaviour adjusting to both internal and external (both autonomous and state-induced) forces of change, are producing spaces which are increasingly diverse, in both geographical scale and structural characteristics.

One element of particular interest in the emerging mosaic of territorial imprints is the phenomenon of Regional Economic Zones (REZs). Existing REZs can be characterized as cross-border regions, with substantial recent manufacturing growth in territories adjacent, or in close proximity, to longer established nuclei of export-oriented industrial production, predominantly industrial regions in the Asian NIEs.

151

They reflect the increasing economic integrative tendencies across national boundaries, partly associated with the regionalization process evolving at a sub-regional scale, to a differential degree supported by increased cooperation between national and/or regional governments. However, the term is also applied to various recent initiatives to economically integrate nearby regions of several neighbouring countries. The regions involved are of widely varying 'size', regional economic structures and levels of development. The economic integration aimed for usually, but not necessarily and exclusively, is private investment driven, usually with a focus on manufacturing. The role of government in the initiatives to establish new REZs varies. REZs basically seem to be dissimilar with respect to the prevailing conditions and stage of development, the mechanisms, processes or forces at work, and the dominant actors. Thus, when one considers the present status of areas spoken of as new growth areas or REZs, a kaleidoscopic picture emerges.

This chapter considers the emergence of Asian Pacific REZs. After a brief outline of the background to the dynamics of the industrial landscape, three REZs are discussed, the South China-Hong Kong-Taiwan Economic Zone (SCHTEZ), the Singapore-Johor-Riau (SIJORI) Growth Triangle, and the Yellow Sea Rim (refer to Figure 1.2 for location details). For each of these cases the pattern of development, as well as the processes of integration and regionalization are outlined. Subsequently, these REZs are considered comparatively as to the mechanisms and factors underlying the emergence of the zones, the role of the state, the interpretation of the phenomenon and prospects for future development. Finally, in the conclusion, the spectrum of REZs is briefly reconsidered.

Background: an emerging new industrial landscape

Since the 1980s the NIEs have increasingly faced tight labour markets and rapidly rising wages. This has put pressure on labour costs, which have risen to a level too high to support low-cost labour-intensive manufacturing. The competitive position for this type of production was also severely affected by the appreciation of currencies. In addition, external forces have started to threaten continued foreign investment in, and sustained growth of, the manufacturing sector. In Malaysia, Thailand, Indonesia old policies in which ISI still played a role, were de-emphasized, in favour of more rapid EOI. Among the range of policy measures was a substantial liberalization of the economy and of the foreign investment regime. The policy changes have greatly increased the competitive position of these countries as far as investments in labour-intensive production are concerned.

In the 1980s the global trading environment deteriorated significantly. The gradual decline in industrial competitiveness of the US and the EU, as revealed in a worsening trading position, saw protectionist pressure mount. Changes in the geopolitical context made it easier for the US and Europe not to exclude the NIEs from protectionist measures. In the period 1950-80 the ideological confrontation between the Soviet bloc and the Western capitalist bloc made it imperative that the

NIEs be viewed as successful models of free market development. Hence they needed nurturing, encouragement and support on technology transfer, capital inflows and market access from the part of the capitalist industrialized countries. The post-Cold War era in the late 1980s and early 1990s has, however, resolved the economic development war between the two blocs decisively in favour of the capitalist camp. There is no longer a need to hold up the NIEs as models of Third World success to prove the superiority of the capitalist system for economic growth and development. With the Western industrialized countries facing lower growth, rising unemployment and structural problems in industrial upgrading, the success of the NIEs, particularly in their market penetration in North America and Europe, is increasingly seen as a threat to stable employment and the standard of living of the people in these countries. Consequently, during the 1980s, a proliferation of trade restrictions against NIEs' products occurred.

The deterioration of the global trading environment in the 1980s is also reflected in the difficulty of bringing the Uruguay round of GATT to a conclusion. The materialization of the EU and NAFTA has undermined the belief in the establishment of a more liberal multilateral trading system. Notwithstanding the successful conclusion of the Uruguay Round of GATT, these factors have led the Southeast and East Asian States to a re-orientation towards their own region, and towards each other. The larger regional integration resulting from this, which is already becoming visible in the larger volume of intra-regional trade, is complemented with initiatives towards more intensive economic cooperation between national and regional governments, multi-lateral (e.g. AFTA, APEC, EAEC) and bi-lateral.

Larger regional integration also reflects the changes in the economic and geo-political environment in the region. After the collapse of the Soviet Union, the world order is moving away from a bipolar structure wherein alliances were centered upon the US and the Soviet Union. The communist alliance has deteriorated into one of political insignificance (except for the China-North Korea alliance). The triangular strategic alliance among Washington-Tokyo-Seoul is also been undergoing transformation due to a changing international political and economic environment. In this period of flux, China and Japan are foreseen to assert their role as regional powers. China, being apprehensive of Japan's increasingly hegemonic position in Asia, strives for rapid economic modernization. The decline of the bipolar order has meant the lowering of barriers between the socialist and the market economies. Asian socialist economies, in the transformation towards 'socialist market economies', seek closer economic relations with neighbouring economies for their development. China and Vietnam have opened their door for foreign investment and trade. As the trend towards larger regional integration testifies, economic transactions driven by pragmatic interests rather than political ideology occur increasingly across national boundaries.

The Southeast and East Asian NIEs have responded to the internal and external pressures in several ways. The initial response has been an attempt to alleviate the labour shortage by 1) measures aimed at increasing participation in the labour force, especially of women, 2) stimulating more rapid transfer of labour out of agriculture (particularly Korea and Taiwan), 3) taking in migrant labour (particularly Hong Kong and Singapore), and 4) increasing the productivity of labour (Kim, 1993). Though these measures have had a positive effect on the labour market situation, they have not prevented a further rapid rise of real labour costs as a result of continuing strong employment growth. Thus, and more significant, the continuing pressures have led the NIEs to initiate a restructuring process of the manufacturing sector and, at a later stage, to adopt new strategies aimed at developing new growth sectors. The ensuing restructuring process aimed at shifting away from labour-intensive and low-technology manufacturing activities to more capital, skill and technology intensive activities. To achieve this shift, a wide range of more specific policies and instruments have been developed and put into operation (though the degree of state direction and guidance has varied between the NIEs). (Ho, 1993; Kim, 1993; Pang Eng Fong, 1991; Rodan, 1989; van Grunsven, 1991, 1992).

The integrative tendencies referred to cannot be separated from the responses of firms towards the set of influences outlined. Indeed, some of these responses are constitutive of the integrative tendencies. In this context continuing domestic pressures (wage increases, currency realignments and appreciation) in OECD Countries has pushed the process of internationalization. In the second half of the 1980s new elements in this process became manifest. Changing competitiveness led to the adoption of new corporate strategies and a widening and deepening of internationalization, involving the redeployment of higher value added production operations, R&D, back office operations and other corporate functions. The Asian Pacific Rim has become an important destination of such redeployment (van Grunsven, 1992). It should be noted that this is 'driven' also by the fact that the Asian Pacific Rim has become an important market in its own right (Rodan, 1993).

OECD firms, and increasingly NIE firms as well, have responded in a variety of ways to changing conditions and policies in the NIEs and the opportunities presented by recent developments (Ho, 1993; Kim, 1993; Lui and Chiu, 1993; Natarajan and Tan, 1992; van Grunsven, 1992, 1994a). Two main responses can be distinguished, the reorganization of production and labour use and rearrangement of the geographical organization of production and other corporate activities. The first includes specific responses: the adoption of flexible labour strategy (e.g. reducing permanent workers and increasing the proportion of temporary/casual employees; subcontracting of production; subcontracting of services; new pay systems), internal training systems to facilitate the redeployment of labour, upgrading the technological level of both processes and products, and automation (capital/labour substitution). The second includes changes in the geographical redeployment of labour-intensive operations from the home-economies, product line substitution and relocation of labour-intensive production to elsewhere in the region (in a variety of ways ranging from physical relocation of assembly lines to new or other existing subsidiaries to outprocessing), and rearranging subcontracting networks. The changed economic and geopolitical conditions in the region have paved the way for significant alterations in the mode of operation of TNCs in the region, e.g. the tendency towards the adoption of a regional mode of operation (Natarajan and Tan, 1992). At the same time there is an increasing involvement of local firms in internationalization processes focused on the region.

Some additional state responses should be referred to. NIE Governments have started to encourage the relocation of labour-intensive operations by both TNCs and local firms. The new geopolitical environment has also allowed, stimulated and indeed led some of the NIEs to engage in the development of new 'spaces' (outside their national boundaries) to accommodate relocated operations by expansion of the hinterland, allowing sub-regional decentralization of economic/manufacturing activities (Chia and Lee, 1993; Ho, 1993; Kim, 1993; Rodan, 1993; Toh and Low, 1993; van Grunsven, 1994a). This has been assisted to a significant extent by the fact that the other ASEAN states (Malaysia, Thailand and Indonesia) and more recently China have been keen to capitalize on the opportunities by capturing much of the investment bypassing, redirected from, or flowing out of the NIEs (with Vietnam about to join the 'flying geese'). Thus, states have not only been involved with restructuring and economic liberalization but also with creating 'new' industrial spaces and/or expanding/transforming existing ones to accommodate, influence and guide firm behaviour. The new climate is conducive for increased cooperation between national and/or regional governments in an effort for new sub-regional and regional economies to take shape. The aim is to create attractive geographical frameworks for relocation and new investment such that (sub-) regionalization (and wider regional growth) results from the more comprehensive and regionally focused operations of firms.

The actions of states and firms (being the dominant actors) not only have significant implications for the structural characteristics of production (or rather firm activities) in a range of industry branches, but also for the territorial structures and the patterns of (urban and) regional development associated with this. Currently we witness a transition from the landscape shaped by the first wave of internationalization to a mosaic of industrial complexes and regions within the Asian Pacific Rim. This mosaic can be 'defined' along a structural dimension and a geographical dimension (van Grunsven, 1994a). As to the structural dimension the production characteristics of the rapidly increased number of 'localized' production complexes have become much more heterogeneous, related to period of establishment and the particular dynamics of firm activity. As to the geographical dimension, the territorial imprints are becoming increasingly complex and are evolving at several spatial scales: not only local, but also national (individual countries), sub-regional (parts of more than one country) and regional (the whole Southeast and East Asian Region). Besides a substantial growth of both existing and new industrial complexes, at the sub-regional level we see the incorporation of localized complexes into larger growth areas (earlier referred to as regionalization) with extensive linkages between the complexes. At the regional level localized complexes and growth areas, located within large areas, are becoming more and more interlinked and are thus evolving into growth corridors. Thus, it is clear that existing REZs are only one element in this mosaic, though an element which seems to gain significance rapidly as new initiatives to establish such growth areas get off the ground.

155

Functioning REZs have emerged through the expansion of existing industrial areas beyond their original boundaries into adjoining territories, usually across regional or national borders. They testify to the formation of transnational economic development occasioned by weakened borders. This has occurred both spontaneously and under the aegis of deliberate integration strategies pursued by national governments. Moreover the rise of REZs reflects the dependence of the Asia Pacific on informal and amorphous economic networks, given the lack of formal multilateral arrangement at the regional level, now and in the near future.

Regional economic zones: three cases

The South China-Hong Kong-Taiwan Economic Zone

Since 1978 when China opened the coastal provinces to foreign trade and investment with the establishment of SEZs, its economic relations with Hong Kong and Taiwan have grown rapidly. The increasingly close economic relations between the three and their enormous economic potentials have led some to foreshadow a Greater China Economic Zone (Harding, 1987, 1993; Shambaugh, 1993). A closer examination of the zone reveals that most of the exchange of economic activities is confined to South China, mainly the provinces of Guangdong and Fujian where the SEZs are located. It is thus more appropriate to refer to the zone as the Greater South China economic zone or more specifically the Guangdong-Fujian-Hong Kong-Taiwan economic zone (Figure 1.2). With a combined population of about 60 million, total foreign trade of over US$400 billion and combined foreign exchange reserves amounting to over US$140 billion, the zone promises growth and expansion.

Although recently the open coastal cities in the north of China are taking an increasing share of FDI, the two provinces in the south and their SEZs, being the pioneer localities, still account for the largest share of the accumulated FDI stock. In 1990, about half of the cumulative total FDI with a value of about US$9 billion is absorbed by the Guangdong and Fujian provinces (Kueh, 1992). Guangdong takes the predominant share, about 55 per cent. Its three SEZs (Shenzhen, Zhuhai and Shantou) in turn accounted for about 40 per cent of the province's total. About 45 percent of Fujian province's FDI is concentrated in Xiamen SEZ. Being the recipient centres of foreign capital and other activities, economic dynamism in South China focuses on these four SEZs. Shenzhen especially stands out from others as in most years its FDI intake was seldom less than that of any single province or municipality including Shanghai and Beijing. FDI in Shenzhen SEZ for instance has exceeded US$400 million annually since 1986. It clearly has benefited from its close proximity to Hong Kong. Enticed by the enormous market opportunities and resources, the strong incentives and political circumstances, the flows of FDI tend to gravitate towards the SEZs and Hong Kong. Since Taiwan bans direct communications with China, Taiwanese trade and investments in China are made through Hong Kong and no mainland Chinese investments are allowed in Taiwan. Taiwan thus mainly plays a supporting role in the zone.

The foreign funded or *sanzi* enterprises in the zone (namely equity and contractual joint ventures and wholly foreign-owned firms) in 1991 contributed 55 per cent of gross value of industrial output in the four SEZs. They also accounted for 46 per cent of SEZ total exports and 53 per cent of SEZ total imports, 41 per cent of Fujian's and 30 per cent of Guangdong's total exports and 63 per cent and 34 per cent of their respective total imports. These enterprises are export-oriented and are strongly skewed towards Guangdong. The *sanzi* enterprises in Guangdong accounted for 66 per cent of the national total. Shenzhen SEZ again contributed a large share of it, about 40 per cent of the provincial total in 1991. In trying to woo foreign investors into the zone China has provided an array of special economic and political incentives (Reardon, 1991). Projects for improving land and water transportation systems between the SEZs and the rest of the country have been started. Imported raw materials or intermediate products used for production or assembly in the SEZs, and for products or semi-products destined for export as duty free. The incentives have attracted a large and steady influx of FDI.

Apart from the significant role of overseas Chinese capital from the US, a substantial part of foreign investment in South China is sourced from Hong Kong and Taiwan. Investments tend to concentrate in the manufacturing and services sectors. Apparently the ready access to external markets through investors from Hong Kong and Taiwan has helped keep FDI in manufacturing. But rising labour and land costs, currency appreciation and problems of environmental pollution are pushing the labour-intensive and some capital-intensive industries out of Hong Kong and Taiwan. To retain comparative advantage there is compulsion to transfer industries to places where the conditions complement with their production factors. The relocation strategy is a means to rationalize growth and development in a period of industrial restructuring. The zone, given its geographical proximity, cultural affinity and infrastructural facilities conveniently functions as the alternative export processing platform for the outgoing industries, while the home front undergoes structural transformation into the more sophisticated types of higher value-added manufacturing that requires a higher level of R&D. The output of the labour-intensive manufacturing activities is destined largely for re-export through Hong Kong, consistent with China's strategy of using foreign investment for export purposes. The products are generally those at the end of the product life cycle produced in the 'sunset' industries of Hong Kong and Taiwan. In channeling trade and investment into the zone, Taiwan and Hong Kong also help expand the marketing network of the zone with the outside world.

Hong Kong firms have capitalized on the incentives given in the nearby SEZs of China by relocating a substantial part of labour-intensive operations there for re-export, via outprocessing, joint ventures and wholly owned subsidiaries. Investments from Hong Kong are from both indigenous Hong Kong enterprises and from the international community in the colony. By 1987 as much as 18.4 per cent of Hong Kong's SMEs had moved to China. In 1991 the realized FDI from Hong Kong in

China was the largest, about US$2,661 million, accounting for about 57 per cent of the total FDI in China. Most of Hong Kong's investments, about 54 per cent, went to Guangdong province especially the Shenzhen SEZ. Hong Kong investment in China now has exceeded US$10 billion. Shenzhen now exports about US$2 billion of goods annually, and over 75 per cent of these are manufactures, accounting for about 40 per cent of China's industrial exports. Most of the manufacturing investments are in labour-intensive industries such as textiles and garments, toys, electronic and electrical parts and consumer appliances. Recently real estate development, particularly housing construction in Shenzhen, has been a major attraction for Hong Kong investors besides collaboration in major infrastructure and service projects such as power plants, transportation systems and hotels. The island is increasingly integrated into the Chinese economy. In 1992, the value of China's trade with Hong Kong went as high as US$57 billion, generating for China a trade surplus of as much as US$16 billion which provides about 40 per cent of China's foreign exchange earnings (EIU,1993a).

Besides actively helping to develop the zone, Hong Kong also plays a vital role as intermediary between China and Taiwan. Since Taiwan only allows indirect trade with China, about three-quarters of its trade with China is via Hong Kong. While many foreign and domestic companies are withdrawing from Hong Kong in anticipation of the 1997 impact, a growing number of Taiwanese companies are entering the British colony. In 1992, the total trade between Hong Kong and Taiwan topped US$17 billion or 10 per cent of Taiwan's total foreign trade with an imbalance of US$13 billion in Taiwan's favour. In 1990 Taiwan's indirect trade with China rose to US$4 billion, accounting for 3.3 per cent of its total trade and earning Taiwan about US$3 billion surplus. Except for 1978 and 1979 Taiwan has consistently enjoyed a large surplus in its indirect trade with China through Hong Kong. This surplus now accounts for an increasing share of Taiwan's overall trade surplus, reaching as much as 26.6 per cent in 1991 (EIU, 1993b). China's indirect trade with Taiwan is also rising but to a much smaller extent. Taiwan's exports to China are about five times its imports from China. Taiwan depends on China primarily as an export market rather than as a source of imports.

Most of Taiwan's indirect trade with China is investment related and consists chiefly of the industrial materials and parts and components imported by Taiwanese firms investing in China. In 1990, for instance, industrial fibers accounted for about 40 per cent of the total value of Taiwan's indirect exports followed by electronic parts and components (11.4 per cent), plastic raw materials (10.9 per cent) and machinery and equipment (8.1 per cent). An integrated network of patron-clientele manufacturing based on outward sourcing is set up between firms on both sides of the Straits. Firms in Taiwan take orders from outside, provide the capital, technology and management expertise while China does the job of manufacturing, supplies cheap and abundant labour and land. Most Taiwanese investors thus prefer wholly-owned ventures which give them the independence in supplying their own industrial inputs and choosing of export markets. The untapped market and resources of China plus the special treatment complement with Taiwan's current economic constraints for further growth and expansion. The rising production costs at home, the shrinking external markets due to currency appreciation and protectionism, and the fear of losing out to competitors like South Korea in penetrating the China market, have compelled Taiwan to move into the mainland. Setting aside the political differences, China has taken the step in 1988 of promulgating the National Regulations on Encouraging Taiwan Compariots Investments which offer special incentives to investors from Taiwan. Some of these include the right to buy and sell real estate, the acceptance of the New Taiwan dollar for conversion into foreign exchange certificates, intellectual property protection for Taiwan investors, and the offering of the same patent rights and status to Taiwanese investors as to mainland nationals. Local authorities such as Fujian province opened Xiamen and Fuzhou as districts specially catering to the interests of Taiwanese enterprises where Taiwan-invested industrial and agricultural projects are given corporate tax exemption for the first four profit-making years.

Since direct investment is banned, Taiwanese investment in China has to go through indirect channels. It uses Hong Kong as the base of operations. There are now more than 2,500 Taiwan-invested companies in Hong Kong, 90 per cent of which are connected with mainland businesses. To help smaller Taiwan investors, the China External Trade Development Council, Taiwan's semi-official trade promotion organization, set up a Taipei Trade Center in Hong Kong in 1991. The British colony provides Taiwan investors with such services as letters of credit and loan extensions, thus overcoming the backward financial, telecommunications and transportation facilities in China. The political uncertainty also makes it safer to use Hong Kong to conduct transactions with China. The rush of Taiwanese investments into China via Hong Kong did not begin until after 1987 when martial law was lifted and people were allowed to visit the mainland and foreign exchange restrictions were relaxed (Liu, 1993). In 1987 only 80 Taiwanese firms invested in China with a contracted total of US$100 million. By the end of 1992, about 10,000 contracts had been concluded with commitments of over US$8 billion. In 1992 alone, Taiwanese capital accounted for about 13 per cent of total FDI projects in China, 9.54 per cent of total foreign capital commitments (Ash and Kueh,1993). As a result, Taiwan has now surpassed Japan and the US and has become the second largest foreign investor in China, after Hong Kong. The Taiwanese investments in China are mostly found in Xiamen SEZ and Fuzhou in the Fujian province due to geographical proximity and historic links. Substantial investments are also made in the Shenzhen SEZ in Guangdong province. Since 1990, Taiwanese investors have diversified into other areas too especially Pudong and Shanghai.

As in the case of Hong Kong firms, initially in the 1980s most Taiwanese firms invested in light and labour-intensive manufacturing such as textile and garments, footwear, toys, food and beverages, leather products, ceramics, woodware, Christmas gift items, home articles and paper products. From the early 1990s Taiwan investment has diversified into more capital-intensive industries such as automobiles and bicycles, chemicals, optical instruments, home appliances, electronic products, metallurgical and building materials, and energy. In addition, since 1991 investment has diversified into the services sector. The latter, particularly real estate, accounted for 12 per cent of all Taiwanese projects and 20 per cent of invested capital in 1991. Most of Taiwanese investments have high export ratios, indicating the attempt to use China as the export platform to third countries in accordance with China's objective of promoting export-oriented industries. In 1990, Taiwanese firms exported about 86 per cent of their total output in contrast with only 35 per cent for non-Taiwanese FDI firms. A large proportion of the exports manufactured by Taiwanese firms are directed to the US. In 1990, products sent back to Taiwan only constituted about 12 per cent of the total export flow generated by Taiwanese firms. These products were mainly precision instruments, mechanical equipment, chemicals, paper products, plastic products, timber and basic metallic products. The scale of operation has also changed from single manufacturing investments made by SMEs to joint investments in manufacturing and service industries by several companies or conglomerates.

The emphasis put on South China has resulted in a widening disparity in growth between regions in China and in some undesirable social and economic consequences. To fuel the economic activities in the zone, China has placed an enormous stake in Hong Kong. In 1993 the Hang Seng Bank estimated that China was the biggest investor in Hong Kong with at least US$12 billion, followed by Japan and the US. China also owns sizeable percentages of important Hong Kong companies, including 20 per cent of Hong Kong Telecom and 12.5 per cent of Cathay Pacific Airways. Chinese-backed banks attract up to 20 per cent of total Hong Kong dollar deposits. The promise of the zone has also led to an enormous exodus of workers from the interior of China to the zone, giving rise to the common problems of uncontrolled urban growth such as inadequate supplies of housing, transportation, water and electricity as the capacity of the zone is stretched beyond its limits. Increasingly there is the criticism that using scarce national resources to propel growth in the zone is wasteful and that heavy reliance on state funds should be corrected. To demonstrate the concern with correcting regional inequality in development, the Beijing government recently has indicated the move to divert its capital from the zone to other areas of the mainland, notably the interior and the north. The government has also taken note of the over-investment in the property market of Hong Kong and has advocated the use of money earned from exports in the zone in other parts of China (*The Straits Times*, 1994).

For Hong Kong the relocation to South China has contributed to remarkable structural changes in its income and employment patterns. In 1991, Hong Kong investors were reported to be employing some three million workers in relocated operations in Guangdong. Relocation has led to a relative and absolute decline in manufacturing employment in the colony. Although a substantial amount of Hong Kong capital has flowed into China for investment, foreign countries continue to increase their investments in Hong Kong. Investments from the US are estimated to have grown to $7.1 billion in 1989 and those from Japan to $8 billion. Consortia involving major US, Japanese and European companies have bid for contracts to build Hong Kong's cable television network and to construct the new airport and port terminal. Confidence is affected by the political uncertainty as indicated by the rising incidence of emigration and capital flight. The Hong Kong and Shanghai Bank's monthly report suggests that the capital outflow may have exceeded HK$32 billion in 1990. Hong Kong government officials have admitted that there has been an increase in borrowing in Hong Kong dollars for financing overseas investments in ASEAN countries. In the first quarter of 1990, Hong Kong projects approved by these countries increased by more than 200 per cent over previous years. Evidently some Hong Kong MNCs are diversifying resources to safeguard their long-term interests in anticipation of possible political instability in China.

For Taiwan the relocation of manufacturing activities to South China has created the fear of a 'hollowing out' of Taiwanese industry. Currently 15 per cent of Taiwanese industrial enterprises are planning to base their operations on the mainland especially industries producing shoes, suitcases, bicycles, tennis rackets, tennis balls and textiles. The plastic footwear industry is affected most. The total number of plastic footwear manufacturing plants in Taiwan has dropped from 1,400 to only 700 in 1990. The determination of Taiwanese firms to sink their investments in China is indicated by the extension of the period of commitment, from 10-20 years to 30-50 years (Luo and Howe, 1993). Nevertheless the relocation has a marginal impact on the GDP and employment in Taiwan. The Taiwanese authorities have effectively restrained the hollowing out of the manufacturing sector through measures such as the banning of overseas investment in industries which are considered important to Taiwan's defence or economic security, the imposition of restrictions on investment in China for 3,764 labour-intensive and low-tech products, control on investment activities by companies listed on the island's stock market, and the banning of Taiwanese banks setting up branches or directly financing Taiwan firms in China. Taiwanese investors have to remit their funds to a third place first in order to be considered as 'indirect investment'. These measures indicate Taiwan's reluctance to help enhance China's competitiveness and the attempt to avoid depending too much on China's market.

The SIJORI Growth Triangle

SIJORI involves the city-state of Singapore and the adjacent areas in the north and the south, the Malaysian state of Johor and the Indonesian Riau archipelago (Figure 1.2). Within the archipelago, development focuses on Batam Island, although increasingly also Bintan and Karimun Islands are becoming incorporated in growth processes occurring within the framework of the Triangle. The Triangle has only a little over 4.5 million people living in its three constituent segments. However, in economic terms it incorporates the economic 'power house' of Southeast Asia, Singapore. The Singapore-Johor connection builds on already strong economic links between the two areas, whereas the Singapore-Riau connection is historically weak. Recent economic integration and regionalization in the context of this zone is, to a significant extent, manufacturing driven.

The origin of the Triangle lies in the autonomous shift of labour-intensive manufacturing activities out of Singapore. This shift began in the early 1980s and can be understood as a market response to the rapidly changing production conditions in Singapore. Soaring production costs as a result of the restructuring policy initiated by the Singapore government at the end of the 1970s made it harder to retain low value-added labour-intensive production in Singapore. New policy under the aegis of the 'Second Industrial Revolution' reflected the perception by the government of the nation's comparative advantage and constituted the initial response to increasing resource constraints, particularly the availability of labour. A set of policy measures was implemented aiming at replacing low value-added and labour-intensive components of manufacturing by higher value-added and skill-intensive components. These policy measures confronted many TNC establishments with severe restrictions on the supply of foreign low-skilled labour and a sharp increase in real labour costs, which threatened their competitiveness in the local market and in export-markets. 'Moving out' was one of the mechanisms by which firms adjusted to the altered conditions, besides automation of production processes and moving into higher value-added product lines. The adoption of the three adjustment mechanisms 'accelerated' substantially in the course of the second half of the 1980s. Conditions in Singapore had by this time become much more favorable for high value-added production. Also, Singapore was in the process of building up an additional competitive edge for other corporate activities. Local (supporting) companies have been faced with a severe competitiveness problem ever since production conditions in Singapore began to alter significantly in the early 1980s. As alternative locations for low value-added labour-intensive operations, areas adjacent to Singapore (initially Johor in particular) were to be included in the newly adopted *regional* mode of operation of TNCs and local firms.

Towards the end of the 1980s the autonomous and market driven responses by firms was taken up particularly by the Singapore government. It sought to establish the Triangle as one investment region and as a sub-regional arena for a range of firms in a range of industries, to carry out diverse manufacturing operations by making use of resource complementarities offered in the Triangle. The strong involvement of the Singapore state became an added factor in the decision of firms to locate manufacturing operations in the northern and southern segments of the zone.

Until the mid 1980s, the economy of Johor was largely based on plantation agriculture and the exploitation of natural resources. However, after the mid 1980s the manufacturing sector grew by on average 12 per cent per annum. The share of this sector in the GDP increased rapidly to 28 per cent in 1990 (Rashid Hussein Securities, 1990). The manufacturing growth is linked to a sudden acceleration in FDI. Over the period 1984-90 M\$ 6.25 billion in approved foreign investments was registered, divided over 877 projects. The role of international capital is illustrated by the fact that 87 per cent of the investment projects approved over this period involved foreign equity; the foreign equity participation in the total equity part of the investments amounted to 68 per cent. Foreign investment in manufacturing has gone on unabated in the early 1990s: over the period 1991-93 an additional 534 projects were approved, involving a total amount of M$ 4.1 billion in foreign investment. A note of caution is appropriate, however. Registered investment in approved projects overestimates actual investment. As at end of June 1993, some 15 per cent of approved projects had not been implemented.

Singapore was by far the largest investor over the period 1984-90, accounting for about half of the total number of approved projects, followed by Taiwan and Japan. However, in terms of capital investment Japan ranked first (around a quarter) followed by Singapore and Taiwan. The category of Singapore investments includes investments by American, Japanese and European TNCs made via the subsidiary located in Singapore (unfortunately this sub-component cannot be isolated from the rest). The role of Singapore became even more pronounced over the period 1991-93. While Japan contributed M$ 0.8 billion to the total registered foreign investment (in approved projects) of the total of M$ 4.1 billion, and accounted for 15 per cent of approved projects (Taiwan M$ 0.4 billion and 11 per cent respectively), Singapore contributed M$ 1.2 billion and accounted for almost 50 per cent of the total number of approved projects.

Potential employment in projects approved over the period 1984-93 amounted to some 215,000 jobs. Approved projects of Singapore origin contributed about half of this, while those of Japanese origin contributed 18 per cent. Comparing the share in potential employment with the share of each country of origin in the total number of projects and total capital investment respectively, it is evident that the Singapore investments were spread over a substantial number of projects, each involving a relatively smaller amount of capital but generating a relatively larger number of jobs compared with Japanese investments. In terms of capital investment, chemical products ranks first among the industry branches invested in, followed by electronics, metal products, non-metallic products and textile/garments. However, in terms of number of projects and employment generated electronics ranks first, followed by textile and garments.

The southern part of Johor still serves as a major source of labour supply for Singapore's manufacturing industries: not only a significant number of guest workers from Johor are resident in Singapore, but also there is a large, and increasing, daily commuter flow across the causeway. The establishment of production units in Johor by Singapore companies has broadened the function of Johor for the Singapore economy by tapping other resources (especially lower-cost local labour and land). Many of the recently established production plants are located on one of the 16 industrial estates developed and managed by the Johor State Economic Development Corporation, which in total occupy some 2,500 ha (Johor Investment Centre, 1991). Some 80 per cent of this land is located in the Johor Bahru District, the southern most part of the State. In the coming five years M$ 900 million will be spent by the State government to develop another 12 industrial estates, covering 2,700 ha. None of the recently developed estates or the estates to be developed has been or will be designated as an EPZ. However, individual plants can operate as a Licensed Manufacturing Warehouse, provided certain export criteria are met (JSEDC, 1993).

The industrial development on Batam Island, recently designated an EPZ by the Indonesian government, has gained momentum only since 1990. Most of the development and management of industrial estates, and factory buildings has been contracted out by the Indonesian government to private developers. Presently, eight industrial estates are being developed or have been completed by a number of consortia. Of those completed, Batam Industrial Park is by far the largest, presently occupying some 500 ha. This has been developed by a consortium of Indonesian and Singaporean investors: the Salim Group, Singapore Technologies (a government-owned company) and Jurong Environmental Engineering (a subsidiary of Jurong Town Corporation, the government statutory board which develops and manages all industrial estates in Singapore). By 1995 some 4,000 ha of industrial land will have been fully developed (BIDA, 1993). Following the completion of several estates, the number of production plants (operational or under construction) has increased rapidly over the past few years, from 22 at the end of 1990 to 82 at the end of 1993 (Table 8.1). Export production has increased rapidly also: the value of exports has jumped from US$151.5 million in 1990 to US$925.8 million in 1993 (BIDA, 1993).

Data on the volume of foreign investment in manufacturing and the structure of manufacturing are still scarce. The latest figures from the Batam Industrial Development Authority show a total capital investment of US$452 million. Private investment constituted some 84 per cent of this. Foreign investment contributed some 45 per cent to the total private investment. Half of the total private investment went into manufacturing, the remainder going into real estate, tourism and hotel projects, trade and services and some agro-business undertakings. Table 8.1 shows information on foreign investors. These data again reveal a substantial 'link' with Singapore. In the case of manufacturing operations from Singapore origin, relocations by Singapore-based TNCs are excluded. A significant part of investment applications in 1989 and 1990 originated from Taiwan, but many of these did not proceed, as Taiwanese companies decided to invest in China instead. About half of the present manufacturing operations on Batam consists of the assembly of electrical and electronic components. Component manufacturing is also typical of production in the metal and plastics industries. Due to the investment regulations, textile and garments will hardly play any role in the manufacturing structure, unlike in Johor.

Due to the small 'indigenous' labour force on the Island, labour for the new industries is largely recruited from other parts of Indonesia, mainly Java (Paradiredja and Yeoh, 1991). The companies managing the industrial estates usually take care of the labour recruitment. They also provide dormitory-style accommodation for the workers within the confines of the industrial estate. The costs are borne by the employers. Batamindo Industrial Management recruits workers from Java and Sumatra on a three year contract for the industries located in the park. Presently, some 27,000 workers, mostly young single females, are working in the 54 plants which are operational. Some 17,000 of these are housed in dormitories located within the park. Besides housing, the workers are also provided with a number of other facilities and amenities within the park, like a market, clinic, recreation facilities and so on. The developers of other industrial estates seem to be adopting the same 'formula'.

Three main underlying processes account for manufacturing growth in the northern and southern components of the economic zone:

1. the cross-border outward shift of particular types of industrial production by *TNCs* operating in Singapore.
2. relocation and expansion of production ('sub-regional internationalization') by *domestically-owned companies* from the longer established manufacturing complex of Singapore.
3. 'long-distance' shift of production (to a significant extent from Japan and the East Asian NIEs through FDI).

Table 8.1
Industrial projects on Batam, operational or under construction, end of 1990 and 1993

Industry/Origin	1	2	3	4	5	Total
1990						
Singapore	1	7	4	1	1	14
U.S.A.				1		1
Netherlands					1	1
Japan		1	1			2
Hong Kong		1		1		2
Panama/Bahamas					1	1
Thailand					1	1
Total	1	9	5	3	4	22
1993						
Singapore	2	17	9	7	10	45
U.S.A.		6		1	1	8
Australia			1			1
Netherlands		1			1	2
Sweden	1					1
Panama/Bahamas					1	1
France		2				2
United Kingdom				1	1	2
Malaysia				1		1
Thailand					1	1
Japan	3	5	2	1		11
Hong Kong	1	1		1		3
Taiwan					1	1
Korea			1		2	3
Total	7	32	13	12	18	82

Note: (1) Electrical (2) Electronics (3) Metal (4) Plastics (5) Other
Source: Batam Industrial Development Authority, 1993

In many cases, the production plant on Batam is a subsidiary of a TNC in Singapore and the relocation of production fits quite well the decanting process. An example is the tuner factory established in 1993 by Philips Singapore Pte. Ltd., a subsidiary of the Dutch electronics company Philips N.V., in Batam Industrial Park. Until the establishment of this satellite operation, the full assembly of tuners (used in television sets) was carried out in one of its Singapore plants. Several years ago, the first stage of the assembly process, the insertion of chips on the small PC board, was automated. The other stages of the assembly process continued to be carried out manually, partly because it is difficult to automate. The Batam facility was set up specifically for the labour-intensive manual assembly part of the production process. Typically, the chip insertion on PCB part of the assembly was retained in Singapore. The partly assembled PCBs and all other subcomponents are shipped to Batam from Singapore for final assembly. The assembled tuners are exported via Singapore. Besides the automated part of the production process, the full assembly of prototypes has been retained in the Singapore plant. In addition, all non-production activities related to tuners are carried out in the Singapore plant. Thus, the Batam facility serves solely as a mass-production unit of several versions of the tuners. The number of assembly-workers in the Batam plant has increased from 300 in June 1993 to 1000 in June 1994.

Decanting from Singapore also lies behind new production facilities by Singapore-based TNCs in Johor. Two cases are illustrative. A National/Panasonic Audio and Video factory was set up by Matsushita in Pasir Gudang Industrial Estate in 1992. In this plant the final assembly of several audio products as well as several types of video recorders takes place for export to the regional market. Until the opening of this new plant, the final assembly of these products was carried out in one of the Matsushita plants in Singapore. While the assembly of the audio products is still in large part carried out manually (and therefore is rather labour-intensive), final assembly of the video recorders is already highly automated, partly because of the required quality standards. Another case is Levitec Electronics Sdn Bhd, located on one of the new industrial estates near Johor Bahru. This plant assembles electric circuit breakers. It is a subsidiary of Levitec (Singapore) Pte. Ltd. which in turn is a subsidiary of the Singapore plant of the Swiss company Meditec Electronics. The Johor plant was set up in 1991, when the company decided to move the labour-intensive assembly out of Singapore. Johor was chosen as the new location because of the ample supply of low-cost labour at that time and the proximity to Singapore which made it possible to maintain face-to-face contacts with Singapore clients. In the Singapore plant the product-lines were changed to low volume high-quality products and further automation led to a substantial drop in the number of employees. Conversely, the number of employees in the Johor plant rose from 40 at the end of 1990 to 800 at the end of 1992.

Whether local Singapore companies follow a similar pattern, that is moving out and simultaneously moving up as far as the operations in Singapore are concerned, remains very much an open question due to the lack of data. However, it can be gauged that SMEs constitute a fair share of those which have set up operations in

Johor or on Batam. Considering also the fact that the industry branch composition of these firms is more diverse compared with the establishments in both areas of Singapore-based TNCs (particularly in Johor), it seems a fair assumption that 'moving out without moving up' has been more common among these firms. Local supply/supporting firms are participating in the cross-border out-movement.

Thus, what is happening in the context of this zone is a process of regionalization, through cross-border sub-regional decentralization (both of/by TNCs and local firms). An added component is new plant openings in the vicinity of the longer established production complex by foreign investors, partly associated with 'regional relocation'. Apart from the production conditions in the northern and southern components of the zone, these production plants could capitalize on the proximity of Singapore with its excellent infrastructure and service-facilities.

Given the structural characteristics of the operations of TNCs and local firms in the zone, it is clear that *segmentation of production* and a clear internal division of labour characterizes the zone. While operations in Singapore are marked by a significant degree of diversity, Johor and Batam can be characterized as 'production-houses' with a predominance of intermediate and low-level operations. In view of the processes at work, the components of the SIJORI zone show strong inter-linkages. Besides capital flows, these inter-linkages involve labour flows (including commuting of management personnel), flows of goods as a result of input linkages between production units (intra- and extra-firm) in the production complexes (it appears that in quite a number of cases inputs/(sub-)components are still supplied from Singapore) and import of inputs and shipment of output via the adjacent complex. Use of financial services and infrastructure in the longer established production complex is another type of inter-linkage. Finally, cooperation between governments in the promotion and further development of the zone should be mentioned. The strong inter-linkages reflect the high degree of segmentation of production which to a large extent is the defining structural characteristic of the SIJORI zone. However, though substantial territorial integration characterizes the zone, not all components are strongly interlinked. There are strong links between Singapore and Johor, as well as between Singapore and Batam, but hardly any links between Johor and Batam.

The Yellow Sea Economic Zone

The Yellow Sea rim covers most of China's northern coastal region from Liaoning down to Shanghai, Korea's west coast, and Japan's Kyushu region (Kim, 1991; Ogawa, 1991). This area is one of the most heavily populated areas in Asia. More than 300 million people live within two hours air distance from Seoul. The size of the population and economic dynamism in the area offer a great potential for an economically integrated zone in Northeast Asia. Industrial structures along the littoral areas of the Yellow Sea also provide an opportunity to form an international network of industrial cooperation through export processing, technology transfer, and direct foreign investment among China, North and South Korea, and Japan. In the late

1980s, the falling political barriers and China's open door policy stimulated interest in reviving the historical trade and cultural exchanges among the littoral areas of the Yellow Sea. With these stimulii trade between China and South Korea has increased from a mere US$20 million in 1979 to US$9.2 billion in 1993. South Korean investment in China has reached a cumulative total of almost US$1 billion in 1993 (Kim, 1994).

Trade and investment between China and South Korea, and the Kyushu region of Japan have also been rapidly expanding. China's Bohai area and northeast provinces have been the main locus of the burgeoning triangular trade and investment among China, South Korea, and Japan (Kim, 1991; Ogawa, 1991). Physical linkages among the littoral areas of the Yellow Sea have been fast forming. Direct sea routes between Pusan-Inchon and Tianjin and between Pusan-Inchon and Dalian were opened in 1989. In addition, charter freighters are running the Pusan-Inchon-Shanghai and Pusan-Inchon-Qingdao routes to carry goods between South Korea and China's Liaodong and Shandong peninsulas. A passenger ferry is running between Inchon and Weihai. Also, container vessels are operating between Kitakyushu and Tianjin and Qingdao. Fukuoka has air connection with Dalian (Wang, 1991).

In addition to obvious geographical proximity, historical connections and cultural proximity account for the concentration of Japanese and South Korean investment and trade (to a lesser extent) along the coastal areas of the Yellow Sea and northeast China. Dalian ranks number one among Chinese cities in hosting Japanese direct foreign investment, reflecting the history of Japanese occupation of Manchuria in the early years of the 20th Century (Haruyama, 1991). Similar to kinship ties that seal many business bonds between Taiwan and China, there is an ethnic component to Sino-South Korean economic interaction across the Yellow Sea. A substantial number of Chinese Koreans of Shandong descent live in South Korea. In addition, about two million Korean Chinese live in and around China's northeast provinces.

Most of all, the emergence of the YSEZ lies in economic complementarity among China, South Korea, and Japan. As revealed in the trade patterns of China, Japan, Asian NIEs, and ASEAN countries, trade complementarity is quite strong between China and the Asian NIEs, particularly South Korea (Lee and Lee, 1991). As China and South Korea seek to lower their import costs and transportation costs, trade with other countries is likely to be diverted and indeed the volume of trade between the two countries has expanded. Trade creation is also possible if both countries substitute imports from each other for domestic production. Further, trilateral trade patterns among China, South Korea, and Japan indicate a strong complementarity and resultant division of labour; China specializing in primary products and component/parts production, South Korea specializing in medium technology manufacturing and commercial subcontracting, and Japan taking a lead in high-tech and capital equipment production. In other words, different resource endowments and industrial structures within the YSEZ provide the foundation for inter-industry cooperation (Kim, 1991). There are, however, some areas of trade competition among the three countries (especially in labour-intensive products between China and South

Korea and in machinery, automobiles and electronic goods between South Korea and Japan (Hwang, 1993).

Increased wages, labour shortage, and currency fluctuation in Japan and the Asian NIEs are forces behind a new international division of labour within Asia including the YSEZ. Intra-industry cooperation within the zone, therefore, enhances the competitive edge of the firms involved through specialization. The economies of scale can also be achieved by intra-industry and/or intra-firm specialization. For example, South Korea, combined with China's Bohai region and its hinterland, which covers most of northeast and north China, provides a large enough market for most consumer durables and some intermediate inputs. Candidate industries for intra-industry cooperation include iron and steel, automobiles, shipbuilding, petrochemicals, and machinery, in which South Korea and Japan have a comparative advantage and an excess capacity. Iron and steel manufacturing is one of the pillar industries in the Bohai region. Although it is growing, it still has an inefficient performance record. Consumption per capita remains small and the existing outdated production facilities are in need of upgrading. In contrast, South Korea has the newest integrated plants and production technology; it could transfer its mid-level technology to China while progressing toward the high-technology end of steel making, as Japan did in the 1980s (Kim, 1991). Joint ventures in iron and steel production between South Korea and China are under discussion. Automobile parts and component manufacturing is another sector where intra-industry cooperation is seriously considered among Japan, China and South Korea. China's Bohai region and northeast provinces has a plan to further develop petrochemical industry and make it a leading industry for the region. For the petrochemical industry, a region-wide perspective is necessary to avoid excess capacity for production. Close cooperation among the three countries could result in more benefits through specialization. In addition, the tourist industry and services have been gradually developing in the YSEZ. With rising income, the demand for tourism is rapidly growing in Japan and South Korea. Common cultural heritage and historical attractions within the zone provide the basis for tourism, although inadequate transportation linkages are still a limiting factor (air and sea connections are well developed between the southern part of South Korea and the Kyushu area of Japan).

Considering the concentration of smoke-stack heavy industry along China's Bohai and Yellow Sea coastal areas, Japan and South Korea are willing to assist China in abating air pollution, which affects South Korea and Japan. At both governmental and private levels, formal organizations have been formed to discuss environmental issues and collaborate on joint management of biosphere in the Yellow Sea area. Maritime cooperation in the Yellow Sea is also advancing between South Korea and China. Lastly, labour flows have started across the Yellow Sea in the early 1990s. There are tens of thousands of Chinese working in South Korea and much greater numbers in Japan, legally and illegally. Although labour migration is still restricted within the Yellow Sea Economic Zone, there is much room for cooperation in the joint use of the available labour pool. China needs high-level labour for growth, while Japan and South Korea need unskilled or semi-skilled labour from China to meet labour shortages in their construction and services industries.

The economic zones in comparative perspective

The characteristics of the zones

Chia and Lee (1993) identify three types of REZs, namely the Metropolitan Spillover into the Hinterland type, the Joint Development of Natural Resources and Infrastructure type, and the Common Geopolitical Interests and Geographical Proximity type. The Greater South China zone and the SIJORI zone are both of the first type. The YSEZ, still being in the formative stage, seems to have been inspired by common geopolitical interests, to exploit economies of scale and agglomeration and to ensure faster economic growth and greater economic security.

The Greater South China zone and SIJORI share the common features of being driven by restructuring and investment. Both are export platforms, unlike the Yellow Sea Rim, which however may become one in the very near future. Both offer attractive advantages to foreign firms in terms of cheaper and abundant sources of land and labour and fiscal incentives. They have already been removed from the preferential trading advantages to developing countries.

A closer examination reveals that each zone has special characteristics. First, the South China zone resembles the Yellow Sea zone in a way in that both do not emerge from any formal arrangement as in the case of the SIJORI zone. It is a natural integration that has grown out of reactions to changing market forces in the internal and international environments. Economic integration in the South China case has a longer history than in the case of SIJORI. Second, the Greater South China and SIJORI have a division of labour which is mainly vertical and inter-industry. The YSEZ has a more complex division of labour. In addition to inter-industry division of labour, intra-industry and even intra-firm cooperation, horizontal cooperation is more likely within the zone because industrial bases along the littoral areas of the Yellow Sea provide an opportunity of industrial complementation. Third, there are differences in the types of investors and investments. Investments in Guangdong and Fujian are dominated by indigenous private investors from Hong Kong and Taiwan. Though indigenous private investors from Singapore play a significant role in investments in Johor, their position is less dominant, while Singapore investments in Riau are dominated by Japanese, European and American multinationals with operations in Singapore. In the Greater South China case, SMEs play a more significant role. Many of such enterprises have engaged in outward processing (sub-contracting of the entire or part of the production process to firms in Guangdong/Fujian). This is much less a feature of production arrangements in SIJORI, where the setting up of joint ventures or wholly-owned subsidiaries are the dominant form of investment. In both cases, the material inputs are brought in from the core area (Hong Kong and Singapore respectively) for processing. Unlike in the

SIJORI zone, very little internal product differentiation is discernible in the South China zone. Most of the products are oriented towards the low end of the production scale. Since labour in the zone is largely unskilled and there is restriction on free movement of labour, it is difficult to carry out the kind of product differentiation found more commonly in the SIJORI zone. Fourth, unlike in the YSEZ and in SIJORI, there is very little labour mobility within the South China zone. The political differences do not allow the free flow of labour between China and Taiwan. Hong Kong opposes the illegal exodus from the mainland though with limited success. Uncontrolled movement of labour is not favoured within the SIJORI zone and the inflow of labour into Singapore is highly regulated. Nevertheless, for obvious reasons, there is a very substantial daily flow of commuters across the causeway. Finally, there are substantial differences as to the level of government commitment and the role of the state.

The role of the State

In the existing conceptualizations of the REZ phenomenon, an important role is assigned to the state. Regional cooperation, embodied in the REZ idea, significantly contributes to the reduction or removal of all barriers, thus facilitating firms to exploit the complementarity by providing simultaneous access to different 'types' of production factors. Despite this logic, in reality the role of the state has been highly differential.

The SIJORI evolved rather *autonomously*, as a market-driven response. However, since the late 1980s governments have played an increasing role in the evolution of the zone. The Singapore government has been a strong protagonist of the growth zone and of 'twinning' with neighbouring areas. Its perception of the role of the state in the development of the industrial zone has not been limited to the joint international marketing of the zone as a single investment region. It has gone as far as direct active involvement in development projects, thus helping to create the necessary conditions which allow firms to use the complementary resource endowments.

The active role of the Singapore State is associated with the new economic strategy adopted following the 1985 economic recession. In the new strategy, Singapore's advantage in the longer run was perceived to lie in financial and business services, rather than in manufacturing. Hence the government shifted its focus of attention towards the further upgrading of the economy. Apart from the strengthening of high value-added elements in the manufacturing structure, the city-state was to become a 'Total Business Centre' with a much larger emphasis on non-production elements of the value chain. The aim was to attract regionally focused non-production operations of TNCs to Singapore, (e.g. the Operational Headquarters (OHQ) Scheme). Moreover, the attraction of R&D functions and the establishment of Singapore as a Regional Coordination and Logistics Node for the internationalizing service-industries should effectively reinforce Singapore's economic structure (Ministry of Trade and Industry, 1991). The new strategy adopted by the

171

Singapore government partly derives from its reading of the tendencies in the operations of TNCs in the region. The promotion of 'twinning' by the Singapore government is an integration strategy allowing a broadening of its international competitive strategy by the incorporation of the resources of adjacent territories. Not surprisingly then, SIJORI has also become a marketing concept, from the Singapore perspective, aimed at attracting the preferred type of corporate activities.

The Malaysian and Indonesian governments have assisted by providing attractive incentives to investors and by investing in infrastructure. Several years ago, the Indonesian government substantially liberalized the foreign investment regime applicable to Batam. Twinning is basically seen by the Johor State government and by the Indonesian government as 'running with the dragon', allowing them to capitalize on Singapore's physical and service infrastructure. The attitude of the Malaysian Federal government towards twinning with Singapore has for a long time been more non-committal than the attitude of the Johor State government and the Indonesian government. The Johor State government, though still committed to the concept, has lately adopted a more distant attitude.

Unlike SIJORI the YSEZ is primarily market driven (Chia, 1993), while in the case of the South China zone government facilitation has been circumscribed by specific constraints. Unresolved political issues have made the direct flows of trilateral economic activities between the three partners in the South China zone less smooth compared to SIJORI. The state plays an important role by prioritizing the economic benefits over the political gains as indicated by the liberalization of the trade and investment conditions and the offering of attractive packages of incentives. The opening of the SEZs in the South China zone and the special treatment given to Hong Kong and Taiwan by China, the gradual removal of constraints to travel to and investments in China as well as the lifting of trade barriers by Taiwan attest to this. Where political sensitivity remains strong the more flexible constituent member plays the intermediary role of facilitating greater cooperation.

A unique feature of the South China zone is the political legacy of the past. The constituent units are historically and culturally related but political ideology and colonial legacy have set them apart. The collapse of world communism and the disintegration of the Soviet Union provide the opportunity to normalize relationships. The process of normalization however is time consuming given the entrenched political and ideological differences between both sides of the Taiwan Straits. To demonstrate the firmness of their stand, China has openly adopted a 'one country-two systems' approach by declaring Hong Kong a Special Administrative District. While this ensures the status quo of the island after 1997 for a period of 50 years, this also holds true for the mainland. On the other hand, there are a number of encouraging signs. To hasten the process of growth and development in the South China zone, greater autonomy has been given to the Guangdong and Fujian provinces in the formulation and implementation of economic and administrative policies. Taiwan has relaxed the rules on visits to China, has lifted the ban on indirect trade and investment and is even in the process of negotiating direct air links with selected areas in China. Such decentralization, state intervention and accommodation lays the foundation for the creation of the conditions necessary for the zone to flourish.

Interpretation: The factors associated with the emergence of REZs

Some consider cross-border complementarity as a sufficient condition for the economic integration of regions of different countries to occur (by inducing intra-firm/industry division of labour). Others (Lee, 1991, 1993) take a broader view and emphasize the role of geographical proximity. The smooth functioning of the sub-regional division of labour does not necessarily augur well with resource complementarity alone. In the SIJORI zone, surveys (Yeoh *et al.*, 1992) show that proximity to Singapore has been significant among the reasons for investing in Johor/Batam (besides the supply and cost of labour). Similarly proximity to Hong Kong and to a lesser extent, Taiwan, has often been cited as the factor that stimulates the growth of the South China zone. Infrastructure, cultural affinity, favourable geopolitical conditions, and the institutional framework are considered important driving forces which allow complementarity and proximity to operate. In the case of the South China zone, close kinship ties have helped promote the Taiwanese and Hong Kong investments in the zone. As much as about US$1 billion has been brought to China since 1987 for investment purposes by Taiwanese during their tours and family visits. The special treatment given to Taiwanese is also one of the strategies used to tap the financial resources of these compatriots of China.

There is no doubt that economic complementarity and geographical proximity have been driving forces behind the emergence of the zones. However, a common interpretation of the emergence of REZs along the lines of economic complementarity and geographical proximity (and the other related factors mentioned above) seems to be insufficient for several reasons. First, the spectrum of REZs is wide. Second, even when only the metropolitan spillover cases are considered it may be noted that the interpretation only considers characteristics of areas, thereby neglecting the main actors involved, in particular the firms operating in the zones. Though the interpretation of forces leading to the formation of REZs has been made from the perspective of cost minimization and market maximization, the emphasis here has been on complementarity which has very much obscured the possible role of geographical proximity per se. Though it may well be the case that the two factors cannot be separated, consideration of geographical proximity on its own is called for in view of the not insignificant role of 'long-distance relocation' type of investment by Japanese and East-Asian NIE firms in the industrial growth of Johor. Perry (1991) has correctly observed that it would have been cheaper (and substantially so) for these firms to locate their production further away from Singapore. Ongoing research shows that in the SIJORI case geographical proximity plays a significant role, other than the availability of low-cost labour in an area contiguous to the previous production location. Some operations are intimately linked to Singapore and/or to other operations in Johor/Batam through sourcing and supply-relationships. In other cases the practicing of a JIT system requires proximity to client firms or easy access to efficient shipping facilities. In these and yet other cases the easy accessibility of Singapore's excellent infrastructure seems to be essential also. As far as local Singapore companies are concerned, these considerations seem to add to the relevance of proximity besides cultural similarities which make it easier to internationalize production (Lee, 1991, 1993). It appears then that the role of geographical proximity cannot be understood in isolation from the characteristics and organization of production. It does not seem incorrect to suggest that the metropolitan spillover type of REZs may be partly linked to firms operating in a specific way in specific industries or which are engaged in specific product-branches, requiring proximity to specific elements of the core area.

Conclusion

In the course of the 1980s a profound process of industrial change in Southeast Asia has begun. While this process is still evolving and new structures are still in a formative stage, it is clear that adjustments at firm/corporate and industry levels over the past decade have impressively changed the manufacturing landscape, both structurally and geographically. The tendency has been towards much stronger territorial integration. In the process of change a new territorial configuration, the cross-border economic zone, has emerged in which the increased economic integration and regionalization in a sub-regional framework is manifested. The spectrum of REZs in the Southeast and East Asian region currently comprises zones which are established and others in a formative stage. Regionalization and sub-regional economic integration should be seen against the background of not only the pressures of industrial restructuring but also the dramatic alterations over the past decade in the geopolitical situation in the region.

The Greater South China Economic Zone and SIJORI have already evolved into major manufacturing complexes in the Asian Pacific Rim. Both are restructuring driven, private investment driven, initially market forces driven and at a later stage also government-driven (though this is much stronger in the SIJORI case). Yet, both have developed along a different path and in a different 'local' context. Though a number of issues surround their future development, there is no doubt that their current status will be maintained in the immediate future. New initiatives to a large extent aim to emulate the development experience of these zones. Differences in context and conditions should warn us against a uniform 'formula' or 'model' for regionalization, sub-regional integration and the development of cross-border economic zones. Whether the new initiatives will succeed in 'coercing' investors into the zones and developing into new growth areas seems to critically depend less on the type of development than on whether the success factors are present and can be effectively put into operation. The range of new initiatives is rather bewildering. As has been stated in the introduction, the REZs involved are of widely varying 'size', have widely varying regional economic structures, levels of development, and conditions. Some of the new initiatives are largely political metaphors. Though employed to encourage investors, they may well remain political metaphors.

References

Ash, R. F. and Kueh, Y. Y. 1993: 'Economic Integration Within Greater China: Trade and Investment Flows between China, Hong Kong and Taiwan'. *The China Quarterly*, 710-745.

Batam Industrial Development Authority 1993: Development Data. Jakarta, BIDA.

Chia, Siow-Yue 1993: Motivating Forces in Subregional Economic Zones. Pacific Forum/CSIS Conference on National Economic Territories and Challenges to the Nation State. Honolulu, 30 November - 2 December 1993.

Chia, Siow-Yue and Lee, Tsao Yuan 1993: 'Subregional Economic Zones: A New Motive Force in Asia Pacific Development', in Bergsten, C. F. and Noland, M. (eds) *Pacific Dynamism and the International Economic System*, Washington DC: Institute for International Economics, 225-269.

Dicken, P. 1992: *Global Shift: The Internationalization of Economic Activity* (2nd edition). London, Paul Chapman Publishing Co.

EIU (The Economist Intelligence Unit), 1993(a): Country Profile: China 1993/94. London, EIU.

EIU (The Economist Intelligence Unit), 1993(b): Country Profile: Taiwan 1993/94. London, EIU.

Harding, H. 1987: *China's Second Revolution*. Washington, The Brookings Institution

Harding, H. 1993: 'The Concept of Greater China: Themes, Variations and Reservations'. *The China Quarterly*, 661- 686.

Haruyama, H. 1991: 'Kyusu-Yamaguchi Economic Area and External Relations', in Nishimura, A. and Watanabe, T. (eds) *Kankoukai Keizaiken*. Kyushu, Kyushu University Press.

Ho, K. C. 1993: 'Industrial Restructuring and the Dynamics of City-State Adjustments'. *Environment and Planning A*, 25 (1), 47-62.

Hwang, In-Joung 1993: 'Prospects for Economic Cooperation in the Yellow Sea Rim Bloc and its Future Direction', in Won Bae Kim et.al. (eds) *Regional Economic Cooperation in Northeast Asia*. Proceedings of the Vladivostok Conference. Honolulu, Northeast Asia Economic Forum.

Johor State Economic Development Corporation 1993: Johore Investment Guide. Johor Bahru, JSEDC.

Johor Investment Centre 1991: Directory of Foreign Companies operating in the JSEDC Industrial Estates. Johor Bahru, JIC.

Kim, Doo-Hyon 1994: 'Present Status and Prospects for Trade between Korea and China'. Economic Bulletin, Economic Planning Board, Republic of Korea, No. 94 03.

Kim, Won Bae 1991: 'Yellow Sea Economic Zone: Vision or Reality'. *Journal of Northeast Asian Studies X*, 35-55.

Kim, Won Bae 1993: 'Industrial Restructuring and Regional Adjustment in the Asian NIEs'. *Environment and Planning A*, 25 (1), 27-46.

Kueh Y. Y. 1992: 'Foreign Investment and Economic Changes in China'. *The China Quarterly*, 637-690.

Lee, Keun and Lee, Chung 1991: 'Future Dynamics in Sino-South Korea Relations'. *Journal of Northeast Asian Studies IX*, 15-35.

Lee, Tsao Yuan (ed) 1991: *Growth Triangle: the Johor-Singapore-Riau Experience.* Singapore, Institute of Southeast Asian Studies.

Lee, Tsao Yuan 1993: 'Sub-Regional Economic Zones in the Asia-Pacific: A Conceptual Overview', in Toh, Mun Heng and Low, L. (eds) *Regional Cooperation and Growth Triangles in ASEAN.* Singapore, Times Academic Press, 9-58.

Liu, P. 1993: 'Mixed Diagnosis for Mainland Fever'. *Free China Review*, September, 42-47.

Lui, T. L. and Chiu, S. 1993: 'Industrial Restructuring and Labour-Market Adjustment under Positive Non-Interventionism: the Case of Hong Kong'. *Environment and Planning A*, 25 (1), 63-80.

Luo, Qi and Howe, C. 1993: 'Direct Investment and Economic Integration in the Asia Pacific: The Case of Taiwanese Investment in Xiamen'. *The China Quarterly*, 746-769.

Malaysian Industrial Development Authority, Statistics on the Manufacturing Sector in Malaysia. Several Issues. Kuala Lumpur: MIDA.

Ministry of Trade and Industry 1991: *Singapore Strategic Economic Plan.* Singapore: National Printers.

Natarajan, S. and Tan, Juay Miang 1992: *The impact of MNC Investments in Malaysia, Singapore and Thailand.* Singapore, Asean Economic Research Unit, Institute of Southeast Asian Studies.

Ogawa, Y. 1991: 'Asia's New International Division of Labor', in Yuhei, O. (ed) *Ajia Kyoseino Jidai.* Tokyo.

Pang, Eng Fong 1991: 'Singapore: Market-Led Adjustment in an Interventionist State', in Patrick, H. and Meissner, L. (eds) *Pacific Basin Industries in Distress, Structural Adjustment and Trade Policy in the nine Industrialized Economies*, New York, Columbia University Press, 215-256.

Paradiredja, A. and Yeoh, C. 1991: Migrant Workers in a Corner of the Growth Triangle. Faculty of Business Administration, National University of Singapore, mimeo.

Perry, M. 1991: 'The Singapore Growth Triangle: State, Capital and Labour at a new Frontier in the World Economy'. *Singapore Journal of Tropical Geography*, 12, 138-151.

Rashid Hussain Securities 1990: Johor the Newly Industrialising State. Kuala Lumpur.

Reardon, L. C. 1991: 'The SEZs Come of Age'. *The China Business Review*, November-December, 14-20.

Rodan, G. 1989: *The Political Economy of Singapore's Industrialisation: National State and International Capital*. Hampshire, Macmillan Press.

Rodan, G. 1993: 'Reconstructing Divisions of Labour: Singapore's New Regional Emphasis', in Higgot, R., Leaver, R. and Ravenhill, J. (eds) *Pacific Economic Relations in the 1990s: Cooperation or Conflict?*. St.Leonards, Allen and Unwin, 223-249.

Scalapino, R. 1993: 'The Politics of Development and Regional Cooperation in Northeast Asia', in Won Bae Kim et.al. (eds) *Regional Economic Cooperation in Northeast Asia. Proceedings of the Vladivostok Conference*. Honolulu, Northeast Asia Economic Forum.

Shambaugh, D. 1993: 'The Emergence of Greater China'. *The China Quarterly*, 653-659.

The Straits Times, June 1 1994.

Toh, Mun-Heng and Low, L. (eds) 1993: *Regional Cooperation and Growth Triangles in ASEAN*. Singapore, Times Academic Press.

Van Grunsven, L. 1991: 'Staat en Vrije Markt in Singapore'. *Derde Wereld*, 10, 91-3, 63-85.

Van Grunsven, L. 1992: 'Industrial Change in Southeast Asia: Perspectives for Geographical Research', in *Proceedings of the International Conference on Geography in the ASEAN Region, Yogyakarta, August 1992*. Yogyakarta, Facultas Geografi, Gadjah Mada University.

Van Grunsven, L. 1994a: 'Industrial Change in Southeast Asia: New Spatial Patterns of Division of Labour', in Custers, G. and Stunnenberg, P. (eds) *Processes of Incorporation and Integration in Developing Countries*. Nijmegen Studies in Development and Cultural Change 16. Saarbrücken, Verlag Breitenbach Publishers, 65-103.

Van Grunsven, L. 1994b: 'Industrial Regionalization and Urban-Regional Transformation in Southeast Asia: The SIJORI Growth Triangle Considered'. Paper presented at the Fifth Asian Urbanization Conference, Taipei, January 1994.

Wang, Xiao Ping 1991: 'Economic Development of Tianjin and Bohai Economic Zone Plan', in Nishimura, A. and Watanabe, T. (eds) *Kankoukai Keizaiken*. Kyushu, Kyushu University Press.

Yang, Dali 1990: 'Patterns of China's Regional Development Strategy'. *China Quarterly*, 122, 230-57.

Yeoh, C., Lau Geok Theng and Funkhouser, G. R. 1992: Summary Report: Business Trends in the Growth Triangle. Faculty of Business Administration, National University of Singapore, mimeo.

9　Conclusions

Richard Le Heron and Sam Ock Park

The Asian Pacific Rim and Globalization is an argument about the interpretation of geographically and historically specific patterning of industrialization, enterprise and state policy and integration and regionalization. This concluding chapter briefly restates the argument which the book as a whole presents and comments on implications for method and policy which stem from the theory and evidence included in the book.

The book's argument is built on several foundations. First, globalization is viewed as a category summarizing the emergence of *pluralistic, open-ended and indeterminate processes* directed to purposive functional integration of activities. The processes may or may not be primarily economic in character. This conception has major consequences for the interpretation of industrialization experiences in the Asian Pacific Rim. Instead of regarding a priori, that there is a single or unchanging or unmodifiable model of industrialization, the form and nature of mid - and late twentieth century industrialization is seen as beginning in and constructed from the historical and geographic circumstances of different nation-states. The chapters proceeded in a fashion consistent with this position, situating and discussing industrialization trajectories of different nation-states in relation to wider globalization forces and tendencies. As well, the theorization has some corollaries. It rejects the notion of industrialization as the sole ingredient of globalization, and by implication, the generally unstated view that globalization is principally a Western-inspired phenomenon. It means, moreover, that the Asian Pacific Rim should be seen as only *possibly* having some 'internal' unity of economic interaction, with any claim of this kind requiring, empirical confirmation. Furthermore, the way is opened up for a consideration of *different* developmental paths in the Asian Pacific arena, made up of processes whose history and geography is still little known and poorly comprehended from a Western standpoint. These qualifications are embodied in part of the methodology adopted by contributors, where most chapters effectively map industrialization from local knowledge of global processes. The chapters thus stand as very tentative examples of territorial knowledge. This knowledge is attuned to extra-national hierarchies connected with the spatiality of production and consumption and comes from contextualizing local attempts to offer something internationally which might be valorized in global networks and circuits. In acknowledging different origins and trajectories of industrialization, the way is opened for investigation, explanation and translation that *might* present industrialization as less nation-state bounded than has hitherto been thought.

Second, industrialization is conceptualized as an outcome of governance and enterprise policies and strategies, themselves the product of ongoing *politics and power-relations*, springing from diverse sources but cohering within frameworks of state policy about economic and industry growth and enterprise structure and strategy. Detail found in the chapters provides insight into the social relations of efforts formative of industrialization policies. From this view the potential *interconnectivity* of industrialization experiences in the Asian Pacific Rim becomes a matter of great interest. In part this follows the diffusion of industrialization models, when various nation-states tried to copy from other contexts elements of policy perceived to be offering competitive advantages in the global economy. But more crucially the interconnections need to be examined as a probable *blend* of 'western' and 'eastern' conceptions about industrial and firm policy relevant to situations in the Asian Pacific Rim. In addition, the notion of *interpenetrating* structures is particularly pertinent to how integration is viewed. In the book's introduction integration was discussed as a distinguishing feature of contemporary capitalist globalization. This representation draws heavily on the *relational* Geography of Accumulation and Regulation framework proposed by Australasian economic geographers (Fagan and Le Heron, 1994). Thus, although this framework itself is a synthesis of Anglo-American ideas, restated in a broader and more 'globalized' format, it has not been subjected to critical application and evaluation in other geographic contexts. The main case for utilizing the framework in the book rested on the general propositions contained in it's conceptualization, especially the recognition that the internationalization of capital, the changing role of the state and the social relations of consumption and production are intertwined. Capitalist globalization is therefore in part an elaboration of new forms of organization of capitalist production and consumption, manifest in internationalization trends, governmental norms and enterprise strategies. In as much as industrialization where ever it has been experienced and encouraged involves the emergence of organizational forms and inter- and intra-organizational arrangements, there is a direct connection to the framework. Because the framework is *nondeterministic and nonhierarchical*, indeed largely suggestive in formulation, no special primacy is given to which of internationalization, the state or social relations will be avenues of greatest change. Shifting *power-relations* in and between each of these spheres will inevitably alter and new organizational forms and links will appear, rearranging power balances amongst actors, thereby changing the nature and dynamics of experiences in different settings. Chapters 3, 4 and 8 in particular offered treatments that broadly correlate with the ideas incorporated in Figure 1.1.

Third, just as the integrative tendency can be characterized as a dimension of capitalist globalization and industrialization (a point which is central to much theorization in economic geography in the 1990s), so too can patterns of regionalization be included in discussion on this subject. In the book the term regionalization is mainly employed with reference to the rise of clusters of economic activity which are *inter-nation in reach, but consist of groupings of proximate sub-national areas.* Chapters 6 and 8 approach regionalization in this fashion whereas Chapter 7 considers regionalization more conventionally, as a phenomenon to be explained in a national setting. A number of points already made about integration inform the discussion of regionalization. The appearance of distinctive regional concentrations of investment, attitudes towards investment in particular areas, government policy aimed at attracting investment into areas, corporate organization of investment into systems incorporating particular places and so on can all be reassessed in terms of possibilities for cross-border investment, labour and trade flows wherein the particularities of industry and enterprise in a place derives, to use Doreen Massey's general phrasing, from 'the *mixture* of wider and more local social relations' (Massey, 1993,240). A significant conclusion to be drawn is that the social origins of any regionalization are varied and may be explored through analysis that attempts to portray the range, interests, discourses, imaging, actions and interactions of public and private sector stakeholders, from many territories. The ensuing territoriality is a refashioning of places-to-places, very often transcending and criss-crossing existing administrative units such as nation-states.

What implications might follow from the interpretive shifts explicated in the book? In a far reaching and provocative paper Pieterse (1994) suggests that the nature of many disciplines will be markedly changed as a result of any reinterpretation of globalization. He remarks that a global sociology 'is taking shape around notions such as social networks (rather than 'societies'), border zones, boundary crossing and global society' (Pieterse, 1994, 179). In his conception conventional sociology conceived within the framework of nations and societies is making place for a sociology of hybrid formations, times and spaces. Although his conclusions with respect to sociology give some feel for pressures upon researchers in other disciplines they are at best suggestions about the objects likely to attract interest in geography over the next decade or so. Given the major contributions geographers have already made to the debates about globalization and localization it is probably reasonable to anticipate that a remaking of contemporary economic geography is in progress. However, there is only limited indication that economic geographers have begun to regroup around the possible ingredients of some vaguely sensed 'new' economic geography. Nonetheless, *The Asian Pacific Rim and Globalization* reveals *some* elements of different research practice and questioning which underscore the different understandings of geographies of industrialization discussed in the book.

The capacity of researchers to develop theoretical, empirical and policy statements about dimensions of globalization depends heavily on the development of a broadly shared vocabulary of concepts to guide research inquiry. Progress in this direction cannot be separated from empirical work; both theoretically-informed analysis and empirically-referenced theorisation are required. One of the more pressing matters needing early resolution is the status and interpretation of global processes. To settle the confusion which often accompanies discussion of global processes a distinction must be made between general processes (these are really abstractions, devised to help figure out system developments which in practical terms can only be summarised in theoretical language) and processes operating at various spatial scales (these being very directly the products of investigation and analysis of actual changes/developments/events and can readily draw upon and incorporate everyday language). The interest in the contemporary economic geography literature on production-consumption systems (Dicken, 1994) prompts some comments on how global might be included in discussion. Indeed, Gereffi and Korniezwincz (1994) propose the wording *global commodity system*, acknowledging the spatiality or territoriality of all commodity systems. Their argument, grounded in historical analyses informed by world-system theory, appropriately defines commodity systems, under capitalism, as *potentially* global (see Fagan and Le Heron (1994) for a similar view). It is a mistaken view however to assume that the abstract concept of a global commodity system automatically means the existence of totally global systems of commodity production and consumption or that only global processes underpin the emergence of global commodity systems. Neither of these views are tenable. The scope of actions and interactions may not embrace or originate at a global scale. Likewise, the constitutive processes of commodity systems will always involve some local processes as all production and consumption is territorially grounded. The general concept of a global commodity system instead should be seen as a conceptual architecture to guide research into how specific (or collections of) commodity systems continue to emerge as part of contemporary capitalism. At the level of specific systems the architecture is an attempt to show how the relational character of global commodity systems is both a product of and is influenced by the spatiality and territoriality of production-consumption links and networks. *Local linkages and international networks are intertwined with international linkages and local networks*, forming circuits and channels through which interactions may be pursued. Accordingly in general theoretical discussion the phrasing 'global processes', 'national processes' or 'local processes' represent signals that *some* processes of the world capitalist system may require theorization and empirical treatment, because the scales in question are perceived to be consistent with the actuality of action and interaction.

The above interpretation needs further qualification. We can identify in general theoretical discussion, for instance, that processes of particular forms and character are discernible but the next step of orienting enquiry to the particularities of given global commodity systems can only be adequately achieved through a combination of related theoretical and empirical effort. In all likelihood, investigations will involve consideration of the 'scale at which pertinent processes are operative'. This wording stands in sharp contrast to the less helpful phrasing, 'processes at different spatial scales', which tends to encourage thinking which automatically castes global processes in a premier or overarching position of influence. The preferred wording attempts to highlight that *any* representation of the spatiality of processes placing places into the context of other places is intended to be *a* representation of the actualities of experience. This means that most economic geography, in practise, might take the form of enquiry into the territoriality of economic activities, as seen from a situational perspective, shaped in one or more territories. This idea is advocacy of analysis which is neither hierarchical nor deterministic, because investigation of actual processes is needed. Only when this has been completed should some determination be made of which processes are more or less important, in what mix and under what conditions. Thus, in problematizing industrialization and globalization and exploring facets of integration and regionalization through a different lense, *The Asian Pacific Rim and Globalization* has opened a door on the possible practise and emphasis of future work by economic geographers.

References

Dicken, P. 1994: 'The Roepke Lecture in Economic Geography: Global-Local tensions: Firm and states in global space economy', *Economic Geography*, 70 (2), 101-128.

Fagan, R. and Le Heron, R. 1994: 'Reinterpreting the geography of accumulation: the global shift and local restructuring', *Environment and Planning D: Society and Space*, 12, 265-285.

Gereffi, G. and Korzeniewicz, M. (eds) 1994: *Commodity Chains and Global Capitalism*. Westport, Connecticut, Greenwood Press.

Massey, D. 1993: 'A global sense of place', in Gray, A. and Mc Guigan, J. (eds) *Studying Culture*. London, Edward Arnold, 232-240.

Pieterse, J.N. 1994: 'Globalisation as hybridisation'. *International Sociology*, 9 (2), 161-184.

Index

strong transition thesis 56-7
structural coherence 5
Sumitomo 95

Taitung 22
Taiwan 27,29,32,61-82,107,110,116-
    26,156-61,165,172
Taiwan Cement 22
**Teco Electric and Machinery
    Company** 78
territorality 5,13,78,182
Thailand 19,25,33,107,110-11,116-20,
    155,165,
**TNT (Thomas Nationwide
    Transport)** 28
Toyota 47,95,148
Toyotism 45-6,54-7
Toyotist 43,45,47,49,52,54

United Kingdom 20,93,139
United Parcel Services 28
United States of America 19-27, 29,
    40, 70, 76-7, 82, 87, 89-90, 93, 98,
    107-9, 113-15, 117, 121, 129, 151-2,
    159-60,165

Vietnam 27,79,107,119,153

weak transition thesis 54-5

Yellow Sea Rim 167-74
Yue Loong Motors 21

Zaibatsu 57,63,95,132-6
Zhejiang (China) 107